Celebrating 100 Years of Minor League Baseball in Greater Binghamton: Tales from the Binghamton Baseball Shrine

GREATER BINGHAMTON

100

YEARS OF BASEBALL

CRICKETS • BINGOS • TRIPLETS • METS

Jim Maggiore

Let's Go Mets!

Jim Maggiore

All My Best!

Michael J. McCann

Michael McCann

2/14

ISBN # 978-0-615-96636-6

Cover Design courtesy of Greg Smith (greg@gregksmith.com)

Cover Photos: All photos courtesy of the Binghamton Mets Baseball Club, unless otherwise indicated. Top Photo is aerial shot of NYSEG Stadium, provided by the Binghamton Mets and taken by Ed Aswad. The aerial shot of Johnson Field in the middle of the diamond is provided courtesy of the Broome County Historical Society. The photo of the Johnson Field Façade, in the lower-right corner, is provided with the courtesy of the family of Frank Saraceno. Photo inserts on the bases: home plate is Thurman Munson; first base is Whitey Ford; second base is Edgardo Alfonzo; David Wright is at third. NYSEG Stadium is pictured in the lower left of the front cover.

Back Photo shows game being played at Johnson Field in the 1940's. Note the hills beyond the center field fence, there are no houses dotting the landscape as there are today. Photo courtesy of the family of Frank Saraceno.

Printed in U.S.A.
Superior Print on Demand
165 Charles Street
Vestal, New York

First Edition: April 2014

Acknowledgements

With the publication of this book, it is safe to say that "It takes a community to publish a book!" Thanks goes to the following people for making this book possible; they are listed in no particular order:

- o B-Mets General Manager Jim Weed and his staff, who opened their photo vault to the authors and provided numerous proof copies; special thanks to Heith Tracy-Bronson and Ed Saunders
- o The Board of Directors of the Binghamton Mets Booster club, who were supportive every step along the way—Vince Fiacco, Diane Kalmen, Doug Johnson, Eileen Plunkett, Jeff Smith, Alan Stockholm, and Denis Wickham
- o The people who donated their time to and offer comments on the drafts of this work: Kevin Healy, Doug Johnson, Diane Kalmen, Alice Maggiore, Joseph McCann, Susan McCann, Jeff Smith, Alan Stockholm, and Denis Wickham
- o The staff at the A. Bartlett Giammati Center at the Baseball Hall of Fame
- o The baseball enthusiasts who donated their pictures that appear in this book: Frank Saraceno and family; John Nuzzela and family; Colleen Zuhone ,daughter of Gilbert DeClerq)
- o The people who gracefully gave of their time to be interviewed for material in this book, including Lisa Cox (daughter of Wally Burnette), John Fox, Rob Gardner, Lou Howell, Frank Keetz, Charlie Keller III, Steve Kraly, Gene Monahan, Larry Pitler, Ralph Terry, and Michael Urda
- o The people who helped with the final formatting of this work, including Robert Blakeslee (see his work at cwbattlefieldimages.com), Eileen Plunkett, and Kevin Shoemaker.

-- Jim Maggiore and Michael J. McCann
April 2014

Dedication: This book is dedicated to you, Dad. You gave me the gift of the fever on that September afternoon long ago—Jim Maggiore.

This book is dedicated to my wife and two children. Thanks for all your support—Mike McCann.

Author's Notes:

- • The majority of the statistics used in this book are from the baseball reference web site (www.baseball-reference.com)
- • All web sites listed in this book were current as of this printing.

A Few Words about the Binghamton Mets Booster Club…

This book is sponsored by the Binghamton Mets Booster Club, which has paid for all publishing and printing costs. The authors, Jim Maggiore and Michael McCann, have written this book on behalf of the Booster Club and all proceeds from the sale and distribution of this book go to the booster club. The Binghamton Mets Booster Club is a not-for-profit organization that was formed in 2013 whose mission includes:

- Providing community support for the Binghamton Mets and the minor league players of Greater Binghamton
- Enhancing the overall fan experience for the baseball devotees of Greater Binghamton.
- Promoting sportsmanship and community pride

The booster club fulfills its mission by providing welcome packages for all team members, providing snacks and refreshments for team road trips and, where appropriate, providing team meals for the Binghamton Mets Baseball Club. Throughout the course of the season the booster club holds memorabilia raffles at NYSEG Stadium, as well sponsoring theme nights (i.e., "Booster Club Night," "Make Some Noise Night," etc.).

Additional information on the booster club and its activities can be found on facebook (binghamtonmetsboosters.com) and on bmetsboosters.wordpress.com. Additional copies of this book can be ordered by using the order form at the back of this book or contacting the booster club via facebook or the bmetsboosters.wordpress.com blog.

A Booster Club Meeting Started it All: It was during a booster club meeting in September of 2013 where the idea of writing this book was first discussed, as part of a larger discussion of what the booster club could do to help commemorate the 2014 Binghamton Mets as the 100th minor league baseball team in Greater Binghamton. The Binghamton Baseball Shrine became the bedrock upon which to build the story, as by writing a short profile for each Shrine member, the story of baseball in this area could also be told. Because of the dedicated efforts of scores of people, this book has come to fruition in a remarkably short timeframe. The 99 teams that preceded the 2014 team are listed in Appendix B and are based on the *baseball reference* web site (www.baseball-reference.com). The book is priced at only $10.00 because the booster club wanted to put the baseball story of Greater Binghamton in as front of as many eyes as possible.

Table of Contents

Foreword by Steve Kraly 7

Introduction 9

Greater Binghamton's Baseball History 10

Tales From the Shrine 18

    "Welcome to the Big Leagues, Johnny" 20

    When Terry Strutted Like a Peacock 22

    "Mr. Norman, My Husband Is Not Going to Believe This" 24

Shrine Spinoff: The Fan of the Year Award 26

Binghamton: The Core of Big Apple Baseball 33

Shrine Profiles 39

    George F. Johnson: A Lifetime of Giving Back 40

    Johnny Logan: Endicott Gave Him His Name—"Yatcha" 41

    "Wee Willie" Keeler: "Gentlemen Don't Do That" 43

    No Matter the Moniker, Ford is Truly the "Chairman of the Board" 45

    Tommy Holmes: "Mr. Clutch" Redux 47

    When "Wild Bill" Put Binghamton at the Center of the Baseball World 49

    Eddie Sawyer: "I'm 49 Years Old and I Want to Live to 50" 53

    Ron Luciano: "My Voice is Perfect for Mime and My Face is Made for Radio" 55

    In Binghamton, "Johnny Mac" Has Nothing to Do With Tennis… 57

    Stephen "Bud" Souchock: From the Triplets to the Big Leagues and Back Again 59

    Deron Johnson: "I Need Hittin!" 61

    Why Kraly Wasn't Getting the Corners… 63

    Thurman Munson to Ron Guidry: "Trust Me" 66

    John H. Johnson: From Johnson Field to Kuhn's Right-Hand Man 68

    Lee Thomas: "Carter's Bat Was Like a Hammer" 70

    Bill Virdon: "Will It Mean Something to You?" 71

    James Whitney: A Grasshopper Hails From Conklin, N.Y. 73

    Bud Fowler: "A Dandy in Every Respect" 74

    Vic Raschi: From the Cellar to the Penthouse 76

    Steve Swisher: Father Knows Best 78

    Spud Chandler: 'I'll Be Pitching in this Lot!" 79

    Al Downing: "I Never Say 7:15 Anymore, I Say It's a Quarter After Seven" 81

    Bobby Richardson: The Link From the Best to the Worst 83

    Bob Taylor: Henry Street Hero 84

    Clete Boyer: "Brooks Beat Me Out of About 7 Gold Gloves" 85

    Fred Norman: "I Didn't Think it Would Go Past 5, but it Did" 87

    Eddie Farrell's Journey From Dentistry to the Diamond 89

    Ralph Terry and the Hall-of-Fame Heart of the Order 90

    Pete Suder: On Second There Stands the Man with the Hands 93

    John Montgomery Ward: A Baseball Pioneer 95

    Johnny Blanchard: Raconteur Extraordinaire 97

    Frank Verdi: Another "Moonlight" Graham 100

    Ken Harrelson, "The Hawk," and the "Wild Thing" 102

    Jerry Toman: Leader in the Best and the Worst of Times 103

Rob Gardner: 15 Innings of Fame Instead of 15 Minutes 105
Bob Grim: Hometown Hero.. 107
Jake Pitler: Binghamton was "Home Sweet Home"...................................... 108
Bert Campaneris: "His Nickname Was Dagoberto but His Real Name is Campy" ... 111
Lefty Gomez and the Night He Screamed, "Turn off the Water!" 113
Bill "WB" Kay: Binghamton's All-Time Hit King 116
Bobby Jones: September 12th–Prelude to a Pennant................................... 117
Brook Fordyce: A Roll of the "Dyce" Pays Off 119
Charlie Keller III: A Promising Career Cut Short 121
Cory Lidle: An Eerie Echo 123
George McQuinn: No Depression When He was at Bat............................... 125
Edgardo Alfonzo: "Fonzie" in His Happy Days.. 126
Gene Bearden: A Golden Arm and a Purple Heart...................................... 129
Dan Casey: You Be the Judge—The "Mighty Casey" or Not? 130
Joe Pepitone: Playing in His Back Yard... 132
Dale Long: Lefty Catcher and a Hefty Hitter 134
Danny McDevitt: Closing Time Was His Time, and Not Only at Ebbetts Field........ 136
Quilvio Veras: July Was His Month 138
Wally Burnette: "A Good Ol' Boy and a Real Good Pitcher" 140
John W. Fox: His Magic Number was 61! 141
Harry Lumley: Home Run King in the "Dead Ball" Era 144
Gene Monahan: "It Really Is a Wonderful Life"... 145
Curtis Pride: The Pride of the B-Mets 147
Bill Skowron: A Moose Is On the Loose.. 149
Willard Hershberger: A Heavy Cross to Bear 150
Tom Tresh: Carrying on the Family Business 152
Pete Van Wieren: The Old Professor and He's Not Casey Stengel! 154
Shrine On Deck Circle… 157
Epilogue 161
A Photo Gallery of Baseball in Binghamton 162
Appendix A. Shrine Statistics.. 177
Appendix B. Teams of Binghamton 183
Notes 186
Bibliography 194
Mail Order Form 197

Foreword

When I returned home from my first day of work for IBM in 1962, my wife, Irene, greeted me with her usual warm smile. Then she told me my old friend, Casey Stengel, the manager of the New York Mets, had left me a message to call him back. When I returned Casey's call that night I learned he wanted me to go to spring training with the Mets, and he had a contract for me to sign for $25,000. During the past five years Irene had followed me from New Orleans to Lancaster to Nashville to Indianapolis and now, after having just landed a secure and exciting job with IBM, baseball was calling again.

I told Casey I needed a day to think it over as it would mean giving up my IBM job. I went off to work the next day and after a day of deep thought and consultation with friends, I returned home with a smile on my face. Irene greeted me at the door and asked, "Are we leaving?"

I looked at her and smiled. "Are we going out to eat?"

No, aren't you going to go play?"

"No." I said as I took her hands in mine. "I'm not. You and our two children mean more to me than my baseball career."

You did that for me?"

"Yes."

When I called Casey that night and told him I was staying put, he said he understood. "You know, Kraly, you're probably going to win a lot more up there with IBM than you would down here with me and my Mets!"

Casey was right. I have never looked back.

I am proud to have called the Greater Binghamton Area my full-time home since 1956, after I completed my second tour of duty with the Triplets. I have so many fond memories of this area, from having my best season in professional ball in 1953, to marrying the woman of my dreams and raising our four wonderful children—Kathleen, Steve, Tom and Bob. After finishing my playing career I left behind one great organization, the New York Yankees, to work for another one—IBM. Like many people in this area, I am the descendant of immigrants from Eastern Europe and baseball was the road I traveled to assimilate into the culture of small town America. Today I still get to go to the ballpark on a regular basis, serving as the official home scorekeeper of the Binghamton Mets.

If you have a fondness for baseball or an affinity for the Greater Binghamton Area, you will enjoy turning the pages of this book. You'll learn about Hall of Famers like Whitey Ford and Lefty Gomez, as well as players like myself, who had a sweet and lengthy "cup of coffee" in the big leagues. You'll also read about how and why Endicott became known as the "Magic City" and you'll come to appreciate the era when Johnson City was the prototypical "Main Street, USA."

You'll travel along the historic crossroads of both Binghamton and baseball as you read the stories of the members of Binghamton's Baseball Shrine. I hope and trust that a smile will be your companion as you learn about the rich tradition of baseball in Binghamton and its ultimate effect on the game in the Big Apple.

Steve Kraly,
Pitcher for the 1953 World Champion New York Yankees
April 2014

Steve Kraly

Introduction

Whether you read this book from front to back or by selected chapters, or by player profiles, you will learn not only about baseball in Greater Binghamton, but about the area's history as well. Turning these pages will remind you of how important baseball was in assimilating immigrants into the everyday life of America in the first half of the twentieth century, when baseball, boxing, and horse racing dominated the sports headlines, with baseball clearly leading the way.

You will be entertained as you travel along this literary road, because Binghamton Baseball Shrine members such as Lefty Gomez and Ron Luciano were stand-up comedians even though they chose the diamond as their stage. Nuggets of information too will fill your trivia basket. Uncover which member of the Shrine saved Whitey Ford's life and why Johnny Logan once walked from Endicott to Johnson City in the spring of his twelfth year. Discover why raconteur extraordinaire Johnny Blanchard once hung up the phone on George Weiss, then general manager of the New York Yankees. You simply won't believe what George F. Johnson thought should happen when a major league owner wanted to purchase one of his minor league players and you'll wish there were more corporate leaders like him today. You'll learn about heroes between the lines as well as those who gave up their prime baseball years to become heroes outside the lines.

The Shrine supports the argument that baseball is a reflection of life. Interwoven in these stories of triumph are equally dramatic stories of despair and tragedy. While four members of the Shrine are also in Baseball's Hall of Fame, two members of the Shrine committed suicide, and another two were killed in crashes of small planes that they owned.

You'll come to also appreciate how a minor league team can serve as a community gathering place, where the entrance gates serve as common denominators and a ticket gives you a seat to a reality show every night. Juxtaposed against today's world, with information, communication, and sporting events of all sorts seemingly ubiquitous, you'll sense how the playing of a baseball game dominated an area's thoughts and how a professional team signified community prosperity and growth. You'll also come across a restaurant a long foul ball from where Johnson Field once stood that is the longest family-owned restaurant in the Greater Binghamton Area and whose original owners served as a second set of parents to the young men who came to Broad and Brockton Streets, home of Johnson Field.

Most of all, as you turn these pages, you'll come to appreciate the rich tradition of baseball in this area and see how the game has reflected the personality of its patrons. Through good times and bad, on warm summer nights and frigid spring evenings, the players have played and the fans have cheered, forging a partnership of perseverance and pride, providing bedrock for the area's peaks, plateaus, and valleys.

Enjoy the Read!

Greater Binghamton's Baseball History

Greater Binghamton's baseball roots can be traced to the 1860's, when amateur and semi-pro baseball gained popularity after soldiers returned from the Civil War. The earliest professional team in Binghamton that was part of a professional league played in 1877, when the Binghamton Crickets were one of 28 teams in the League Alliance, which had no major league affiliation. Baseball was in its nascent stages then, with the National League only being formed the previous year. The teams in the Alliance were largely in the Northeast, though teams ranged as far west as the Minneapolis Browns and as far south as the Memphis Reds.

Legend has it that Binghamton's team became known as the Crickets largely due to the influence of the Hayes brothers—Henry and Joseph. On their return to Binghamton from a trip to the British Isles, they brought back an extensive outfit for playing cricket. This led to a cricket club being formed and when it came time to select a name for the baseball team, Hayes and their friends displayed a distinct lack of imagination by coming up with the name "Crickets."

The association with the League Alliance lasted only one year. In 1878 Binghamton placed a team in the International Association for one year and then the area went without an organized team until 1885. During much of the last two decades of the nineteenth century this was a pattern that repeated itself: Binghamton would have a team for a few years, then suspend operations, then begin operation again. It wasn't until 1899 that Binghamton started an extended streak of continuous baseball.

From 1899 through the 1919 season Binghamton housed a minor league team, giving it a string of twenty-one consecutive seasons. After not having a team from 1920 through 1922, Binghamton started a string of 45 consecutive seasons with a baseball team from 1923 through the 1968 season. In 1969 Binghamton was again without a team until the New York Mets brought baseball back to Binghamton in 1992. April of 2014 introduced the 100th year of a minor league team in the Greater Binghamton Area.

During the area's five score years of hosting professional baseball, the list of notable baseball personalities calling Binghamton home have included "Wee Willie" Keller, who played for the Binghamton Bingos in 1892 and hit .373 on his way to the Hall of Fame; Daniel Maurice Casey, who claimed to be the "Casey" in Ernest Thayer's *Casey at the Bat* iconic poem; Whitey Ford, who won 234 big league games while being the ace of the Yankees throughout the 1950's and early 60's; and such modern big league stars as Matt Harvey, David Wright, and Jose Reyes.

A few major league teams have been affiliated with the minor league franchises in the Binghamton area through the years, but until the arrival of the Mets, the area's baseball heritage was synonymous with the Yankees, which served as the parent affiliation of the Binghamton Triplets from 1932 to 1968, with the exception of the three years from 1962 through 1964. The Triplets played their home games at Johnson Field, which stood from

1913-1968. The Yankees took an active interest in Binghamton, often sending the major league team to play an exhibition game at Johnson Field.

In 1923 the Binghamton area baseball team became known as the "Triple Cities Baseball Club," in honor of the communities of Binghamton, Johnson City, and Endicott. In the 1920's newspapers referred to the team as the "Binghamton Triplets" and the moniker stayed with the team until baseball left the Greater Binghamton Area after the 1968 season.

Binghamton's prominent place in baseball history can be directly attributed to George F. Johnson, who, along with Henry B. Endicott, incorporated the Endicott Johnson Shoe Company in 1920. The company's headquarters was in Johnson City and its factories dominated the Greater Binghamton Area in the early twentieth century. In addition to being an astute businessman, George F. Johnson was a philanthropist, who believed not so much in accumulating wealth as dispersing it. In 1935 the *New York Times* reported that when Endicott Johnson was incorporated, Johnson's wealth was seven million dollars. In 1942, it had gone down to two million dollars, with much of it going back to the community, as Johnson explained his philosophy:

"The use of my own private wealth, in the building of hospitals, churches, community betterments of every kind, shape or nature, and encouraging all things which help the people to a happier existence – has been of great use and benefit. I have dispersed most of my fortune…largely in this community. I have plans which will dispose of practically all the balance. Believing wealth received by the consent of society and the cooperation of the community, rightly belongs to that community in the final distribution, I have acted on this belief."

It was in 1912 that Johnson became the sole owner of the Binghamton team and one of the first things he did was to commission his brother, Charles Fred Johnson, to build a stadium for his team. The stadium was open for competition in 1913, at the corner of North Brockton and Broad Streets, and appropriately enough, was named Johnson Field. Up until this time, professional baseball games had been played in an area of Binghamton called "Stow Flats," which was near the Stow Manufacturing Company (Binghamton's State Plaza shopping center now resides in this spot). The opening of Johnson Field put a stamp on Lestershire as a growing community and when the community renamed itself Johnson City in 1916, it marked not only an appreciation of the growing shoe factory and the entire Johnson family, but also signified the start of a golden era for the village.

Johnson Field was built to fit within the existing contours of the area, which meant it had to fit between existing houses and streets, giving it quirky field dimensions. When players first set foot on Johnson Field, the 318-foot distance straight down the left field line caught their attention almost as much as the center field fence, which was only 340 feet away! In a sense, the field was the antithesis of such stadiums as Yankee Stadium and the Polo Grounds, whose deep dimensions to the center field fence made players refrain from hitting fly balls to straight-away center.

The 1920's saw the addition of CFJ Park (named for Charles F. Johnson) and the Endicott Johnson Pavilion (used for dinners, dancing, boxing matches, and a performance arena for prominent entertainers), as well as the electrification and expansion of Main Street. Almost a half century before Rod Serling brought national attention to Greater Binghamton with his "Walking Distance" *Twilight Zone* episode (episode # 6 in 1959, the first season) the community of Johnson City had many of its businesses, churches and attractions within walking distance of each other. In the ensuing years, players for the Triplets lived and socialized in the immediate vicinity of Johnson Field as well, taking advantage of not only being able to walk to the ballpark, but also of being able to walk to churches, businesses, and such restaurants and watering holes as "Frankie's" (later "Zopp's," now closed, though the building still stands), "Mickey's Blue Haven" (now "Giblin's"), and "Red's Kettle Inn."

Today the Johnson City Senior Citizen's Center sits where baseball fans once cheered hometown heroes such as Lefty Gomez, Tom Tresh, and Vic Raschi and such exhibition game opponents as Joe DiMaggio, Lou Gehrig, Mickey Mantle, and Babe Ruth.

When the Binghamton Baseball Shrine opened its doors in 1993, perhaps they opened widest for George F. Johnson. Without Johnson, Binghamton's baseball history would only have turned out to be a shadow of what it has become. Ironically, if Johnson were alive today, because of current business practices, he might not even be a baseball fan, though it was his favorite game as a youth and he enjoyed taking his friends to the World Series every fall during much of his adult life.

Can you picture a major league owner selling a baseball player to another team and then insisting that the player keep the money? Or an owner refusing to display advertising that bordered the playing field? Well, those were two things that Johnson firmly believed in when he was the owner of the Binghamton team. He did not believe in advertising adorning the outfield walls because it took attention away from the game as he felt baseball was not so much a business as a community asset. In 1919 when Philadelphia A's owner and manager, Connie Mack, agreed to pay $2,500 for Patrick Martin, the star left hander of the Binghamton team, Johnson insisted Martin keep the money!

Johnson became so disgruntled with the business practices that were beginning to influence baseball that after the 1919 season he allowed ownership of the Binghamton franchise to revert back to the International League (then AA) and he wanted no money for doing so. Indeed, when the franchise was awarded to Akron for $25,000 Johnson was incensed. He was angry that the $25,000 did not go directly to the players; he felt it was unfair that they be automatically assigned to the Akron team without remuneration.

Johnson's magnanimity extended well beyond the baseball fields. Today Greater Binghamton still has a plethora of homes that were built and subsidized by the Endicott Johnson Corporation, as employees shared in the cost of building a home through payroll deductions. Along with these "EJ houses" are an abundance of parks that were built by the company as well. Among the parks that George F. Johnson gave to the area besides CFJ Park in Johnson City are Recreation Park in Binghamton, West Endicott Park and Enjoie Park in Endicott.

Johnson's disgruntlement with the business of professional baseball explained the absence of minor league baseball from 1920 through the 1922 season. But when the American Legion Posts of Endicott, Binghamton, and Johnson City brought baseball back to the area with the 1923 season, Johnson became a key financial supporter of the team, though he preferred to stay out of the day-to-day operations of the team.

Johnson was instrumental in getting the Yankees to purchase the Binghamton team in 1932. As the depression took foothold in the nation, the Yankees were interested in developing a farm system and the Binghamton community was interested in getting a major league affiliation. Johnson opened discussion with the Yankees and made improvements to Johnson Field to solidify the area's negotiating position.

In July of 1932, the New York Yankees became official owners of the Binghamton Triplets. In the accounting offices of the Yankees and the Triplets, the Binghamton franchise became incorporated as the *Binghamton Exhibition Company* and 5,000 shares of stock of the company were issued, with each share having a value of one hundred dollars. These shares were then transferred to George Weiss, who represented the New York Yankees and at the time was charged with creating and running the farm system for the parent team. With this transaction New York City became irrevocably linked with the Greater Binghamton Area.

The Yankees would remain affiliated with the Triplets until the end of the 1968 season, with the exceptions of the three years from 1962-1964, when the Triplets team was an affiliate of the Kansas City Athletics in '62 and '63 and an affiliate of the Milwaukee Braves in 1964. The Yankees resumed affiliation with Binghamton in 1965 and remained the parent club until professional baseball ceased operation after the 1968 season.

1992: Baseball Returns after 23 Years

Baseball returned to Binghamton in 1992 after a 23-year absence. For the residents in the Binghamton area, the surprise was not that it took so long for baseball to return; rather it was that baseball returned at all. Although from the moment baseball left town its return was generally discussed, for over two decades the talk reflected a low simmer, never reaching a boil.

In the mid 1960's, while the nation was roiling over political assassinations and the seemingly unending Vietnam war, the Greater Binghamton Area seemed serene as the SUNY Binghamton campus and industry stalwart IBM gave it a strong sense of stability, even as Johnson Field was targeted for demolition and the Endicott Johnson Corporation was fading. In order to fulfill its goal of expanding State Route 17, New York State needed to cut through the outfield of Johnson Field, requiring its destruction.

In 1966, two years before the Triplets played their final game at Johnson Field, a Broome County Sports Authority was formed to convince county government to purchase a 60-acre parcel of land for the building of a new stadium. This movement never gained momentum, however, as the topic of baseball brought with it visions of a few hundred fans attending games at Johnson Field in the late 1960's.

Once Johnson Field was gone, so too was minor league baseball as there were no more George F. Johnsons in the community to step forward and build a stadium. Without a stadium, the Greater Binghamton Area could not attract an owner or a professional league to bring baseball back.

In 1977, Binghamton City Council even established a 9-member commission to study the feasibility of building a sports stadium at the corner of Henry and Water Streets in downtown Binghamton. This stadium would house a semi-pro football team as well as a baseball team, but this too failed to gain any traction. Eventually, this site would be developed, but not for baseball; the Binghamton Regency Hotel was erected in 1990 (now known as the Doubletree Hilton Hotel).

And in 1978 then Binghamton Mayor Alfred J. Libous, given the choice of spending $30,000 for the purchase of five new police cars for the city or using the money to conduct a feasibility study for constructing a downtown stadium, opted for the police cars.

It took Mayor Juanita Crabb, who took office in January of 1982, to bring the baseball discussions to a heated debate in the late 1980's. From the start, as Crabb rekindled the area's baseball fever, three things rang true about the prospects of a stadium:

1. Most politicians did not want to build it.
2. Prospective owners did not want to build it
3. Tax payers did not want to pay for it.

The story of the building of Binghamton's NYSEG Stadium (originally called Binghamton Municipal Stadium) is a tale replete with hotly debated city council meetings, visions of doom and eventually the arrival of a knight in shining armor. Gerry Hunsicker, now Senior Advisor of Baseball Operations for the Los Angeles Dodgers and then the Minor League Director for the New York Mets, summed it up succinctly during the ground-breaking ceremony in the summer of 1991 when he said "without Juanita Crabb, this deal simply would not have been done."

In discussing the story of Binghamton's stadium, woven throughout the twists and turns of the plot, Mayor Crabb is omnipresent, a bright beacon for stadium supporters and a voice of unrestrained enthusiasm for baseball. Why her efforts have not yet put her into the Binghamton Baseball Shrine can be almost as hotly debated now as the building of a downtown stadium was in her days as mayor.

Her hard work ultimately convinced the New York Mets to step up and do the unorthodox by purchasing the minor league franchise and delivering the funds to build Binghamton a stadium in 1992.

The Mets not only financed $3.1 million dollars toward the building of a stadium, but they also bought the AA Eastern League Williamsport franchise to move it to Binghamton in time for the 1992 season. In the end, the Mets partnered with Binghamton for many reasons, not the least of which was that the cost of the stadium would be shared, as the city had a $1.4 million grant from the state's Urban Development Corporation to spend on the stadium. Williamsport mayor Jessie L. Bloom had made it clear that his city would not build a new stadium. Hunsicker stated, "We took probably a little more risk than we usually take." But the Mets wanted to come to Binghamton, as its geographical closeness to Shea Stadium was a big factor as well. Hunsicker let it be known that eventually the Mets would look to sell the franchise to local ownership.

The New York Mets organization retained ownership of the Binghamton franchise in 1992 and 1993. In 1994 five businessmen in Greater Binghamton came forward to purchase the Binghamton Mets for $4 million dollars. The group was comprised of George Scherer and two sets of brothers—Michael and Chris Urda and David and William Maines. Scherer had been a boyhood friend of Mike Urda's as they had been schoolmates all through the Binghamton school system and at Broome Community College and SUNY Binghamton as well. An executive officer for Binghamton Savings Bank arranged for the trio of Mike, Chris, and George to meet with the Maines brothers and, after a single meeting, the group agreed to join forces in becoming AA baseball owners. The sale of the franchise was completed in 1994.

The opening day ceremonies for the new stadium in 1992 actually took four days to complete, as Binghamton denizens suffered through three consecutive rainouts. But what were a few rainouts when they had already endured 23 years? Opening day ceremonies for Binghamton Municipal Stadium began on Thursday, April 12, 1992, when the Binghamton Mets were scheduled to take on the Harrisburg Senators, the farm club of the Montreal Expos. A steady rain fell from a low slate sky that enveloped the city.

Mayor Crabb had fought for this stadium for ten years and with such dignitaries on hand as Governor Mario Cuomo, who once played center field for St. John's under the tutelage of Louie Carnesecca; ex-Met shortstop Buddy Harrelson; and various New York front office personnel, as well as a sold-out crowd screaming to hear the yell of "Play Ball," Crabb was not going to be denied.

In late afternoon, under a steady rainfall, with the infield tarp-covered, Crabb approached a microphone behind home plate and started the ceremonies by praising the fans for their support and saluting their pride in being part of the historic return of baseball. She noted that the community's enthusiasm for baseball could be seen by the fans and their respective families who visited the field at various points of the stadium's construction during the year. She smiled recalling the weekend visitors to the construction site and the handful of people who ran the bases and roamed the outfield grass while the concrete and steel façade stood opposite the backdrop of the city. Crabb went on to thank the New York Mets' organization for being the official owners of the AA franchise.

Governor Cuomo was announced to a chorus of boos, but he quickly turned them to cheers when, under an umbrella while the rain steadily fell, he closed by exhorting, "I don't know about you, but I came here to see a ballgame. Let's play ball!"

After the opening comments, Cuomo, Crabb, and NY Mets co-owner Fred Wilpon all threw out ceremonial first pitches. The game, however, was officially called off at approximately 3:30 PM. Rain canceled Opening Day on Friday and Saturday as well. On the fourth day the Binghamton Mets defeated the Harrisburg Senators, 1-0, in the first game of a doubleheader on Easter Sunday. Baseball was finally back in Greater Binghamton and with the return of baseball, the Binghamton Baseball Shrine was soon to be born as well.

Greater Binghamton's Baseball Timeline...

Date	Event	Significance
1877	First Professional baseball team plays under the name of the Binghamton Crickets in the League Alliance.	This marks year #1 of minor league baseball in the Greater Binghamton Area. Team disbands in middle of the season.
1885	Binghamton Awarded franchise in New York State League	7-team league
1887	John "Bud" Fowler plays games for the Bingos before teammates and opposing teams object.	Fowler would later go on to start up Negro baseball teams at the turn of the century.
1892	Bingos win Eastern League Championship in its first year in the Eastern league	"Wee" Willie Keeler is the star player.
1913	Opening of Johnson Field in JC	George F. Johnson is primary team owner
1920-22	No organized team in Binghamton	Johnson disillusioned with selling players for a profit and lets team disband.
1923	The Eastern league (Class B) formed in Binghamton's Arlington Hotel and the city is given a franchise.	Johnson sells team to three American Legion Posts— Binghamton, Johnson City, and Endicott, hence the Triple Cities (a.k.a Triplets) name.
1932	New York Yankees buy franchise	Yankee Teams often play exhibition games at Johnson Field throughout next quarter century
1962-63	Kansas City A's affiliate for 1962 and 63	Ken 'Hawk" Harrelson and Tony LaRussa are teammates on the 1962 team.
1964	Binghamton joins Class A NY PENN League as Milwaukee Braves affiliate	Andy Pafko is the manager and Mike Lum and Cito Gaston are prominent players.
1965	Yankees return as affiliate	Triplets finish first with 81 wins
1968	Final year of baseball at Johnson Field	Thurman Munson is the star player
1992	Baseball returns to Binghamton with the AA Mets in Eastern League (Champions)	NY Mets own the franchise, pitcher Bobby Jones, catcher Brook Fordyce and manager Steve Swisher lead team to EL Title.
January-1994	NY Mets sell franchise to local Binghamton ownership	Brothers Michael and, Chris Urda, and partners George Scherer, and David and William Maines are the new local owners.
September 1994	Eastern League Champions; AA All-Star Game held in Binghamton	Team members include Edgardo Alfonzo, Rey Ordonez, Jason Isringhausen, Jay Payton, Bill Pulsipher
March, 2001	Binghamton Municipal Stadium gets renamed to NYSEG Stadium	B-Mets negotiate a more favorable lease agreement with state officials. State forgives the $1.4M stadium debt largely due to efforts of State Senator Tom Libous.
2002	10th-year Anniversary All-Time Binghamton Mets team named	C: B. Fordyce; 1B: B. Daubach ; 2B: E. Alfonzo; SS: R. Ordonez; 3B: B. Huskey; OF: J. Payton; OF: J. Tyner; OF: A. Escobar; RHP: B. Jones; LHP: B. Pulsipher; reliever: J. Riggan
2013	Binghamton Mets finish 1st in Northern Division, but lose in first round of playoffs	Team finishes with 86-55 record. Number of wins second in area history, to the 96 wins of the 1953 Triplets.

Tales From the Shrine

The Binghamton Baseball Shrine began as a joint effort among a group of local baseball fans and the Binghamton Mets. In forming the Shrine committee in 1992, the goal was to include local baseball historians as well as representatives of the Binghamton Mets. The original committee included:

- RC Reutemann, general manager of the Binghamton Mets
- John Fox, veteran area sportswriter
- Linda Mapes, local amateur baseball historian and author of "Johnson Field: A History," available from the Broome County Historical Society
- Jerry Toman, ex-general manager of the Binghamton Triplets

Over twenty years later the Shrine is still going strong, with its committee looking remarkably similar to the one in 1992:

- Jim Weed, general manager of the Binghamton Mets
- John W. Fox, sportswriter emeritus for the *Binghamton Press & Sun-Bulletin*
- Mike McCann, local amateur historian and co-author of "Baseball in Broome County"
- Joe McCann, local amateur historian
- Lou Howell, catcher for the Triplets from 1966-1968 and coach at Susquehanna Valley High School for a number of years
- Carl Gaffney, Section IV Hall of Fame member for longtime basketball officiating, and season ticket holder since 1992

Shrine Rules for Election

In forming the Binghamton Baseball Shrine, the founders wanted to not only recognize those athletes who contributed to the Binghamton baseball legacy, but also desired to pay tribute to the area's deep roots in the development and popularity of the sport in the twentieth century. In devising the criteria for election to the Shine, the constant was on the athlete's connection to the Binghamton area.

In order to be elected to the Binghamton Baseball Shrine, the inductee must no longer be an active player and have accomplished at least one of the following:

- Played for a Binghamton professional baseball team and performed in outstanding fashion or went on to achieve success in major league baseball after playing in the Binghamton area. If, while playing in Binghamton, a player has led the league in batting average, home runs, or runs batted in, the player becomes a strong candidate.

- Been born and/or raised in the Greater Binghamton Area and went on to achieve success in major league baseball OR a Binghamton Professional Team (i.e., Bingos, Crickets, Triplets, Mets, etc.)

Note: The same general rules apply for non-playing members of the Shrine (e.g., George F. Johnson, John H. Johnson, John Fox, and Jerry Toman).

The Shrine committee generally meets three times a year to conduct its business, with numerous e-mails exchanged in between the meetings. The first meeting often occurs in November, which essentially serves as a nominating meeting. Then the committee gets together in the spring, usually at the beginning of the season to hear oral arguments on the merits of election for each nominee. Then a final meeting, usually conducted by the end of June, is held to finalize the inductees and finalize the plans for the induction ceremonies. Usually the vote is unanimous, but on some occasions a majority vote has proven to be sufficient.

All expenditures for the event are paid by the owners of the Binghamton franchise, which generally include all the expenses incurred by the inductees (e.g., travel, hotel and meal costs).

When it comes time to recognize those players who excelled while playing for Binghamton, it is easy to understand why so many of them return for their Shrine induction. Besides coming back as a way of thanking the community for their development as players and men, they come back to rekindle friendships and visit old stomping grounds. In coming back to Binghamton they return not in their youth, but as seasoned veterans who are proud to recognize their stay in Binghamton as a key part of their professional and personal growth. Though this may be their first visit since they left, the memories of their stay have always been within "walking distance" from any point in their memories.

Theirs is a happy story, and their induction is a day of smiles. They come to remember, and in doing so, they echo the lessons learned by Martin Sloane, the protagonist of the Twilight Zone episode "Walking Distance." Rod Serling, the creator of the "Twilight Zone," was proud to call Binghamton his hometown, as his family moved this area when he was 3-years-old.

In "Walking Distance," Gig Young portrays Martin Sloane, who has his car break down outside his hometown; Sloane decides to walk back to where he grew up, hoping to gain a respite from the pressures of his adult life. Serling based this episode on his memories of growing up on Bennett Avenue on the West Side of Binghamton, just a few blocks from Recreation Park. Ironically Serling's boyhood home is only a five-minute walk from the Davis Street home of "Wild Bill" Hallahan, clearly the most famous baseball player who called Binghamton the city of his birth. If Serling's canvas had been baseball instead of words, he too would be in Binghamton's shrine. In his introduction to "Walking Distance," Serling proudly stated "Everyone has to have a hometown, and mine is Binghamton, NY."

David Wright, captain of the New York Mets, called Binghamton his home for two months in the 2004 season. In a radio interview he had with Boomer Esiason and Craig Carton (hosts of the "Boomer and Carton" morning radio show on WFAN) after he was an established star, he said it was in AA baseball that he first realized he had a real shot to make it to the big leagues. As a teenager playing in amateur baseball leagues in Virginia he mostly played against top talent in the Northeast and did not have the chance to play against the elite athletes from California and Texas. At Binghamton in 2004 he played against top talent from all over the nation and he dominated the league during his short stay, hitting .363 with 10 home runs and 40 RBIs in only 223 at bats. The momentum from Binghamton carried him to the big leagues by July of 2004. The most important thing he learned was that his talent could take him to the big leagues.

Bill Virdon, 1960 World Series Champion, 1955 NL Rookie of the Year, and a big-league manager for 13 years from 1972 to 1984, credits the Binghamton area as an essential step in his development as a player, saying that playing at Binghamton was a step he needed to take along the way to the major leagues. He has always cherished the wonderful treatment he received from the community and the fans during the summer of 1952, when he played center field for the Triplets.

In the next few pages we recount a few of the more memorable stories of the "walk home" that the inductees experienced during their induction weekend. While these stories are not as dramatic as that of Martin Sloane, they are full of humor and small moments, portraying the importance of the everyday moments that add up to the living of a life and the development of a professional ball player.

"Welcome to the Big Leagues, Johnny"

In 1955, Johnny Blanchard had just completed the best year he would ever have in his professional career. As the first string catcher for the Triplets in 1955, he hit .281 with 34 home runs and after the last game of the year he went with a few teammates to "Mickey's Blue Haven" (now called "Giblin's"), a restaurant and bar on Main Street in Johnson City, a short walk up North Broad Street from Johnson Field.

While he was hoisting a few and having a late-game snack, he heard the bartender call out, "Is Johnny Blanchard here? Phone call for Johnny Blanchard." Blanchard was wondering who would be calling him at that late hour. He picked up the phone and said "Hello, Blanchard speaking."

'Hello, Johnny. This is George Weiss and I want to congratulate you on being called up to the Yankees!"

Suddenly it was clear to Blanchard why he got called to the phone. His teammates were playing a gag on him. Blanchard's face twisted in annoyance as he looked into the phone. "Yeah, you're George Weiss, and I'm Babe Ruth. Good-bye!"

Blanchard emphatically hung up the phone and rejoined his buddies, determined to show he was too smart to be suckered into such a banal prank.

"Who was that on the phone, Johnny?"

Blanchard barked, "Aw, just some wise guy saying he was George Weiss."

Blanchard resumed his eating and drinking and having merriment. After about 15 minutes, Zeke Bella, his roommate on the road, came through the doors, looking for Blanchard.

'Hey, Johnny, the Yankees have been trying to get hold of you. George Weiss just called the stadium!"

Blanchard's eyes became wide. He shook a bit.

"Uh, uh, someone called me a while ago and said he was Weiss. I hung up on him!"

Bella looked at Blanchard, smiling broadly. 'Oh man, c'mon, let's get back to the park so you can talk to him."

When Blanchard again got on the phone with Weiss, Weiss told him he was coming up to the Yankees to finish the season. He wanted him to report to the stadium as soon as possible. Blanchard stammered an "OK, that's great" over the phone and then got directions to Yankee Stadium. When he reported to the stadium the next day, after he and his wife drove all night and checked into a hotel in the wee hours of the morning, Blanchard was surprised to see an older man waiting for him.

"Hello, I'm Johnny Blanchard. I've been told to report here."

"Yes, I know who you are. I'm George Weiss. Don't ever hang up on me again!"

"No, no sir. Again, I apologize. I had no idea…"

"One more thing, Blanchard, before I fill you in on some administrative details."

"Yes sir?"

Weiss held out his hand. Then he smiled from ear to ear.

"Welcome to the big leagues!"

When Terry Strutted Like a Peacock

Another one of Blanchard's Yankee teammates from the 1960's with a self-deprecating sense of humor was ex-Triplet starting pitcher Ralph Terry, who fondly remembers his minor league playing days.

During his Shrine induction weekend in 2002, Terry remembered spending time with Ralph Houk and Tommy Lasorda with the Denver Bears in the 1950's, which was then a Triple-A farm club of the Yankees. One game the team was playing listless and player-manager Houk (he would get 4 at bats that year) murmured, "I wish we could do something to get these guys started, we need a fight or something."

Lasorda looked at him and said, "Yeah, what inning would you like it"

Houk smiled at him and said "I've always liked the third inning for a ruckus."

Lasorda was coaching first base at the time and in the third inning, a foul ball came to him. When he threw the ball back into play, he made sure to put something on it and he hit the first baseman, Stan Jok, in the foot! Within seconds he and Jok were exchanging words and rolling around the ground.

Lasorda looked into the dugout and gave Houk a big smile!

Ralph Terry was a teenager when he pitched for the Triplets in 1954. On July 22nd before that night's Triplets game, he drove up to Cooperstown, NY, to see the Yankees play the Hall of Fame game against the Cincinnati Reds. In those days, the Hall of Fame ceremonies took place in the morning, in front of the Hall of Fame on Main Street and then the witnesses and dignitaries made the short two-block walk to Doubleday Field to watch the annual game. That morning, Bill Dickey, Bill Terry, and Rabbit Maranville had been inducted in the Hall.

Upon reaching Doubleday Field, Ralph Terry got the attention of Jim Turner, the Yankee pitching coach, who told the security guard to let Ralph, clad in street clothes, onto the ball field. After some polite conversation, Turner told Terry "Go take a seat in the dugout next to the old guys." Terry strutted like a peacock to the bench. He was going to sit in the same dugout as his heroes: Berra, Ford, Mantle, and Bauer.

When he got to the bench, he took a seat alongside a frail-looking senior citizen, bedecked in a summer suit. Terry nodded a polite hello and took a seat next to him. The man's hands rested on a cane, he had thin gray hair, a thin face, and ears so large they could have been his wings if he were an angel.

As Terry settled in to watch the game, he noticed two other gentleman sitting to his neighbor's right. He could overhear them talking about batting techniques. Terry found their conversation annoying; he was trying to concentrate on the game, focused on watching the newly acquired Ralph Branca take the mound for the Yankees against journeyman Bud Podbielan of the Reds. Terry was especially excited about watching Branca, an ex-twenty-game winner for the Dodgers. They had more in common than just the same first name. In the late 40's Branca was a fire-balling youngster for the Dodgers, peaking in 1947 when he was 21-12. Terry was now one of the best pitching prospects for the Yankees and like Branca, his best pitch was a fastball.

Ironically, sitting on the bench that day, Terry had no idea how eerily similar their careers would be. Branca, in 1951, with the Dodgers leading the Giants 4-2, relieved Don Newcombe in the bottom of the ninth with two runners on. At approximately 3:30 PM on October 3rd he gave up the home run to Bobby Thomson that gave the NY Giants the pennant over the Dodgers.

Six years removed from his visit to Doubleday Field, on October 8, 1960, Terry would throw a high pitch to Bill Mazerowski and the Pirates would beat the Yanks, 10-9, in the seventh game of the 1960 World Series.

As Terry watched the first inning, he had no thoughts of failure on his mind. He soaked in the sold out crowd at Doubleday Field, and relished securing a seat on the bench to watch the World Champion Yankees.

He was busting with pride as he offered his hand to the senior citizen next to him.

"Hello, I'm Ralph Terry, and I pitch for the Binghamton Triplets, the Class A farm club of the New York Yankees."

The old man took his hand and offered him a frail handshake.

"You are a member of the Yankee organization, is that right? Glad to meet you."

Terry now leaned closer to the old man's ear. "Hey those two guys talking next to you seem to know a lot about hitting."

The old man gave him a wry smile. "Yes, they do." The old man was now looking directly at Terry and Terry could not take his eyes off the man's enormous ears.

"I'm Cy Young, nice to meet you."

Terry practically fell over. He was sitting next to baseball royalty. Cy Young won 511 games!

Cy saw Terry's shock. He would now go for the knockout.

"Ralph, let me introduce you to two of my buddies. The fella on the right is Zack Wheat and the fella holding the bat is Ty Cobb."

Cobb had a lifetime batting average of .366 over 24-year career and Zack Wheat hit .317 during his 19-year career, 18 of them as star outfielder for the Brooklyn Dodgers.

Terry's reply was a stammer. "Uh, uh.....glad to know you Mr. Cobb. Gl...gla...glad to know you Mr. Wheat."

"Mr. Norman, My Husband Is Not Going to Believe This"

In 2003 Fred Norman, a mainstay on the staff of the Big Red Machine of the 1970's, returned to Binghamton to be inducted into the Shrine, along with Pete Suder and John Montgomery Ward. Norman won 16 games during his two-year stay in Binghamton in 1962 and '63 when the Kansas City Athletics were the major league affiliate. Though he made his major league debut for the A's in 1962, he is best remembered for being part of the starting rotation of the Cincinnati Reds (a.k.a. the 'Big Red Machine") in 1975 and 1976.

The day after he was inducted he became animated when he was driven around the neighborhood that once housed Johnson Field. In an eager voice, Norman asked, "I used to live right around here. Do you mind if we drive around a bit to find the house I used to live in?"

Sure enough, his weekend host and driver, Mike McCann, found the blue house on 37 Plymouth Street, right behind the Johnson City Senior Citizens center. In the days of Johnson Field, the house sat behind the first base parking lot.

Norman broke a huge smile as he spotted the brick front porch.

"That's it! That's it! I used to sit on the porch all the time. Let's walk up and get a picture!"

As McCann scanned the porch he noticed a woman looking at him quizzically from the garage, which was behind the house. He got out of the car but looked toward Norman

"We better introduce ourselves first," stated McCann.

McCann slowly walked up the black asphalt driveway, pausing about two feet from the porch, as the woman met him in the middle of the driveway. He introduced himself and his companion, being sure to play up the point that Norman was a celebrity of sorts, having been inducted into the Shrine the previous night.

'Hello, I have Fred Norman with me. He used to play baseball for the Triplets and he lived in this house back when he played in the early 60's. He got inducted into our Hall of Fame last night."

The young lady now wore a wide smile. "My husband and I were at the game last night," she said as she looked at Norman. "He remembered watching you play in the majors." Her smile grew as wide as a half moon. "He's not going to believe this!"

Norman nodded, smiled, and asked, "Would you mind if we got a picture of me sitting on your porch?"

"No, no, of course not!"

As Norman took a seat on the porch, the woman asked Norman, "Would you mind signing the program we got last night? Oh, my husband is going to be so disappointed he missed you, he had to work today."

"I'd be happy to sign your program," Norman answered. Then he sat on the porch with a huge smile. McCann took his picture as he signed the program under the inscription, "Thanks for coming to the induction!"

Later that day Norman was driven the 90 or so miles to the Hall of Fame in Cooperstown and he delighted in touring the Cincinnati exhibits honoring the championship teams of 1975 and 1976. He asked specifically to see Sparky Anderson's plaque. After silently reading the text on the plaque, Norman said "he was a great manager, but an even greater person." Norman later became animated when he passed a picture of Pete Rose. "Just a great player, a great teammate, one of the greatest players ever to play the game," he said.

No doubt part of Norman's recollection focused on Rose's desire to do anything to win on a baseball field. In the mid-1960's Rose had established himself as an all-star second baseman, but in 1967 he became a left fielder to allow Tommy Helms to break into the lineup at 2B and in 1975 Rose moved back to the infield, becoming a third baseman, to give George Foster a chance to become a regular in LF. Rose's move to third paved the way for the Cincinnati Reds to dominate baseball in 1975 and 1976, becoming The "Big Red Machine," as Foster hit 52 HRs and knocked in 199 runs over those two years.

In a radio talk show in 2013, Rose said he felt that 1975 was his best year because he was able to change positions during the season without any preparation and doing so made the team that much stronger. He hit .317 that year, with 7 home runs and 74 RBIs. Though he won the MVP award in 1973 and had better statistical years than he had 1975, Rose marks 1975 as his best season because of the effect his change of positions had on the team.

Visiting Cooperstown often results in a day of reflection. As he left Cooperstown that day, Norman explained his own success in a humble and sincere manner. "I was fortunate to be born with a live arm."

Shrine Spinoff: The Fan of the Year Award

A significant byproduct of the Shrine has been the establishment of Binghamton's annual Fan of the Year Award, which was instituted in response to questions from community members as to why there weren't any fans in the Binghamton Baseball Shrine. "Fans are the core of the game," reasoned the advocates for recognizing the Binghamton baseball fan through a formal award.

Bill Terlecky, general manager of the Binghamton Mets from 2000 to 2005, instituted the "Fan of the Year" award in 2005 and named it after Joe Genneralli, who was a long-time Binghamton businessman who organized yearly baseball bus trips and hot stove dinners when the Triplets were the "toast of the town." Joe and his wife hosted scores of dinners for Binghamton players and coaches through the years and their home was the favorite destination of Lefty Gomez after Sunday afternoon games at Johnson Field when he managed the Triplets in 1946 and 1947.

Appropriately enough, the first winner of the award went to Joe's son, Fran, then a season ticket holder of the Binghamton Mets and ex-bat boy for the Triplets. You can find his name inscribed on the plaque for winners of this award in the concourse area behind home plate at NYSEG Stadium, which is also where the plaques for the Shrine inductees are located. The nine winners of this award thus far include: Fran Gennarelli, 2005; Denis Wickham, 2006; David Spence, 2007; Tom Miller, 2008; Ron Winn, 2009; Bob Crouse, 2010; Rich Perrin, 2011; Eileen Plunkett, 2012; and Carolyn Laskoski, 2013.

Denis Wickham, retired engineer, has been a season ticket holder since baseball returned to Binghamton in 1992. Upon receiving the Fan of the Year in its second year of inception, in 2005, he profoundly uttered, "What an honor to receive this award!" For many years, his season tickets were in the first row behind the visitor's dugout, giving him a direct view of the Mets dugout. His wife, Jean, has been with him every step of the way—along with his baseball glove, which he always keeps on his left hand, ready for action. During a game in 2009 a Mets batter hit a screamer—a line drive that made it to the stands almost before any fan could turn a head. Denis was sitting to the left of his wife as the ball streaked straight for her head. Jean was bending down to get her drink and the only warning Jean had that a missile was tracking her was a low buzz from the crowd that started as soon as the ball left the bat.

Denis, though, had seen the ball from the moment it left the bat and with graceful aplomb he reached around her, stuck out his glove and snatched the ball out of the air! The sound of ball hitting leather was soon accompanied with loud applause. Muttered more than one fan, "That ball was headed straight for her head, what a great catch!" Jean now turned her head toward Denis, "Somebody actually caught that ball?"

Denis slowly opened his glove and showed her the ball, a smile creasing his face.

Denis turned and gave a quick wave of his hand to the crowd, all the while his wife looking at him in shock. Denis had a huge smile, knowing he had made the catch of his life. While Wickham was acknowledging the crowd's applause, the visiting players turned their heads into the stands to see what happened. Wickham's pride was high, as he made eye contact with members of the visiting team and they pointed and smiled at him in acknowledgement of his great catch. Denis had become a real-life Walter Mitty.

Wickham refocused his eyes on the field for the next pitch, all the while lying to Jean, telling her the ball wasn't hit as hard as hard it looked and she was never in danger. Wickham's downplaying his feat did not have the intended effect on his wife, however. Though Denis loved those seats, the next season Jean demanded they move their seats to an area that was well above the dugout.

Denis still yearns for the day they can return to their original season seats.

Eileen Plunkett was voted Fan of the Year in 2012 and upon hearing her name announced as the winner of this award during the final home stand of the season, she turned to her season-long comrades and quipped, "OK, who's the wise guy who put the Mets up to this?" Being a middle/high school teacher for thirty years has left its mark on Eileen—she sees sophomoric tendencies in all of us. Today she can still be found sitting between home and the third base dugout and is often wearing a jersey of her favorite Binghamton player, Mike Nickeas, who played for Binghamton from 2006-2010.

Besides being a retired ninth-grade science teacher, Plunkett can also bake a "mean" batch of cookies. In 2013 she started baking cookies for the Mets players to take on their road trips and the cookies have been a huge hit. Cory Vaughn, an outfielder for the 2013 Eastern League Northern Division Champions, smiles broadly when he remembers one of the themes of those AA road trips—"We crush those cookies!" Cory Mazzoni, Vaughn's teammate, explained how they made him think twice about where he sat on the team bus. "If I sit in the back, the cookies are all gone by the time the snacks make it back to me!"

"Every time I go to a B-Mets game, I get to see the affiliate of MY team and it reminds me of my grandpa," says Plunkett, who grew up on Long Island. "He was the one who taught me about baseball and his Mets!" Eileen has had a season ticket since 2007 and cherishes how close the seats are to the field. "It may not be helping the pitchers, but I love the fact that the foul territory is so small here. You get to see all the action up close and I get the biggest kick out of seeing the guys play here and then getting to catch up with them again at Citi Field!"

NYSEG Stadium and Citi Field are not the only places Eileen catches up with her Mets; one of the benefits of being retired from the classroom trenches is that she now is able to go to Port St. Lucie every year to see "her boys" play in the spring as well. Jack Leathersich, lefty reliever for the Binghamton Mets in 2013, praised her knowledge of the game after eating dinner with her at a promotional event. "This woman really knows her baseball. Hats off to her," he tweeted to all his followers.

Perhaps the best known winner of the Fan of the Year Award is David Spence, who sits behind third base for all the Binghamton Mets games. Fans do not know him by name, but they know him by sound. At every game he can be heard yodeling and, at appropriate times, yelling "Let's Get a Dooooouuuuuuble Play! As entertaining as his yodeling and shouting is, though, his piece de resistance is his ability to use spoons as musical instruments. At opportune moments in the game, he can be heard drumming his set of spoons against one another to cheer on his hometown team!

Despite the award having already been given out 9 times, the list of candidates for the annual award is a large one; some of their stories are almost as interesting as the ones from the Shrine. Retired salesman Kevin Healy is emblematic of the scores of diehard Binghamton baseball fans who love to watch their hometown team. He has been a season ticket holder since 2004 and has kept score of over 570 games at NYSEG Stadium. He started keeping score of baseball games in 1964 and, in his own words, "has never looked back." Keeping score of games not only lets him think along with the players and managers as the game unfolds, but it also helps him remember some of the great games at NYSEG Stadium. He accompanies each of his scored games with a short summary paragraph.

Want to know what game Daniel Murphy hit three home runs for the Binghamton Mets? Healy will know Murphy played in Binghamton in 2008 and give him a few minutes and he'll return his scorecard from May 26th, 2008, where he wrote "Daniel Murphy hit three HRs (2-run in 3rd, 2-run in 7th, solo in 9th)." You look at the scorecard and see Murphy hit third and Mike Carp hit fifth that day, and Jon Niese was the starter, but the Reading Phillies beat the Mets, 8-7.

And what if you want to know who pitched the clincher for the Eastern League Championship the Mets won at home in 1992? Healy can answer that one instantaneously, and minutes later can show you the scorecard that shows the Mets beat the then Canton-Akron Indians, 5-2, behind the 4-hit pitching of right hander Bobby Jones. Healy noted at the bottom of his scorecard, "Bobby Jones retired the last 16 batters. Back-to-back errors by Jamie Hoffner in the first and his 3rd error in the second inning led to both C-A (unearned) runs."

Rooting for the B-Mets has been easy for Healy, as the New York Mets have been his favorite team since the team's inception. Healy proudly recalls the first Met game he saw in person. "1962, I saw the New York Mets win their 4th ever game when they tripped up the Phillies at Connie Mack Stadium, 7-5 in 12 innings. The date was May 6th."

When Healy has to take a rest room break, he just hands the scoring duties over to Cyndy, his wife of 41 years. Their motto in life is "The couple that scores together stays together."

The stories of the fans' love of their Binghamton Mets seem endless. On the eve of Memorial Day in 2004, the Binghamton Mets were holding a charity camouflage jersey auction after the game. The players had worn the jerseys during the game, signed them and now they were going to the highest respective bidders. Approximately 50 bidders sat in the stands and, as the auction wound down, David Wright and teammate Wayne Lydon popped out of the dugout and walked through the stands to get a close look at the proceedings, nodding hello to the bidders and smiling broadly.

Wright grew animated as the fans started bidding on #44, his number with the B-Mets. The bids came fast.

Gary Pratt, a retired elementary school teacher and girl's softball coach for thirty years for the Deposit, NY school district, sat in his seat but did not raise his bid card. Though Pratt was a Wright fan, he had promised himself before the game that he would not bid on #44. "The bids will go too high," he told himself.

He tried to block out the auctioneer's barking. "This is the final jersey of the night! I have $300, do I hear $350.00? Now I've got $350.00, I've got $400.00....I've got $450.00, who has $500.00?"

Suddenly, Pratt was holding up his bid card. He already had won bids for three jerseys; he did not need a fourth. The bids reached $700.00 and Pratt's right hand was still going up! What was he doing?

When the auctioneer paused ever so slightly at the $900.00 mark, Wright put on his jersey and then pranced in the concourse, slowly taking the jersey off to humorous hoots from the stands. Wright's dance worked—now the bids approached one thousand dollars!

The bidding was down to two people.

The auctioneer, looking at Wright, then at Pratt, shouted out, "C'mon, all the money goes to charity, do I hear a thousand dollars? Wright looked into the stands and yelled, "If the bid goes over a thousand dollars, I'll take the winning bidder to lunch!"

Pratt's arm shot up once again. He had bid one thousand dollars! Wright was all smiles, nodding his head in support.

The auctioneer was not done, however. "I've got $1,000 dollars! Do I hear another bid? Will anyone go higher? C'mon, we're at one thousand, do I hear $1,010.00? You can't let it get away for just ten dollars!

Six-foot four-inch Bob Topa fidgeted in his seat as the auctioneer looked at him and then he raised his hand to increase the bid to $1,010.00. Topa was bidding for his then 12-year-old son, Justin, a diehard fan and ironically, almost a decade later, a 2013 draft pick and signee of the Pittsburgh Pirates.

The auctioneer now looked at Pratt.

Wright looked at Pratt.

Squirmed in his seat did Pratt.

Pratt raised his hand one final time and then, after waiting for one of the longer moments of his life, the jersey was his for a winning bid of $1,020.00, which is still the all-time record for a jersey auction held by the B-Mets!

Wright was all smiles and stayed to sign autographs and talk to the fans. He and Pratt exchanged small talk and Wright gave him his cell phone number so they could firm up the lunch date. Gary asked him for one favor—did he have an extra cap? Wright said "Sure, give me a minute, I'll be right back." A few minutes later Wright handed Pratt his game cap from that night, which contained the inscription "Nena and Pops Forever" on the underside of the bill, in honor of his parents.

By the time Wright left the stadium it was close to midnight. Pratt went home with four jerseys, a tentative lunch date, and lifetime memories.

The next day, however, Wright was called up to Norfolk for a six-week sojourn before he made his debut with the Mets on July 21st.

Gary still has Wright's phone number in his cell, but has never called to collect his lunch. He often goes to watch the Mets in spring training, and one of these days he just might try to get the attention of Wright and ask for a quick lunch in St. Lucie!

Mark Berghorn has made all twenty-two opening days for the Binghamton Mets and even remembers being the 256th person in line when tickets for the first opening day went on sale in the winter of 1992. He got on line at 5 AM that day as the line stretched for a quarter of a mile up State Street and extended eastward along Court Street, almost reaching the court house. The closest he came to missing an opening day game was when his son, Scott had a game on the same night. Mark got him to change out of his uniform in the car and father and son made it inside the stadium for the 5th inning.

Despite all the opening days he has attended, none of them compare with his most memorable game, which occurred on May 19, 2000. That was the night Mark proposed to his girlfriend. At the time the B-Mets had a promotion called "Lady Fan of the Game" and it was sponsored by a local florist. One of the team's mascots, "Buddy the Bee," would bring the lucky female a rose with a card that read, "Congratulations on being selected as the Lady Fan of the Game." Well, before the game started that night, Mark arranged for "Buddy" to select his girlfriend as the "Lady Fan of the Game" and got Buddy to deliver a special card that asked, "Debbie – Will you Marry Me?"

The rest, as they say, is history.

Mark and Debbie will be celebrating their 14th wedding anniversary during the upcoming season. Ironically though, Debbie is not the only relative that Mark can directly trace to the baseball diamond. As a season ticket holder, Mark often takes advantage of getting to the park long before the gates officially open so that he can see batting practice and informally chat with the players. During the 1994 season he chatted so often with backup catcher Tony Tijerina that they became fishing buddies. Late in the season Mark's sister, Linda, who was working in Washington, DC, came to visit him. Mark introduced her to Tony and once again, the rest, as they say, is history. Mark was the best man at their September wedding in 1997.

Mark is quick to point out that one of Tijerina's proudest baseball moments was being a member of the 1994 Eastern League Championship team where he played alongside such players as Edgardo Alfonzo, Rey Ordonez, Bill Pulsipher, Jason Isringhausen, and Ricky Otero. After that '94 season was over, Tijerina would often mention to Mark that he couldn't wait to receive his championship ring. Well, that was the only opening Mark needed and pretty soon Mark "the miscreant" was writing a letter to Tony that went something like this—

```
Dear Player:

Congratulations on winning the Eastern League title this year! Due to
unforeseen costs, however, we are asking each player to contribute to
the cost of his championship ring. Please submit a check for $354.62 if
you would like a ring.

Regards,


Binghamton Mets Ownership
```

Shortly after sending the letter, Mark received a phone call from Tony, where Tony fumed over having to pay for his ring.

"Can you imagine that?" Tijerina exhorted to Berghorn. "A form letter asking me to pay for my ring—right down to the penny! Now I know why this is called the Bush Leagues!" After letting Tijerina vent for a while, Berghorn confessed to writing the letter. They still laugh about it today, brothers-in-law and best friends that they are.

How many fans do you know have ever been a candidate to have a bobble head doll made of them and given away as a promotion? Well, in 2008 that is exactly what happened to long-time Binghamton Mets fan, Mike "Jingles" Rubino. He still loves being called "Jingles," which was his nickname as a kid playing ball on the sandlots, when the change in his pocket would jingle as he ran.

The Binghamton Mets offered fans a voice in selecting the personality for a bobble head night in 2008. The voting took place online and at the stadium over a span of approximately six weeks. Fans submitted 18,433 votes and had the option of voting for several local personalities. Though Rubino lost in the fan balloting (former Binghamton Triplets and New York Yankees pitcher Steve Kraly won), his nomination just increased his celebrity status within the gates of NYSEG Stadium, where he is widely known as the "dancer during the seventh-inning stretch." When the music starts to play, Rubino is often seen dancing in the aisle behind home plate.

Rubino has been known to voice his displeasure with both umpire and player performance from time to time. On his more nettlesome nights, he can be heard yelling criticism at both manager and player, home and visiting team alike, holding his ticket high, showing everyone that he paid his way into the game and has the right to point out poor play. Rubino is often part of the memories that the players take with them from Binghamton. In 2004, Benny Agbayani, when asked what he remembered most about his time in Binghamton, was quick to mention to Scott Lauber, reporter for the *Binghamton Evening Press,* that he got a kick out of "Jingles, that fan who danced in the stands." Brian Daubach, who has been a minor league manager in the Nationals' system for the past few years, brought up Rubino in a conversation he had with Binghamton area fans during spring training 2012. "Is 'Jingles' still going to the games?" Daubach wanted to know. In 2014 Daubach will be able to answer his own question when he visits NYSEG Stadium as the manager of the Harrisburg Senators.

No discussion of the baseball fans in Greater Binghamton can close without mentioning Mike Urda, who is President of the Binghamton Mets and also serves as the spokesman for the local ownership group. Mike is one of those guys with whom you can sit and talk baseball for hours and have it seem like minutes. Some of his best childhood memories are of watching his hometown Triplets play against such future major league stars as Bobby Bonds (Barry's father) and Jerry Koosman, and of getting to see the likes of Thurman Munson and Horace Clarke play every day.

His memories of his B-Mets are bountiful, but one story that he especially likes to tell is when he and Steve Phillips, then general manager for the New York Mets, were watching Jason Isringhausen make an early season start in 1995. "It was in April and it was one of those bitterly cold days. Steve Phillips was sitting next to me and we were seated right behind home plate," Urda explains as he sets the stage. A smile crosses his face as he continues, "Isringhausen was unbelievable that day, he struck out 13 of the first fifteen batters he faced! But around the fourth inning, I was freezing so I asked Steve if he wanted to move up to a skybox. Phillips looked at me and said he was freezing too, but there was no way he was going to move and risk jinxing Isringhausen. So we just sat in amazement at Isringhausen's performance!"

Phillips was so impressed with Isringhausen that day that by July he was in the New York Mets' rotation and wound up winning nine games for the big league team in less than half a season.

The common theme running through these stories of making a catch, baking cookies, yodeling, keeping score, winning a bid, making a proposal, dancing in the aisle, and sitting in the freezing cold is the pleasure of weaving baseball into everyday lives for these fans. Just as stories unfold on the diamond, they unfold in the stands as well. The Fan of the Year Award allows the fans to take a well-deserved bow.

Binghamton: The Core of Big Apple Baseball

In looking at the minor league history of both the Yankees and the Mets, Binghamton is a common denominator. From 1932 until 1968, with the exception of 1962 through 1964, Binghamton was a key cog in the Yankees' minor league system and since 1992 Binghamton has been the AA farm club of the New York Mets, giving the Greater Binghamton Area a total of 64 years of sending players to the Big Apple. Because of this lengthy pipeline to New York City baseball, Binghamton can arguably claim the title of being the most influential minor league city for New York City baseball.

The only other region in America that can come close to Binghamton's 64 years of sending players to the Big Apple is the area in and around Norfolk, Virginia. Norfolk was a low-level minor league team of the Yankees from 1934 through 1955 before becoming the AAA affiliate of the Mets from 1993 until 2006. After you add in the years that Tidewater was also a AAA farm team for the Mets (from 1969 to 1992), the Tidewater region has sent ball players to the Big Apple for 59 years.

In reviewing the history of the Mets and Yankees, you not only come across hundreds of players who called Binghamton their home before performing for the Yankees or Mets, but you also learn how the Binghamton franchise has supplied its parent club with players at an unprecedented pace. Also, in closely looking at Binghamton baseball, you can make a strong case that events in Binghamton in 2004 cost the NY Mets post-season appearances in 2007 and 2008. Finally, it is worth noting the important, though indirect, role Binghamton played in restoring baseball to Brooklyn.

One of the most successful periods for the New York Yankees was the early 1960's; from 1960 through 1964, the Yankees won five American League pennants and two World Championships. The Binghamton Shrine includes no fewer than nine players who played pivotal roles for the Yankees in those championship years; infield starters included Moose Skowron, Bobby Richardson, Clete Boyer, and Joe Pepitone. Starting pitcher Whitey Ford won 94 games during those five years while Ralph Terry won 76, and Al Downing won 26 for the Yankees in 1963 and '64. The 1962 Rookie of the Year, Tom Tresh, was a star outfielder for the '62-'64 teams, hitting 61 home runs and knocking in 237 runs. Backup catcher and outfielder Johnny Blanchard hit 61 home runs and knocked in 170 runs from 1960 through 1964.

One member of those 1960-era Yankee teams even played a pivotal, though indirect role in the 1969 championship and 1973 pennant-winning seasons of the Mets. Ralph Terry was finishing his career in 1966 when he ran across Tug McGraw that fall; Tug was in the instructional league and Terry was working on his knuckleball and playing a lot of golf. It was here that Terry taught McGraw how to throw the screwball, as McGraw recapped in his book, *Screwball*:

"…we played a lot of golf together in the sun that fall. And he started to suggest that I turn the ball over when I pitched it, taking something off my fastball and turning my wrist in toward my body when I released that pitch. He showed me how it would spin, using a golf ball as a prop, and right there my screwball was born—on a golf course in Florida."

McGraw returned to pitch in AAA in 1967, and the improvement from his prior season in AAA was remarkable. His E.R.A dropped from 4.22 to 1.99 and he won ten games, pitching 167 innings for Jacksonville that year. It took him one more year of mastering the pitch and his control in the minors, but in 1969, when he rejoined the NY Mets, he became a reliever, saving 12 games and teaming with Ron Taylor to give the Mets an unmatched lefty-righty combination out of the bullpen.

In 1973 McGraw's performance both on and off the field became legendary in Mets history. He coined the phrase "Ya Gotta Believe" as the Mets struggled through most of the year, then got hot in the last month to win the NL East crown with only 82 wins. That team beat the Big Red Machine in the NL playoffs, but lost to the Oakland A's in a seven-game World Series. McGraw was the closer and was sensational during the months of August and September. After that '73 season, McGraw wrote his autobiography, called it "Screwball," and sent one of the first copies to Terry with the inscription "Ralph, thanks for giving me a career!"

The Mets and Yankees have met only once in the World Series and when this occurred in 2000, Binghamton's presence was prominent in the Mets lineup. Of the 48 players the Mets used that year, 14 were ex-Binghamton players, including six pitchers and eight position players. Bobby Jones, Shrine member and the ace of the 1992 Binghamton Mets, won 11 games in 2000 and authored the best post-season pitching performance in Mets history when he threw a one-hit shutout against the Giants in the National League Division Playoffs.

Second baseman and Shrine member Edgardo Alfonzo hit .324 with 24 home runs and 94 RBIs for the National League Champs, providing an RBI target for cleanup hitter Mike Piazza. Benny Agbayani, Binghamton alumnus from 2006, had a .386 on base percentage for the NY Mets that year and played alongside Jay Payton, who hit .291 and smashed 17 home runs while knocking in 62 runs and playing an excellent center field.

Roger Neel, noted sports broadcaster in the Binghamton area, feels that Payton was one of the most impressive players he saw come through Binghamton. In talking to the Binghamton Mets Booster Club in 2013, he explained that "When people think of the best players to come through Binghamton, and who had the great years, you always think of David Wright, but I often think of Jay Payton as well. I really think Payton could have achieved greatness in the major leagues as well if he did not get hit with so many injuries during his career."

Even with his injuries, Payton had a solid 12-year major league career, hitting .279 with 119 HRs and 522 RBIs. His best year was 2003 when he hit .302 and socked 28 home runs for the Colorado Rockies, while knocking in 89 runs. As the Shrine committee considers naming future inductees, Payton's credentials, as both a B-Met and major leaguer, will garner him a lot of votes.

The "core four" of the Mets in 2000 of Agbayani, Payton, Alfonzo, and Jones clearly did not have the staying or performance power of the core four of the Yankees that year— Andy Pettite, Bernie Williams, Jorge Posada and Derek Jeter, but without the contributions of that quartet from Binghamton, there would have been no playoffs for the Mets. Interestingly a number of ex-Binghamton Mets were involved in trades that brought key players to that 2000 team, including:

- Pitcher Ed Yarnall and center fielder Preston Wilson for Mike Piazza (from the Marlins)
- Pitcher Jesus Sanchez was part of the deal for Al Leiter (also the Marlins)
- Octavio Dotel was part of the trade that brought Mike Hampton and Derek Bell from the Astros
- Mike Kinkade and Leslie Brea were traded as part of the Mike Bordick deal with the Orioles

Since that 2000 season, the Binghamton franchise has provided the parent team with players at a steady and unprecedented pace. While the AAA affiliation has moved from Norfolk to New Orleans to Buffalo to Las Vegas since 2006, the Binghamton franchise has remained constant. In 2012, the NY Mets, on multiple occasions, fielded nine starters who spent significant time in Binghamton along the way. The first occurrence took place on July 7th, when Dillon Gee beat the Cubs and Jeff Samardzija, 3-1 at Citi Field. Gee pitched eight innings, giving up one run and getting the win while Bobby Parnell got the save. Ike Davis hit a two-run home run in the third inning and Jordany Valdespin hit a solo shot in the fourth to account for all the runs for the Mets. The starting lineup for the Mets that day, complete with their batting averages after the game's completion:

Batting	AB	R	H	RBI	BA
Ruben Tejada SS	4	1	2	0	.327
Daniel Murphy 2B	4	0	1	0	.289
David Wright 3B	3	0	1	0	.352
Ike Davis 1B	4	1	1	2	.205
Lucas Duda RF	3	0	1	0	.253
Jordany Valdespin LF	3	1	2	1	.254
Scott Hairston PH-LF	1	0	0	0	.249
Josh Thole C	3	0	0	0	.269
Kirk Nieuwenhuis CF	3	0	1	0	.268
Dillon Gee P	3	0	0	0	.148
Bobby Parnell P	0	0	0	0	

If Scott Hairston had not pinch hit for Valdespin, the entire game would have included all ex-Binghamton Mets!

The second time the Mets started a team of all ex-Binghamton players was on Sunday, July 22nd, when the Mets lost to the Dodgers, 8-3 in a 12-inning affair on a Sunday afternoon at Citi Field. Jonathon Niese started for the Mets, going seven innings and exiting the game trailing, 3-2. The Mets tied the game in the bottom of the ninth, as Ike Davis got an RBI groundout after Ruben Tejeda and Daniel Murphy had singled. Ramon Ramirez, acquired by the Mets from the Giants in the offseason for Angel Pagan, took the loss as he surrendered five runs on five hits in the 12[th inning]. The lineup that day:

Batting	AB	R	H	RBI	BA
Ruben Tejada SS	6	1	1	0	.309
Jordany Valdespin LF	5	0	2	0	.299
David Wright 3B	6	0	3	0	.349
Ike Davis 1B	5	1	1	1	.207
Daniel Murphy 2B	5	1	4	1	.306
Lucas Duda RF	6	0	1	0	.241
Kirk Nieuwenhuis CF	6	0	2	0	.261
Josh Thole C	4	0	2	1	.273
Jason Bay PH	1	0	0	0	.194
Jonathon Niese P	2	0	0	0	.207
Justin Turner PH	1	0	0	0	.288
Mike Nickeas C	1	0	0	0	.172

Twenty-two of the forty-nine players who donned a uniform for the Mets in 2012 passed through Binghamton. The only regular that year who did not come up through Binghamton was center fielder Andres Torres, as the players who started the most games at the other positions all called Binghamton their home at some point: Josh Thole, catcher; Ike Davis, 1B; Daniel Murphy, 2B; David Wright, 3B; Ruben Tejeda, SS; Jason Bay, LF; Lucas Duda, RF.

When so many organizational players find themselves in the everyday lineup, it is usually a sign that the major league team is having its problems. Indeed, the 2012 Mets only won 77 games. The NY Mets can only hope 2012 planted some seeds for fruition in later years, similar to the foundation their cross-town rivals put in place in 1991 when Bernie Williams became the first member of their "core four" to establish himself as an everyday impact player, a full four years before his first World Series win.

Ironically, if things had broken differently for the Binghamton franchise on Friday, July 30th, 2004, the NY Mets might have already garnered a championship or two in the twenty-first century. Binghamton's diehard denizens still refer to this day as its Black Friday. On that day the NY Mets traded away 60% of Binghamton's starting rotation:
- Starters Scott Kazmir and Jose Diaz were traded to the Marlins for Victor Zambrano and Bartolome Fortunato
- Matt Peterson, along with Jose Bautista and Ty Wigginton were sent to the Pirates for Kris Benson and Jeff Keppinger.

With Kazmir, Diaz and Peterson departing, manager Ken Oberkfell lost 12 wins and 213 innings from his rotation, with the most painful loss being Kazmir, the 2002 first-round pick. Kazmir had joined Binghamton a few weeks earlier and had dominated in his four starts, throwing 26 innings, striking out 29 and allowing only 16 hits and 5 earned runs. (Amazingly, Oberkfell replaced his starting trio with Brian Bannister, Wayne Ough, and Ken Chenard and managed to bring home enough wins to get his team into the 2004 playoffs, finishing second with a 76-66 record.)

Kazmir made his debut with Tampa Bay later that 2004 season and from 2005-2008 he was a mainstay on the Tampa staff, winning 45 games and never posting an ERA above 3.77, leading the American League in strikeouts (239) and games started (34) in 2007. When the Mets lost to the Cardinals in the seven-game National League Championship Series in 2006, Met fans mused about the difference Kazmir might have made in the season and the series, as catcher Yadier Molina hit a two-run homer off reliever Aaron Heilman (another ex-Binghamton Met) in the top of the ninth, to beat the Mets, 3-1, and send the Cards to the World Series.

In 2007, while manager Willie Randolph was being forced to use a still-developing Mike Pelfrey in the rotation and Jorge Sosa was filling in for an injured Orlando "El Duque" Hernandez, Met fans once again commiserated about how different things might have been if Kazmir were still wearing orange and blue. The Mets faded miserably in September that year and finished in second place, one game behind the Phillies in the Eastern Division of the National League. In September, when only one win would have made a difference, journeyman Brian Lawrence got 5 starts – he threw 29 innings, posting a 6.83 E.R.A. Rookie Phillip Humber was asked to make a crucial start in September as well, after getting very little work for the first three weeks of the month. Humber would throw seven innings in September with a 7.71 E.R.A.

The miseries of Mets fans continued in 2008, as the team blew another division lead in September and finished 3 games behind the Phillies with a record of 89-73. Nelson Figuerora, Claudio Vargas, Brian Stokes, Brandon Knight and Tony Armas combined for 14 starts, essentially replacing starts not made by the injured Pedro Martinez, who only made 20 starts that year. Kazmir's 12 wins and 3.49 ERA that he had for the Rays would have been welcomed by Willie Randolph.

While the results between the lines have been disappointing for Mets fans since 2006, off-the-field developments have been encouraging. Citi Field, a state of the art ballpark that brings back memories of Ebbetts Field is opened in 2009 and baseball continues to thrive in Brooklyn, where the N.Y. Mets have a short season team.

Baseball returned to Brooklyn in 2001, when the Brooklyn Cyclones became the short season class A affiliate of the New York Mets. R.C. Reutemann left his post as the Binghamton general manager to serve in the same position for the Cyclones in their inaugural season. "My experience in starting up the Binghamton franchise helped to prepare me to start up the Cyclones. There are so many things to do in starting a new club, from the logos to the uniforms," Reutemann explained to Ed Shakespeare, the author of the book, "When Baseball Returned to Brooklyn." Though Reutemann enjoyed his stay in Binghamton, he was ready for the challenge of bringing baseball back to Brooklyn.

Interestingly, in order to bring baseball back to the Brooklyn borough, the NY Mets also purchased a minor league franchise and relocated it, just as they had done with the Binghamton franchise a little more than a decade earlier. Using their experience with the Binghamton franchise as a model, this time the Wilpons bought the Pittsfield franchise of the New York-Pennsylvania League. Operating and owning a franchise in Brooklyn was especially rewarding for New York Mets' owner Fred Wilpon, who had grown up in Brooklyn and played on the same high school baseball team as the legendary Sandy Koufax. Fred Wilpon's fond memories of baseball in Brooklyn can be seen in the many elements of Citi Field that bring back memories of Ebbetts Field, including the brick edifice, rotunda behind home plate, and the tribute to Jackie Robinson as you enter the stadium.

Brooklyn followed in Binghamton's footsteps on the playing field as well, finishing in first place in the Stedler Division of the NY-Penn League, with a record of 55-24. Prominent big leaguers who played on that inaugural team included Mike Jacobs and Angel Pagan.

Given Greater Binghamton's history of sending players to the Big Apple, it comes as no surprise that current and future hopes for the New York Mets rest heavily on the shoulders of those who received their baseball education at the corner of Henry and Lewis streets, as Jon Niese, Zack Wheeler, Dillon Gee, Rafael Montero, Noah Syndergaard, and Matt Harvey are being counted on to become one of baseball's best pitching staffs in the ensuing years.

Two decades earlier the story was the same as New York Mets fans were hoping for great things from ex-Binghamtonians Bill Pulsipher, Jason Isringhausen, and Paul Wilson. Injuries derailed the careers of Pulsipher and Wilson, while Isringhausen overcame a series of injuries early in his career to become one of baseball's best closers, though not for New York, as he was traded away in 2000. As Harvey recovers from Tommy John surgery in 2014, Mets fans are hoping that history does not repeat itself regarding promising prospects who dominated Eastern League batters while pitching for the Binghamton Mets. Binghamton is a beacon of hope for Mets fans and the legacy of Sandy Alderson, general manager of the New York Mets, rests heavily on the shoulders of the young men that Binghamton has recently developed for playing baseball in the Big Apple.

Shrine Profiles

This chapter discusses each Shrine member, organized in alphabetical order within the year the member was inducted. The players in **bold** also are members of Cooperstown's Hall of Fame; underline indicates the player was a Binghamton Met. Note that no inductions were held in 1994 (due to AA All Star game festivities) and 2010 (front office transition activities).

Class	Inductees	Class	Inductees
1993	1. George F. Johnson **2. "Wee" Willie Keeler** 3. Johnny Logan	2003	28. Fred Norman 29. Pete Suder **30. John Montgomery Ward**
1994	None—1994 AA All-Star Game	2004	31. Johnny Blanchard 32. Ken Harrelson 33. Frank M. Verdi 34. Jerry Toman
1995	**4. Whitey Ford** 5. Wild Bill Hallahan 6. Tommy Holmes 7. Eddie Sawyer	2005	35. Rob Gardner 36. Bob Grim 37. Jake Pitler
1996	8. Ronald Michael Luciano 9. John Francis McNamara 10. Steve Souchock	2006	38. Bert Campaneris **39. Vernon "Lefty" Gomez** 40. W.B. Kay 41. Bobby Jones
1997	11. Deron R. Johnson 12. Steve C. Kraly 13. Thurman L. Munson	2007	42. Brook Fordyce 43. Charles Keller III 44. Cory Lidle 45. George McQuinn
1998	14. John H. Johnson 15. Lee Thomas 16. Bill Virdon 17. James E. Whitney	2008	46. Edgardo Alfonzo 47. Gene Bearden 48. Daniel M. Casey 49. Joe Pepitone
1999	18. Al Downing 19. John W. "Bud" Fowler 20. Victor J. Raschi 21. Steve Swisher	2009	50. Dale Long 51. Danny McDevitt 52. Quilvio Veras
2000	22. Spurgeon "Spud" Chandler 23. Eddie Farrell 24. Bobby Richardson 25. Bob Taylor	2011	53. Wally Burnette 54. John Fox 55. Harry G. "Judge" Lumley
2001	None—All Decade Team	2012	56. Gene Monahan 57. Curtis Pride 58. Bill "Moose" Skowron
2002	26. Clete Boyer 27. Ralph Terry	2013	59. Willard Hirshberger 60. Tom Tresh 61. Pete Van Wieren

George F. Johnson: A Lifetime of Giving Back

George F. Johnson was an obvious inductee into the inaugural Shrine class, for without his financial and emotional support for baseball at the turn of the twentieth century, baseball might never have taken root in the Greater Binghamton Area.

Johnson was born in 1857 in Plymouth, Massachusetts and the Civil War years left an indelible mark on him as his childhood years were lived with little money. At the age of 13 he quit school at 13 and went to work in a local shoe manufacturing company. Though he did not know it at the time, this proved fortuitous as it was shoes that would bring him unparalleled industrial success and enable him to be a benefactor for his workers and neighbors throughout his professional life.

Johnson started working for the Lester Brothers Boot Company in 1881, in Lestershire (now Johnson City), NY. Johnson advanced steadily in this firm, first becoming a foreman, then rising to co-owner with Henry B. Endicott and then, upon Endicott's death, gaining full ownership and seeing the company be renamed the Endicott Johnson Corporation by 1920. Along the way he accumulated enough wealth to be able to purchase part ownership of the Binghamton Bingos in 1899. When Johnson became sole owner of the team in 1912, he put his brother, Charles F., in charge of building Johnson Field, which became home to professional baseball in Binghamton for fifty-six years.

After opening the 1913 season on the road in Scranton, PA, against Joe McCarthy's Scranton Miners, the Bingos played their first game in Johnson Field on May 6, 1913. The day was proclaimed "George F. Johnson Day" and the headline in the *Binghamton Daily Republican* that day treated George F. Johnson as if he were royalty:

The Old King is Here and Ready to Reign Supreme: Monarch of Baseball's Broad Expanse to Be Honored as Never Before in History of Binghamton—All Fandom Out for Holiday

Most area businesses closed for the day so employees were free to attend the gala event. Taking advantage of the press coverage for Opening Day, and knowing that the day was appealing to men and women alike, the *Callahan & Douglas Hardware and Sporting Goods Store* advertised "Leonard Cleanable – One Piece Porcelain Refrigerators starting at $20.00, with Alaska Refrigerators starting at $11.00." On May 7th accounts of the game and holiday took up two entire pages of the 14-page edition of the *Daily Republican*.

George F. Johnson was never one to back down from an issue that he felt needed to be addressed and the controversial topic of the day at the time Johnson Field opened was the playing of baseball on Sundays, as many people felt it should truly be a day of rest, even for ballplayers. New York State even had laws on the books, outlawing professional games in New York State on Sunday afternoons. Johnson, however, was a staunch advocate of Sunday baseball, not because of potential ticket sales, but because he felt it provided an ideal source of entertainment for many of his workers who toiled six days a week. In a letter to the *Binghamton Press* in 1913 he stated:

"It is rather inconsistent for those who ride Sunday afternoons in their automobiles or drive their horses and carriages or go boating on our beautiful Susquehanna River or have a number of other pleasant but harmless recreations to say that is wrong for others who are not as fortunate as themselves to go to a Sunday baseball game."

Johnson supported his case by donating all ticket sales from the Sunday, May 11th contest. He went on to stage free Sunday baseball games to demonstrate his commitment for providing Sunday entertainment for his workers. Eventually, though, he had to stop his team from playing on Sunday until the New York State laws were changed in 1917, allowing Sunday professional baseball.

Johnson saw baseball as a sport to be enjoyed by the community; owning a team was an extension of the social contract he established with his workers, where he provided parks, carousels and subsidized housing in exchange for dedicated workers in his factories. His was a model also followed by his friend, Thomas J. Watson, who was establishing IBM as an international business at the same time that Endicott Johnson dominated the shoe industry. While Johnson provided numerous public parks for the local denizens, Watson was providing a country club, golf course, and a pool for his employees. A few years later, when the nation would suffer from the severe depression of the 1930's, area residents were beneficiaries of full employment practices instituted by Johnson and Watson.

Ironically, George F. Johnson passed away on a Sunday – November 28th in 1948. Funeral services were held on December 1st at Enjoie Park. All EJ and IBM facilities were closed, along with many stores, schools, and government centers. The funeral services were broadcast over the three major radio networks: ABC, CBS, and NBC. Twenty-five thousand people attended the services at Enjoie.

Johnny Logan: Endicott Gave Him His Name—"Yatcha"

Johnny Logan played in 1,503 major league games and that number gives him the distinction of playing in the most major league baseball games by a Broome County native. Johnny would often return to his native Endicott stomping ground to visit with his mother and friends. Endicott was proud to claim him as a native son, as the Little League complex on the north side of Endicott was named after him in the 1950's.

Logan was a star athlete at Union-Endicott High School during most of World War II, graduating in January 1945 after excelling in football, baseball, basketball and track for the U-E Tigers. He signed with the Boston Braves in 1947, but not before both the Yankees and Dodgers passed on him in his teenage years.

During Logan's high school years, Eddie Sawyer, fellow Shrine inductee and future big league manager of the 1950 Phillies, got Logan a tryout with the Binghamton Triplets, as Sawyer was managing the Triplets in 1942 and 1943. While growing up in Endicott, Logan's childhood dream was to play for the Triplets as, with most other youths of the day, the Yankees were his favorite team. Unfortunately, Sawyer could not convince the Yankees to sign Logan; the Yankees felt Logan, at 5'11" and 160 or so pounds, could not withstand the daily grind of professional baseball.

Perhaps the Yankees might have thought differently if they had known that in May of 1938 Logan walked from Endicott to Johnson City to catch a glimpse of his hero, Joe DiMaggio, play center field against the Triplets in an exhibition game. Logan didn't have the nerve to tell his parents he wanted to skip school to see a baseball game so instead of going a few blocks to school he walked approximately 11 miles instead. He did not have a ticket to the game, so he watched the game from a hole in the outfield fence (a true member of the "knot hole" gang). He was not disappointed, as DiMaggio hit a homer in the Yankees win against the Triplets.

Amazingly, the Brooklyn Dodgers also had a chance to sign Logan as he was invited to work out for them at Bear Mountain, where the Dodgers conducted spring training in the early 1940's due to the war. Jake Pitler, Binghamton Shrine Class of 2005, was a minor league manager in the Dodgers organization during the early 1940's and arranged for Logan to work out with the Dodgers, but he too could not convince the Dodgers to sign Logan.

As was the case with so many high school graduates of his era, Logan grew up in a hurry, as he was drafted and joined the army immediately after his graduation in January of '45. After his stint in the army, Logan was signed to a minor league contract to play baseball in the Boston Braves organization. He was signed by Braves scout Dewey Griggs, who also signed Hank Aaron and Wes Covington.

Logan was the starting shortstop for the Braves throughout the 1950's, with the highlight of his career coming in 1957 when the Braves won the World Series and Logan hit the first home run in the series. Logan accomplished many feats during his 13-year major league career, including being named to the National League All Star team four times (1955, and 1957-59), playing in another World Series in 1958, and never striking out more than 59 times in a season, despite displaying enough power to hit 93 home runs and knock in 547 runs in his career. He also still holds the World Series record for most assists by a shortstop in one game—ten.

A fiery and scrappy competitor, Logan was always looking for a playing edge, and was known for doing things that did not necessarily show up in the box score. Five times he finished in the top ten of National League batters for being hit by a pitch and was in the top 10 for sacrifice hits seven times.

Bob Uecker, a longtime announcer for the Milwaukee Brewers was good friends with Logan and marked Logan's passing in August of 2013 with praise, "He was one of the toughest players I've ever been around. And a really good shortstop, too. He had a guy alongside him in Eddie Mathews, who was another fireball, you know what I mean? A guy who wouldn't take anything from anybody, and Johnny was the same way. Johnny has been such a great friend and I can think of hundreds of things that have happened with him."

Logan and Eddie Mathews spent a lot of time together off the field during their playing days and were known to get into a scrape or two both between and outside the white lines. Logan explains how even Joe Louis, one of the greatest boxing champions of all time, was familiar with the exploits of Logan and Mathews:

"After winning the World Series in 1957, I met Joe in Las Vegas, where he was a host at Caesar's Palace. He told me, `I've done a lot of reading about you. I hear you and Mathews like to fight. I could beat you two guys one on one, but if you two ganged up on me, I wouldn't stand a chance.' "

Logan was always popular with the fans and throughout his career would receive requests for autographs in the mail. He was happy to oblige and was thrilled that fans remembered the Braves from Milwaukee. He was instrumental in forming *the Milwaukee Braves Historical Association*, which still preserves the history of the Milwaukee Braves today.

Logan's Milwaukee legacy includes a star on the Walk of Fame at Miller Park. When the star was unveiled, his good friend, Bob Uecker, served as the master of ceremonies. In Endicott, people still refer to Logan as "Yatcha." It is a nickname his Russian mother gave him; Logan elaborated in an interview with Bob Buege:

"I must have been very active, and in the Russian language, to settle a young kid, they'd say "Yah-shoo, yah-shoo. Just be quiet.' The word is a combination of Russian and Croatian. A guy on my street took that and gave me the name Yatcha, or Yatch. The name became very popular in Endicott."

Today Endicott has a little league baseball field named after Logan and a five-foot stone marker serves as a sentinel to the field. The stone marker is engraved with the following:

- Johnny Logan # 23, SS
- Nickname: Yatcha.
- Born and raised in Endicott, NY.
- Graduated from U.E.H.S.in 1945.
- Lettered in Baseball, Football, Basketball, Track, Golf.
- Played ML Ball 13 Years.
- 9 years with Milwaukee Braves.
- N.L.'s # 1 shortstop first three years-52, 53, 54.

"Wee Willie" Keeler: "Gentlemen Don't Do That"

Baseball great Ted Williams succinctly summed up Willie Keeler's baseball life with 14 words, saying "He may have been small in size, but he was huge with the bat!" At 5' 4" inches and 140 pounds, Keeler may very well have been the greatest hitter, pound-for-pound and inch-for-inch, who ever played. He was signed to his first professional contract in 1892 after he was seen playing semi-pro ball for a Plainfield, New Jersey team. In 1892 Keeler hit .392 for the Bingos before being signed to a major league contract to finish the year with the New York Giants, where he hit .321 (53 at bats). In a series of letters that Keeler wrote to his brother Joe while playing for Binghamton in 1892, Keeler touched on his joy in getting to explore the cities he visited, his opinion of his manager, and the trouble a ball player has in dating.

In a June 9th letter to his brother, Keeler wrote "I was down to see the Niagara Falls this morning, it is the greatest sight you ever saw in your life, it is only about an hour ride from where we are – it cost me about three dollars to see it all—we were on the Canadian side and were taken all over in the *Maid of the Mist*—it cost one dollar to go on that."

Keeler apparently had a tougher time adjusting to the game outside the lines than he did on the diamond. In the same letter he praised the beauty of Niagara Falls, he did not hide his disdain for the curfew established by his manager, Frank Leonard, "This manager is a stinker, and we got to be in at 11 every night. Mike Lehane and Mike Slattery, and Bill Daley and myself was (sic) out looking at the sights the other night until about 12 o'clock— you ought to have seen the look he gave us when we came in."

And as with many ballplayers in his day, Keeler had a tough time convincing the parents of lovely young women the worthiness of a ballplayer as a beau. In another letter he wrote to his brother on August 3rd, he stated "You don't want to say a word about that girl of mine though her old man raised an awful stink about her going with a ballplayer."

Born in Brooklyn, NY on March 3rd, 1872, Keeler managed to play 14 of his 19 years in his hometown, playing for the NY Giants, the Brooklyn Grooms and Superbas, and the New York Yankees. He had his best years with the Baltimore Orioles, however, where he posted the following string of batting averages from 1894 through 1898: .371, .377, .386, .424, and .385.

Bunting was a specialty for Keeler; he loved to draw the corner infielders in close as they anticipated a bunt and then Keeler would often chop the ball over their heads or slap the ball by them for base hits. He was also known to tire out pitchers by consistently fouling off pitches that he did not like – in 1903 he saw his average drop to .313 from .333 and part of this was attributed to the new rule that counted foul balls as strikes at the start of the 1903 season.

Keeler played in the major leagues for 19 years, compiling a batting average of .341 with 2,942 hits. He was elected to the Baseball Hall of Fame in 1939, his fourth year of eligibility, with 75.5% of the vote. When the Baseball Hall of Fame formally opened its doors in June of 1939, Keeler was one of 26 players inducted at the inaugural ceremony.

When asked by *Brooklyn Eagle* writer Abe Yager to explain his hitting success, Keeler inadvertently gave himself the nickname of "Hit 'Em Where They Ain't" when he explained that "I have already written a treatise and it reads like this: 'Keep your eye clear and hit 'em where they ain't; that's all.' "

Keeler's most memorable feat was hitting safely in 44 straight games in 1896 while playing for the Baltimore Orioles. Joe DiMaggio broke this record in 1941 when he hit safely in 56 games, and DiMaggio's record still stands today, with most baseball fans feeling this record is unassailable. Pete Rose tied Keeler's mark in 1978, when he set a new National League consecutive game hitting streak. Ironically, before Rose established this new record, the holder of the National League record for most consecutive games with a hit was ex-Binghamton Triplet and fellow Shrine member, Tommy Holmes, with 37.

Keeler was always popular with his teammates and was admired for his style of play. After Ichiro Suzuki broke Keeler's record of getting 200 hits for nine straight years in 2010, Charlie Keeler, the grand nephew of Willie, recalled a story that his father, also named Willie, told of visiting the Yankee locker room with the fabulous hitter. While touring the locker room he noticed players sharpening their spikes and asked his uncle why the players were doing that.

Shaking his head, Willie simply replied, "I don't know. Gentleman don't do that."

No Matter the Moniker, Ford is Truly the "Chairman of the Board"

In a minor league career that lasted a little over three years and saw Whitey Ford win 51 games, perhaps the most prominent memory of his minor league years was that Ford couldn't wait to leave them! Though he enjoyed playing baseball in each city in his minor league sojourn and his confidence grew with each stop along the way, the bus trips were anything but fun. "We'd sit on that bus anywhere from ten to 12 hours. Then, after we played, we'd climb back on the bus for another 12-hour trip home. We might get in at 7 AM, then right away have to play a day game."

Bus trips notwithstanding, Ford will never forget his stay in Binghamton. He made sure he did not have far to travel for home games, as he lived within a block of Johnson Field, renting an attic room on Broad Street. It was while he played for the Triplets that he started to throw his curveball more, mixing his pitches better than he ever had, demonstrating an increased ability to get strikeouts. Years later Ford recalled his stay in the Triple Cities. "I was starting to strike out six and seven guys a game now, and for the first time I began to think I had a chance to make it to the big leagues."

Ford earned his entry to the Shrine in 1995 for both his major league and Triplet success. During his Shrine induction speech in August his eyes grew moist as he recalled his years of being a teammate of Mickey Mantle, who was then dying of cancer. Ford closed his speech with perhaps the most poignant remark of any Shrine induction statement as he asked the fans, "When your knees hit the ground tonight, say a prayer for the Mick."

Mantle passed away a few days later, on August 13, 1995. Ford was one of the pallbearers, along with Yogi Berra, Bobby Murcer, and Hank Bauer.

In 1949, despite missing the first six weeks of the season with remnants of amoebic dysentery that he caught while pitching in the Mexican League that winter, Ford posted a 16-5 record for the Triplets, leading the league with 151 strikeouts and posting an ERA of 1.61. Though the Triplets finished in fourth place, they swept through the two playoff series and were the 1949 Eastern League Champs.

Ford lost his first name of "Eddie" while a member of the Triplets; in his autobiography, "Slick," Ford explained how he gained the moniker of "Whitey":

"It was the great Lefty Gomez, of all people, who stuck me with the name 'Whitey.' Lefty was managing the Yankees' Binghamton club in the Eastern League, and I was assigned to spring training with his team in 1947. They trained at Edenton, NC, and there were so many players down there, I guess Lefty had a hard time remembering all their names, so he just gave them nicknames. I was 'Blondie' or 'Whitey' for obvious reasons. Eventually, he settled on 'Whitey.'"

"Whitey" was just the start of nicknames for Ford. After he reached the big leagues, Billy Martin and Mickey Mantle bestowed on him the nickname of "Slick" due to his being born and raised in Queens. After Ford went 24-7 in 1963, catcher Elston Howard started to refer to him as the "Chairman of the Board" due to his mound excellence and presence and this phrase is second only to "Whitey" when Ford's name is mentioned in baseball circles.

After his brilliant season in '49, Ford displayed his confidence by calling Paul Krichell, the scout who signed him, asking if Krichell could arrange for a call up to the Yankees for the end of the season. The Yankees were locked in a close duel with the Boston Red Sox for the pennant and Ford felt he could be a difference maker. What the heck, he was on top of the world, ace of a championship team with an Eastern League check for $223.00 in his pocket as his minor league championship share.

Krichell conferred with George Weiss and they politely decided to turn down Ford's request in 1949. Krichell responded, "But, if you behave yourself, we'll take you to spring training with the Yankees next year."

The rest, as they say, is history.

Ford was a key element of the Yankee pitching staff in 1950, winning 9 games and starring in the World Series against the Philadelphia Phillies. He became the ace of the New York Yankee staff from 1953 through the mid 1960's, winning 236 games and compiling a 2.75 ERA over 3170.1 innings. His teammates during those years read like a "Who's who" of Binghamton Shrine members: Johnny Blanchard, Clete Boyer, Al Downing, Bob Grim, Deron Johnson, Danny McDevitt, Joe Pepitone, Bobby Richardson, Moose Skowron, Ralph Terry, and Tom Tresh.

Ford was elected to the Baseball Hall of Fame in 1974 in his second year of eligibility, being named on 77.8% of the ballots. He won six World Championships with the Yankees and in 146 innings of World Series play he won 10 games and posted a 2.71 ERA.

Ford's penchant for enjoying a good laugh was evident in the opening of his Induction speech for Baseball's Hall of Fame on August 12, 1974, a few days after Gerald Ford took over in Washington for the exiled Richard Nixon:

"Thank you, Commissioner. I tell you, I walked down the aisle three weeks ago with my daughter, she got married, and I thought I was nervous then, but I think this tops it today. Between what happened in Washington last week and up here in Cooperstown today, I'd have to say it's a pretty good week for the Fords."

Tommy Holmes: "Mr. Clutch" Redux

Accompanying Ford into the Shrine in 1995 was Tommy Holmes, a lefty hitting and throwing outfielder who had a lifetime batting average of .302 over 11 seasons in the majors. He was one of the most popular players in Boston Braves history, having a career year in 1945, when he hit .325 with 28 HRs and 117 RBIs. He earned his election to the Shrine not only for his major league career, but also for his outstanding minor league season of 1938, when he hit .368 for the Triplets, patrolling center field with aplomb and leading the Triplets to a first place finish.

Robert Merrill, the renowned baritone opera singer who was also known for his singing of "The Star Spangled Banner" at Yankee Stadium, often liked to tell of his growing up with Holmes in Brooklyn: "I played baseball as a kid in Brooklyn with a fellow named Tommy Holmes for a church team. I could see he had that big league swing! Me? I wanted to be a pitcher. The problem is I had a forty-mile-per-hour fastball."

Holmes spent the 1938 season batting leadoff and he started hitting from the first day of the season, which was only his second of professional ball, after having been signed by the Yankees in 1937 while he played semi-pro ball in Brooklyn. The *Binghamton Evening Press* called attention to Holmes' torrid first week of hitting in a three-column headline in its sports pages on May 4th:

Holmes hits .430 to lead Triplets in First Six Games

47

Under the banner headline was a two-column picture of Holmes settling under a fly to make a catch at his hips, long before Willie Mays made the basket catch a household word. The article pointed out that his teammates from the 1937 Norfolk team marveled not only at his hitting prowess, but at his ability to "run far and wide to snag fly balls" as well.

The exploits of Holmes and his teammates in 1938 provided a day-to-day respite from the daily headlines that warned of increasing tensions in Europe. In the late 1930's residents of the Triple Cities looked to the sports pages to divert their attention from the ominous front pages. In the *Binghamton Evening Press* syndicated columns such as Walter Winchell's "On Broadway" and Grantland Rice's "The Sportslight" provided news and features that stood in stark contrast from what was going on across the Atlantic and Pacific.

The brightest moment for Holmes that year came in the first semifinal playoff game against the Elmira Pioneers on Thursday, September 8th. Holmes was "Mr. Clutch" in that game and it stands as one of the best games ever played at Johnson Field, perhaps the best ever. The 3,395 fans in attendance that afternoon not only saw a great playoff game, but also witnessed a preview of the heroics Holmes would later author in the majors.

Entering the bottom of the ninth, the Triplets were trailing 1-0 and Pioneer starter Lew Krausse was in command. After Krausse quickly retired the first two batters, Johnson Field took on a funereal presence, as the fans feared defeat was seconds away as 21-year-old first baseman Ed Levy stepped in the batter's box—no matter that Levy hit .318 and hit 12 home runs during the season.

But when Krausse tried to sneak a curve past the six-foot, five-inch first baseman, Levy put the barrel of the bat on the ball, sending it over the center field fence to tie the score!

But the best was yet to come.

After the Triplets held the Pioneers scoreless in the top of the tenth, in the bottom half of the inning Tommy Holmes came up with Garton Del Savio at second. Holmes hit a double to center, scoring Del Savio and giving the Triplets a 2-1 win, sending the Johnson Field faithful into a frenzy.

Holmes and Levy were hometown heroes and no one thought finishing off the Pioneers in the next two games would be anything but a formality. But a few days later the Triplets season was over, as the Pioneers took 3 of the next 4 games.

Amazingly, 10 years later, in 1948, Holmes would find himself in a similar situation—only this time it was on baseball's biggest stage, the World Series.

In Game 1 of that series, at Boston Braves Park, Johnny Sain dueled Bob Feller of the Cleveland Indians. Sain had held the Indians scoreless through 8 innings and allowed only 4 hits; Feller was even better, throwing a one-hit shutout over the first seven innings.

In the bottom of the eighth inning, Holmes was on deck as Johnny Sain was in the batter's box against Feller, with Phil Masi on second and Sibby Sisti on first with one out. Feller looked toward home, peering in for the signs from his catcher. Suddenly Feller whirled and threw to Lou Boudreau, who had snuck behind Masi. It appeared that Masi was picked off, and the hometown fans froze, fearing the worst, but umpire Bill Stewart ruled Masi had gotten back safely. Photographs the next day showed Masi was clearly out, but Feller shook off the disappointment and got Sain to line out.

That brought up Holmes. Runner on second, two outs, tie score, first game of the World Series. As he had done in 1938 for the Triplets, Holmes came through with a hit, hitting a hard ground ball past Ken Keltner at third to drive in Masi with the first and only run of the game, giving the Braves the win and sending the crowd of 40,135 home happy. Feller's two-hitter had netted only a classic World Series loss and the Braves had a quick edge in the World Series.

Holmes would be reminded that history often repeats itself, however. As with the Triplets in 1938, Holmes' team could not make the series lead stand up and the Braves went on to lose to the Indians in six games, winning only one more game in that World Series.

In 1973, Holmes began a 30-year association with the New York Mets, when he joined the front office as director of amateur baseball relations. He lived a wonderful life, dying of natural causes on April 14, 2008, in Florida; he was 91-years old.

Note: If you are a hockey fan you might have a paused a bit at the mention of umpire Bill Stewart's name. His son, Paul Stewart, played hockey for the Broome Dusters and Binghamton Whalers and went on to a long career as an NHL referee after his playing days were over. Paul Stewart is a member of the Binghamton Hockey Hall of Fame, which honors local professional hockey players.

When "Wild Bill" Put Binghamton at the Center of the Baseball World

Bill Hallahan arguably provided Binghamton with its finest baseball moment in this city's history. In October of 1931, thousands of residents of Binghamton and its surrounding areas showed up at the Lackawanna Railroad Station to greet the hero of the 1931 World Series, Binghamton native "Wild" Bill Hallahan, who won two games and saved another one as the Cardinals beat Connie Mack's Philadelphia Athletics, 4 games to 2.

When he returned from the Series, Binghamton denizens gave Hallahan a hero's welcome at the Lewis Street railroad station, treating him to a parade and "Welcome Home" dinner celebration. But while Binghamton was making him the toast of the town, Hallahan was already the toast of the nation. Not since Christy Mathewson had thrown three shutouts against the Philadelphia A's in 1905 had a pitcher been so dominating in a World Series. In 18.1 innings, Hallahan gave up only one run and struck out 12, finishing with a Series ERA of 0.49! This work was even better than what he accomplished in the Cards' losing effort to the Athletics the year before, when he went 1-1, with a 1.34 ERA. As a post season pitcher, Hallahan was the king of the hill.

Hallahan was born on Binghamton's East Side and played for Binghamton High School before pitching semi-pro baseball for *Smith-Corona* (a typewriter Company) in Groton, NY. Johnny Haddock, his manager, saw major league talent in Hallahan and recommended the Cardinals sign Hallahan to a professional contract in 1923.

By 1931, Hallahan established himself as one of baseball's best pitchers, despite his reputation for a lack of control. In 1931 he was Mr. October— long before Reggie Jackson was born. On October 2nd, in Game 2 of the World Series, Hallahan shut out the A's on three hits, beating George Earnshaw, 2-0, while getting the Cards even at 1-1 in the Series. On October 7th, Hallahan won again, beating the A's 8-1, in Game 5 to put the Cards up, 3 games to 2. After only giving up one run in eighteen innings, however, Hallahan saved the best for last. On October 10th, Burleigh Grimes got the start for the Cardinals and he was brilliant, shutting out the A's for eight innings and taking a 4-0 lead into the ninth. But Grimes tired in the ninth and when A's shortstop Williams singled to left with the bases loaded, knocking in two runs, Cardinals manager Gabby Street looked to the bullpen and called for Hallahan to pitch to Max Bishop, the A's leadoff hitter and second baseman.

There were runners on first and second, two out, and Hallahan was pitching on only two days rest. Bishop was so respected for his keen eye at the plate that his nickname was "camera eyes." Hallahan was so well known for his penchant of giving up walks that sportswriters gave him the moniker of "Wild Bill." This was Hallahan's time to shine, however. He got Bishop to fly out to center fielder Pepper Martin and the Cards became the 1931 World Champions!

Hallahan's achievements in 1931 become increasingly impressive when one realizes just how good the A's were that year. They were managed by Connie Mack and compiled a 107-45 record, benefitting from the play of future Hall of Famers Mickey Cochrane, Jimmie Foxx, Al Simmons, and pitchers Lefty Grove and Waite Hoyt. They had been World Champions for the past two years and were favored to win a third in a row.

The Cardinals finished the year at 101-53, led by manager Gabby Street and the quartet of Frankie Frisch, who had a lifetime average of .316 and was elected to the Hall of Fame in 1947; outfielder Chick Hafey, who hit .349 and knocked in 95 runs and joined Frisch in Cooperstown in 1971; "Pepper" Martin who hit .300 and stole 16 bases; and Hallahan, who went 19-9 and led the league in wins and strikeouts while also showing why he went by the sobriquet of "Wild Bill," as he led the league in walks and wild pitches as well.

As impressive as his pitching prowess was in this Series, perhaps Hallahan's greatest feat was saving his catcher, All-Star Jimmie Wilson, from being remembered as one of the all-time goats of the World Series. Hallahan's heroics came in Game 2, as he took the mound after Lefty Grove had won the first game for the A's. Hallahan protected a 2-0 lead as he headed to the mound to start the ninth inning. The leadoff hitter was 23-year-old slugger Jimmie Foxx, who hit 30 home runs and knocked in 120 runs while hitting .291. When Foxx drew a leadoff walk, 37,000 fans in Sportsman's Park squirmed—it was not a good time for Hallahan to show the A's how he got his nickname.

The fans were calmed a bit when 36-year-old outfielder Bing Miller struck out. But Hallahan walked the next batter, third baseman Jimmy Dykes, putting runners on first and second. The fans focused on Hallahan's every move as he faced shortstop Dibrell Williams, the lightest hitter in the lineup. Cheers filled the stadium when Hallahan struck him out. Four hitters up and not a ball put in fair play: two walks, two strikeouts. Now only one out separated Hallahan and the Cards from drawing even 1-1 in the Series. A's manager Connie Mack sent up reserve outfielder Jimmy Moore to pinch hit for pitcher George Earnshaw; Cardinal fans were comforted by Moore's .224 batting average.

Hallahan quickly got ahead in the count, then Moore got it even and on a 2-2 pitch, Moore swung and Wilson caught the ball—an apparent strike three to end the game! But Moore nicked the ball into Wilson's mitt and Wilson could not hold on to the third strike. Wilson grimaced as he threw the ball back to Hallahan. The fans groaned at what might have been.

Now Hallahan had to do it again. Foxx and Dykes would be running as soon as Moore swung. The fans watched with wide and worried eyes while Moore and Wilson focused on Hallahan's left hand, from which a curve ball came. Moore was anxious and though the ball bounced in the dirt, he swung and missed. Game over—again! The crowd erupted in delight as Sportsman's Park turned into the happiest place in the nation. Fans rushed the field to celebrate!

But wait, Wilson was throwing the ball to third! While fans were rushing the field, Hallahan was wondering why Wilson wasn't rushing out to congratulate him, Eddie Collins, Mack's third-base coach, was using his legs as pogo sticks, all the while screaming at Jimmy Moore.

"Run to First! Go to first," Collins exhorted across the diamond; he was a windmill in a hurricane, arms moving around and around, faster and faster.

Collins saw Hallahan's pitch hit the dirt before going into Wilson's glove. The rules called for Wilson to throw to first to retire the batter! Moore, after an initial moment of depression, was now sprinting to first. Wilson was befuddled; he had no ball to throw to first. Moore crossed the bag while first baseman Jim Bottomley looked quizzically at the men in blue.

The umpires got the fans off the field, conferred and ultimately concurred with Collins. Moore was safe at first! The bases were loaded and the A's had a third chance to pull this game out, courtesy of catcher Jimmie Wilson. This was the same Jimmie Wilson who boasted a fielding percentage of .985 and was considered one of the top defensive catchers in the game, who had thrown out over 50% of the runners who had tried to steal against him. Now he had dropped a third strike foul tip and failed to throw to first to secure a putout on a strikeout.

As Max Bishop stepped to the plate, Hallahan focused on getting out of the inning for the third time. Hallahan threw ball one. The fans groaned and flinched.

Bishop swung on the next pitch and raised a fly ball down the first base line, slicing toward the grandstand. Jim Bottomley went into a full sprint after it—he did not stop until he crashed into the grandstand, with the ball in his glove.

This time the game was truly over—Hallahan had his shutout, the Cards had drawn even in the series and Jimmie Wilson heaved a sigh of relief that Hallahan could feel sixty feet away.

Wilson told the Associated Press after the game that he had no excuses.

"If that play were to come up 1,000 times, I believe I'd make it right every time. But this time was the thousand and first, and I just made it wrong….and as Hallahan pitched and I saw Foxx racing for third I was all set to peg to Flowers. The pitch was low and even when Moore swung at the ball, I went through with my previously arranged intention to throw Foxx out at third. I know I should have tagged Moore, or thrown to first base. I could have done that, and have done that very thing many times on similar plays. But I booted this one, and that's one for the error column. I just made a dumb play, and I'm big enough to take some abuse for it."

Hallahan went on to continued glory in the big leagues, winning 16 games in 1933, 8 games in 1934, and 15 games in 1935. Wild Bill started the first ever All Star game in 1933 (opposing fellow Shrine inductee Lefty Gomez) and he gave up the first All-Star home run to none other than Babe Ruth.

"He's the toughest pitcher in the league. He has terrific speed and a mighty tough curve," said standout first baseman Lefty O'Doul of Hallahan in 1933. Catcher Spud Davis felt Hallahan was extra special: "If I was a manager and I needed one ballgame, for a pennant or a World Series, I'd rather have Bill Hallahan than anybody."

Hallahan compiled a lifetime record of 102-94 and was a member of the 1926, 1931, and 1934 World Champion Cardinal teams; it took Dizzy Dean to supplant him as the pitching ace of the Cards. Hallahan won 93 games for the Cards before they traded him to the Cincinnati Reds in 1936. Wild Bill won 9 games for the Reds in two years and then finished his career with the Philadelphia Phillies in 1938, winning 1 and losing 8. Though the end of his career was an effete rendering of his Cardinal years, Hallahan's success in the first part of the decade made him one of baseball's depression-era stars.

After retiring from baseball in 1938, he returned to Binghamton, married, became a father, and lived a wonderfully simple life on Davis Street, in Binghamton's West Side.

He retired from the GAF (General Aniline and Film) Company in 1960, where he worked as a warehouse manager. In his retirement years, he spent most of his winters in southern Florida, but in the spring and summer one of his daily activities included walking to the baseball diamond at Recreation Park to watch the youngsters play baseball. His avuncular nature made him approachable to adults and kids alike. When speaking with adults his succinct sagacity was evidenced in his telling Robert Hood, author of "The Gashouse Gang," that "a hanging curveball is a base hit before it leaves a pitcher's hand."

He was a great neighbor and friend to the residents of Davis Street. Upon his death in 1981, he was remembered as more than just a ball player by one of his neighbors: "He's the kind of person you feel you've gained from by having known him, he was more than a baseball player."

In 1995, Hallahan was a posthumous member of what was arguably the greatest induction class into the Binghamton Baseball Shrine. Joining Hallahan were Whitey Ford, who went 16-5 for the Triplets in 1949 and won 236 major league games on his way to becoming a member of baseball's Hall of Fame; Tommy Holmes, who hit .368 for the Triplets in 1938 and had a lifetime batting average of .302 in 11 major league seasons; and Eddie Sawyer, who starred for the Triplets in 1935 and 1936 and managed the NL Champion 1950 Philadelphia Phillies.

Today, the little league diamond in Recreation Park bears Hallahan's name as well as a stone monument in his honor, praising him as a major league pitcher (though it neglects to mention he also played for the Reds and Phillies). The plaque on the monument behind home plate praises him with the simplest of words, which is just the way Wild Bill would have liked it:

HALLAHAN FIELD
Dedicated in Memory of
WILLIAM A. HALLAHAN
MAJOR LEAGUE PITCHER
ST. LOUIS CARDINALS 1925-1938

Eddie Sawyer: "I'm 49 Years Old and I Want to Live to 50"

Eddie Sawyer served two tours of duty with the Binghamton Triplets, from 1935 to 1938 as a full-time outfielder and from 1942 to 1943 as a part-time player and full-time manager. While doing so he managed to set a record for most career at bats as a Triplet. During his tours of duty with the Triplets, he garnered 1,976 at bats, collecting 606 hits for a lifetime Binghamton batting average of .325. Sawyer never made the major leagues as a player, though he had a career minor league batting average of .319 over 10 minor league seasons.

Sawyer was a graduate of Ithaca College and received his master's degree in biology from Cornell. Paul Krichell, the same scout who signed Lou Gehrig and Whitey Ford, got Sawyer to sign a professional contract with the Yankees in 1934. During his tenure in Binghamton, Sawyer also served as baseball and football coach at Binghamton North

High School. No doubt he did this not only because he enjoyed it, but also because he needed the job; his monthly salary in 1937 playing for the Triplets was $150.00.

Sawyer was known as an erudite manager who also was an excellent judge of talent. He was credited with changing Richie Ashburn from a catcher to an outfielder to take advantage of his outstanding speed. He was also impressed with the exploits of an Endicott youth who dominated the baseball diamond for the Union-Endicott baseball team in the 1940's. He encouraged the Yankees to sign him to a minor league contract, but the Yankees were not impressed enough to request his autograph; instead Johnny Logan became the starting shortstop for the Milwaukee Braves in the 1950s, helping to defeat the Yankees in the 1957 World Series.

Sawyer was a player's manager who would talk his players up in the press and pointed out the mistakes they made in private. His exuberance for his players was seen in his calling his outfielder Ed Sanicki the best center fielder in all of baseball in spring training in 1950. "I mean over the long haul—for the next ten years. Sanicki, in other words, is where Joe DiMaggio was when he came up, He's going to be truly great," gushed Sawyer.

Though 26 when he came up at the end of the 1949 season, Sanicki impressed Sawyer by going 3 for 12, with all 3 hits being homers. Sawyer loved Sanicki's combination of power and gold-glove caliber defense, as Sanicki hit 64 homers in his two previous minor league seasons. Sadly, Sanicki injured his knee in 1951 and was never the same player He only got 5 more at bats in the big leagues and never again hit over .250 in the minors. Sawyer had to "settle" for future Hall of Famer Richie Ashburn as his center fielder in 1950 and it was Ashburn who held down center field for the next decade.

As impressive as his Triplet statistics were, Sawyer's election to the Shrine no doubt was sealed with his success as a major league manager, as he was at the helm when the 1950 Phillies hustled themselves to a National League pennant, becoming known as the "Whiz Kids" along the way. In April of that pennant-winning season, Sawyer had his team thinking big thoughts. "Nobody has told my boys yet that they can't win the flag," Sawyer remarked to a *Binghamton Sun* reporter. "Until they do, I'll be happy to have them thinking they can. They're a wonderful group of boys."

During his eight-year managing career, Sawyer collected 390 wins, with the Whiz Kids accounting for 91 wins in 1950. He started managing the Phillies in 1948, replacing the ex-Yankee Ben Chapman. His experience with the team in '48 and '49 helped him mold it into a pennant winner by 1950. His patience and easy-going manner served the team especially well in the middle of the 1949 season, when he and his team suffered through one of the most bizarre and ugly incidents in baseball history. On June 14, 1949, a deranged woman by the name of Ruth Steinhagen shot starting first baseman Eddie Waitkus. Waitkus survived, but would not play again that year.

The 1950 season came down to the last day of the season, with the Phils holding a one-game lead over the Dodgers. The final game of the season had the Dodgers hosting the

Phils in Brooklyn's bandbox of a ballpark, Ebbetts Field. Robin Roberts bested Don Newcombe, beating the Dodgers 4-1, on a 3-run homer by Dick Sisler in the top of the tenth inning.

Sawyer was at his managerial best in the bottom of the ninth that day. With the score tied 1-1 and runners on second and third and one out in the bottom of the ninth, the Dodgers were sending Jackie Robinson, Carl Furillo, and Gil Hodges to bat.

Even though the Most Valuable Player that year, Jim Konstanty (from Oneonta), was warmed up and ready to come in, Sawyer stayed with Roberts. He came out to the mound and told Roberts to walk Robinson to set up a force at any base. Sawyer told Roberts to keep the ball down on Furillo, who was a high fastball hitter. Years later, Roberts recalled the drama, "Well, my first pitch to Carl was about eye high, but it must have had something on it because he swung and popped it up to Waitkus in foul territory by first base." Sawyer's faith in Roberts was fulfilled when Hodges flew out to right fielder Del Ennis. Roberts had his twentieth win and the Phils had their first pennant since 1915 when Grover Cleveland Alexander was their ace.

Richard Goldstein, in writing Sawyer's obituary in the *N.Y. Times* recalled how Sawyer was known for his intelligence and memory during his major league managing days.

'He's still able to run down the roster of 1,500 former students—first name, last name, hometown— as glibly as he calls off the Phils' batting order," a 1949 Collier's magazine profile of Sawyer observed. "The only thing Eddie couldn't remember was how to hit a curveball." '

Upon his retirement from managing, Sawyer's succinct explanation for his decision showed he hadn't lost a beat. The 1960 season had literally just started and after the Phils lost their first game of 1960, he resigned, stating "I'm 49 years old, and I want to live to be 50."

Ron Luciano: "My Voice is Perfect for Mime and My Face is Made for Radio"

"So what I am doing broadcasting baseball on national TV?" Ron Luciano asked himself as he prepared to make his debut on Major League Baseball's Game of the Week in April of 1980. Luciano could not have foreseen that 16 years later he would be inducted into the Shrine along with John McNamara and Stephen Souchock.

Luciano's path to the broadcasting booth and Binghamton's Shrine was anything but a straight line, but instead a serpentine road, with outward laughter every step of the way. After graduating from Union-Endicott High School he received a scholarship to play football for Syracuse University, where he was a star offensive lineman. He was drafted by the Detroit Lions in 1959 and he thought he was headed to stardom on the football field. Four years later, however, after multiple shoulder injuries, a torn-up knee and only two regular season games, he gave up football and fell into umpiring.

In the winter of 1963, with his football career over before it ever started and while serving as substitute teacher at his old high school, Union-Endicott, Spike Briggs, the owner of the Detroit Lions and Detroit Tigers baseball team offered Luciano a job as the general manager of the Florida State League Lakeland Tigers. Luciano accepted the position eagerly, as it allowed him to reconnect with professional sports. He even went down to Florida a couple of months early to get ready for the season. It was during this time, while he was waiting for the baseball season to start up that he thought he'd enroll in umpiring school. He had dallied a bit in amateur umpiring, being a member of the Endicott Umpires Association in his hometown and he thought at the very least he'd be a general manager who knew the rules better than any of his peers.

After a few weeks of umpiring school he was hooked. He called up Briggs to turn down the general manager job and by the start of the season he was umpiring in the Florida State League. Five years later he would be umpiring in the big leagues.

Steve Pavlovich, an umpiring colleague of Luciano's in Endicott was not surprised at Luciano's choice or his success. "That he went on to umpire in the major leagues was no surprise to me. Sure he was a showman. But he always made the right call. The fun came in between."

During his big league career, one of the things Luciano was known for was his constant battles with Earl Weaver, manager of the Baltimore Orioles. They had known each other from the minor leagues, and their constant battles were also legendary in the minors. In 1965, when Weaver's Eastern League Elmira team was playing against Reading in a four-game series, Luciano and Weaver teamed up to make history.

In the first game of the series, Luciano was umpiring the bases and Weaver got ejected for arguing a call at second base. The second night Lucaino was behind the plate and in Weaver's eyes, he was woeful—Weaver let him know it on every pitch.

When Luciano had enough, he turned to Weaver and asked, "How loud can you yell?"

"Why?" Weaver asked.

Luciano responded, "Because you're going to be doing it from the end of the dugout!" exhorted Luciano as he raised his right hand and threw out Weaver for a second consecutive night.

The third game of the series saw Luciano handling the bases and once again, Weaver came out to let Luciano know that he had missed another call. Once again, Luciano did not appreciate Weaver's whining and ejected him for the third consecutive night.

When it came time to exchange lineup cards the next night, Weaver was already boiling inside as he handed the card to Luciano. When Weaver asked Luciano if he was going to do as bad a job on this night as he did the first three nights, Luciano delivered a riposte as only he could, looking Weaver in the eye and telling him "You're never gonna find out!" And with that, before a pitch was thrown, Luciano ejected Weaver once again.

In his first book, "The Umpire Strikes Back," Luciano notes that after this series, his relationship with Weaver was a downhill one from that moment on.

After the 1979 season Luciano retired from umpiring and in the early 80's he was a broadcaster for NBC's *Baseball Game of the Week*. He also owned a sporting goods store in the Northgate Plaza in Binghamton for a few years, all the time still living in his hometown, on Badger Avenue in Endicott. He was always the comedian in public, poking fun at his favorite target—himself. His self-deprecating one-liners were announced for the masses in staccato fashion:

On his skill as an umpire: "Talking and joking around on the field were my only skills"
On the two things that worried him as an umpire: "Making decisions and working long games"
On his prowess as a hitter: "The day they started throwing breaking pitches was the day I started looking around for someone to tackle"

The humor that Luciano shouted out clearly was a mask for what must have roiled inside. On January 19th, 1995, the main headline on the front page of the local paper was "Japan Quake Deaths Reach 3,100," but the second biggest headline shocked the Greater Binghamton community:

Baseball Celebrity Luciano Dies at 57

Reporter Mark Winheld shook everyone with his opening sentence. "Famed professional baseball umpire Ronald M. Luciano was found dead about 3:50 PM Wednesday in the garage area of his home in Endicott, police said. Luciano had committed suicide, leaving a note and attaching a hose from his muffler to the inside of his car, killing himself of carbon monoxide poisoning."

When news broke of Luciano's death, his sister, Dolores Jester, started receiving condolence calls from all over the nation. She was at a loss for words, mustering only three:

"It's very sad."

In Binghamton, "Johnny Mac" Has Nothing to Do With Tennis…

While John McEnroe dominated the sports headlines of the mid 1970's with both his tennis tantrums and prowess on the courts, Johnny McNamara was carving a name for himself as an astute major league manager. Other than McNamara, the only members of the Shrine who have gone on to manage in the big leagues are Eddie Sawyer and Bill Virdon. These three men form a select group, combining for 2,545 wins. McNamara was at the helm when the Red Sox won the 1986 American League pennant and holds the Shrine record for most managerial wins in the majors; in a 19-year managing career, McNamara won 1160 games. Virdon is second on the all-time list with 995 and Sawyer rounds out the trio with 390.

In 1963 John McNamara served as the player-manager of the Triplets, leading the team to a 65-75 record and a fourth-place finish in the six-team Eastern League. In '63 McNamara shared the catching duties with Neil Junker and though he started off the season well, hitting .291 through early May, by mid season McNamara was hitting only .219 and was on his way to a .226 finish with no home runs and 24 RBIs. McNamara "the manager" did not give McNamara "the player" any special treatment. When Johnny caught, he always hit eighth and when the pitching staff was a bit worn down McNamara even tabbed himself to pitch an inning in mop up duty—ironically, he pitched a perfect inning of relief when he was called on! McNamara's defensive ability overshadowed his hitting, as he lacked power and did not hit for a high average. But while at Binghamton he was honing his ability to motivate a roster of young men while increasing his acumen concerning the strategic elements of the game.

McNamara was only 27 when he first became a player-manager in the minors, finishing in first place with 75 wins for the Lewiston Broncs in the Northwest League in 1959. Binghamton was his first managing job higher than the Class B level, as he came to the Triple Cities after having managed Lewiston from 1959 through 1962. When the Triplets got off to a slow start in '63, going 9-16, no one was more surprised than their manager. McNamara told reporter Lowell Toeniessen of the *Binghamton Sun Bulletin*, "If anyone had told me in Florida that the season would start like this, I would have thought he was crazy. But facts are facts, the record is what counts."

That '63 team never did get on track and dwelled in the second division throughout the season. Despite the lack of success for the Triplets on the field, 1963 was a good year for the local denizens. In early May many went to see veteran stage and film star Tallulah Bankhead star in George Oppenheimer's comedy, "Here Today," at Binghamton's Capitol Theater; and on August 30th thousands of fans honored "Mr. Baseball of the Triple Cities," Pat Kelly, in a celebration at Johnson Field. John H. Johnson, ex-Triplets general manager, gave Kelly a lifetime pass to Yankee Stadium on behalf of the Yankees that night! The night before, Triplets lefty Fred Norman set an Eastern League season strikeout record, as he struck out 14 members of the Springfield Rifles to give him 258 for season! "I just try to throw strikes and let the rest take care of itself," explained Norman.

12 of the 32 players who suited up for McNamara that season went on to play in the big leagues, with two players achieving stardom, as well as joining McNamara in the Shrine. Little Fredie Norman, Shrine class of 2003, won 104 games and earned two World Series rings with the "Big Red" Machine of the Cincinnati Reds in 1975 and '76. Bert

Campaneris played shortstop for McNamara for 48 games, hitting .308 and stealing 17 bases. "Campy" was a mainstay of the Oakland A's teams that won three consecutive World Champioinships from 1972 through 1974, and he went on to play 19 years in the big leagues, accumulating 2246 hits and stealing 649 bases along the way.

McNamara grew up in Sacramento, California, and ironically, he spent most of his 14 seasons in the minor leagues in cities west of the Mississippi, including Fresno, Amarillo, Dallas, and Albuquerque. His best year in the minor leagues came for the Lewiston Broncs, when he hit .267 as the starting catcher for the team that captured the Northwest League title with an 80-win season. McNamara got his first major league managing job in 1969, when he finished the season managing the Oakland Athletics after Hank Bauer was fired. Though he led the Athletics to 83 wins in 1970, McNamara's contract was not renewed and had to wait until 1974 to gain another big-league managing job. Between 1969 and 1996 McNamara managed 7 teams over a 19-year managing career. McNamara won the American League Manager of the Year Award in 1986, as he led the Boston Red Sox to a first place finish with a 95-66 season.

Stephen "Bud" Souchock: From the Triplets to the Big Leagues and Back Again

Stephen Souchock is one of only two members of the Shrine who played for the Triplets, went on to play in the big leagues, and then returned to manage the Triplets after his playing days were over. (Frank Verdi is the other.) In 1942, the Eastern League was Souchock's kingdom as he hit .313 while leading the league both in runs scored (94) and runs batted in (91) and hitting 13 home runs.

From 1946 through 1955, Souchock spent eight years in the majors, hitting .255 as a reserve outfielder and first baseman for the Yankees, White Sox, and Tigers. He had the honor of serving as a teammate of Hall of Famers Joe Luke Appling, Yogi Berra, Bill Dickey, Joe DiMaggio, Joe Gordon, Al Kaline, George Kell, Hal Newhowser, Phil Rizzuto, and Red Ruffing. During his tenure as manager of the Triplets, he guided the 1957 team to a first place finish, helping develop such future big league stars as Clete Boyer, Deron Johnson, and Lee Thomas.

During the spring of 1957, shortly after Deron Johnson was assigned to Binghamton only one year removed from high school, Souchock recognized the star potential that was present in Johnson's bat and the common fault that Johnson would need to overcome so that the potential could turn to achievement. "A kid is so anxious…if Johnson can just make them throw strikes, he'll be all right, but he's so hungry for a fastball, it'll be hard to wait."

The biggest thing that Johnson learned in that '57 season under Souchock's tutelage was the wisdom of not chasing the fastball out of the zone, no matter how many curveballs he would see cross the plate. Johnson had the privilege of learning from a true "baseball lifer" as Souchock spent over 50 years in the game as a player, minor league manager, and scout. In the 1950's spring training for the Triplets was big news and the *Binghamton*

59

Sun and *Binghamton Evening Press* would file daily stories on the battles for playing time. Sportswriters enjoyed conversing with Souchock, as he did not mince words in talking about the team. His management style would not be successful today; he would be accused of throwing his players "under the bus," whereas in Souchock's day it was just telling it the way he saw it.

The first base competition in spring training summed up Souchock's direct approach. First baseman Frank Leja was a late addition to the Triplets in spring training and Souchock made it clear he was happy to see him. "I want to give him a shot at the job, because he shows me the right attitude. He came here to play ball. The way that some of the other first baseman have looked, I wonder what they came for. They look as though they had a job sewn up and I'm here to say none of them has."

Indeed, Leja beat out Jerry Kudajeski and Jimmie Johnston even though both had seen action for the Triplets in 1956; both Kudajeski and Johnston would find themselves playing in lower-level leagues this year, while Leja hit 22 homers for the Triplets, trailing only Deron Johnson's 26.

As significant as Souchock's diamond accomplishments were, however, in reality, his accomplishments off the field dwarfed his achievements on the field. He served over three years in World War II, enlisting in the army after his MVP 1942 season and serving until his release from service on December 6, 1945. He fought in The Battle of the Bulge in 1944, earning a Bronze Star as commander of a five-man gun crew, knocking out two German tanks. The bronze star accompanied a Silver Star, which he had received earlier in his army stint.

Though Souchock's major league statistics fell short of being legendary, his hustling style left him with many fans along his baseball travels. Keith Olberman, sports commentator and journalist immortalized Souchock to a degree in his article, "Where Have you Gone Steve Souchock?" In it, Olberman tells of how the Yankees trading Souchock to the White Sox for outfielder Jim Delsing in December of 1948 caused his father, who was a diehard Yankee fan, to boycott Yankee stadium:

"Unlike other fathers taking their sons to Yankee Stadium for the first time in 1967, he had not seen them all. The style of Ford, the mysteries of Berra, the brooding solitude of Maris — these he had passed by. He had, in fact, been emotionally boycotting the Yankees since Dec. 14, 1948. That was the day they had traded his favorite player, Steve Souchock, to the White Sox. Souchock hit a robust .203 that last season in pinstripes.

'Doesn't matter,' my father said. 'He was my favorite player. I was never the same after that.' "

Souchock had the perfect demeanor to be a manager for the '50's. His war experience helped him keep the game in perspective, and his humility helped him focus on his players. His sense of humor proved to be a strong point as well. Jim Delsing, his former Tiger teammate and outfield partner in '53 and '54, enjoyed playing alongside Souchock.

"I remember Steve as a great hitter, especially against left-handed pitching. He was also great for the team, always encouraging his teammates and helping people with their problems with hitting and fielding. To sum up everything, Steve was a great team player, friend, and teammate, and he always had good stories to tell."

Deron Johnson: "I Need Hittin!"

In 1997, Deron Johnson, Steve Kraly, and Thurman Munson formed an outstanding Shrine class, with Johnson achieving fame while playing for the National League and using his power to propel him to an RBI title in 1965, when he drove 130 runners home.

Upon his graduation from high school in San Diego in 1956, Johnson had a decision to make—accept a football scholarship to Notre Dame or sign a professional baseball contract with the New York Yankees. He chose the latter and got to play in 63 games, hitting minor league pitching as if he were still playing in high school, smashing 24 home runs in only 243 trips to the plate and hitting .329 for the Class A Kearney (Nebraska) Yankees.

In the off season of 1956 Johnson's power was being compared to that of Mickey Mantle, who was coming off his Triple Crown season. The faith the Yankees had in Johnson's ability was displayed when the Yankee front office sent him to play in Binghamton for his first full professional season in 1957. He was seen as a "can't miss" prospect, as evidenced in the following headline from a *Binghamton Press* article heralding his assignment to the Triplets on April 7th:

Stengel's Future Yanks Assigned to Trips

Triplets manager Stephen Souchock was delighted to have Johnson assigned to his club, anticipating an injection of power. He reasoned that even if Johnson's batting average fell off, he'd be an asset to his team. "I'd say if he can hit .265, he'd be helping us with his power," mused Souchock.

Johnson's youthful exuberance for the offensive side of the game provided Souchock with befuddled amusement early in spring training that year. During a routine position switch he motioned for Johnson to come off the field.

"What's the story, Skip?" Deron asked.

"I want you to do some running," Souchock replied.

"Man, I don't need running. I need hittin!" Johnson responded.

The custom of the day in 1957 was to celebrate the opening of the baseball season with local businesses offering prizes to those Triplets who were able to get the season off to a good start. A full page ad greeted the Triplets on April 23rd, which was opening day at Johnson Field and included such notices as:

Johnson started out slowly that day, going 1 for 4 with no home runs, and that performance reflected the need for Johnson to learn patience at the plate and adjust to seeing a lot more breaking pitches. But at season's end, he had learned his lessons well, following his rookie season with another power-laden one, hitting .303 and adding 26 home runs, giving him 50 home runs in his first two seasons.

The next year found him at AAA Richmond, where he hit 27 home runs, with only Rocky Nelson and Luke Easter surpassing his total in the league. At season's end it became apparent his problem was not his talent, but instead the talent the parent Yankees had at the major league level. Front office executives preferred he play everyday in the minors instead of sitting on the Yankee Stadium bench, so in 1959 and 1960 Johnson hit 52 more homers in the minors. In 1961 the Yankees traded Johnson to the Kansas City Athletics along with Art Ditmar for pitcher Bud Daley. It was not until the 1964 season, however, after the Cincinnati Reds purchased Johnson from the Athletics, that Johnson got a chance to play regularly.

On an individual level, the highlight of Johnson's career came on July 10th and 11th in 1971 when he was a member of the Philadelphia Phillies. On Saturday, in the first game of a twinight doubleheader against the Montreal Expos, Johnson supported the 4-hit pitching of Woodie Fryman by going 3 for 4 and hitting a home run in the Phillies 2-0 victory. In the night cap Johnson also was a difference maker, hitting a home run in his last at bat and going 1 for 4 as the Phils beat the Expos, 3-2. Johnson left the ball park in a great mood that night, as his team swept the doubleheader and he had gone 4-8, hitting two homers and knocking in 40% of his team's runs.

But Saturday's output was dwarfed by Johnson's prowess on Sunday, when he went 3 for 5, with three home runs and five runs batted in. He hit his homers in his first three at bats, giving him four consecutive homers and a two-day hitting binge of 5 home runs, 7 hits, and seven runs batted in!

Two years later he would enjoy the highlight of his career, serving as the designated hitter for the World Champion Oakland Athletics, hitting 19 homers and driving in 81 runs; he also hit .300 in that World Series.

In 1975, with a little over a week left in the season and a lead of three and a half games, the Red Sox acquired Johnson from the White Sox as pennant insurance. He provided a veteran presence and an excellent bat off the bench in the waning days of the season, hitting .600 in ten at bats, with a home run and three RBIs. By June 4th of the next season, however, Johnson had only gotten in 15 games and the Red Sox released him on the nation's 100th birthday, leading him into retirement.

Johnson was not out of the game for long, as by 1979 he became a coach for the Angels. From 1979 to 1991, Johnson served as a major league coach for various teams, including the Angels, Phillies, Mets, Mariners, and White Sox.

While on a return tour of duty as a White Sox in 1991, Johnson was diagnosed with lung cancer. He refused treatment, knowing his odds of overcoming the illness were not good and he did not want to undergo a decrease in the quality of his life that the treatment would cause. He did not go public with the diagnosis, finishing out the '91 season. His disease did not become public until he was too weak to resume his coaching duties for spring training in 1992.

In explaining his father's wishes to keep his disease quiet and not to pursue treatment, his son Dominick explained in the spring of 1992: "Dad felt he had a job to do and didn't want to be sidetracked by a lot of well-intentioned sympathy. That's not his style."

Johnson passed away on April 23, 1992.

Why Kraly Wasn't Getting the Corners…

Steve Kraly got the call for the Shrine in 1997 based on his once-in-a-lifetime 1953 season, when he won 19 games for the Triplets in only four months! Kraly was the youngest of five children and grew up in Whiting, Indiana. His parents emigrated from Yugoslavia before he was born and spoke Croatian at home, so Kraly learned how to speak English while attending public schools in Indiana. Whiting's Indiana scholastic teams benefitted greatly from Kraly's presence, as he excelled in baseball, basketball, and track.

Kraly's athletic talent enabled him to receive a scholarship to Indiana University, but when the team's manager told him freshmen were not allowed to participate in the fall baseball program, Kraly decided to sign a professional contract with the Yankees after one year of college. Before he left, however, he organized his freshmen colleagues and challenged the varsity nine to a baseball game. The game turned out to be a going away party for Kraly, as his freshmen team beat the varsity, 9-0 behind an 8-strikeout performance by Steve. Feeling vindicated, Kraly left school and signed with the Yankees for an $800.00 bonus and a salary of $90.00 a month.

The first professional team that Kraly pitched for was the 1949 Independence Yankees, which was a Class D team in the Kansas-Oklahoma-Missouri league. One of his teammates that year was Mickey Mantle, who hit .313 as he started his path to becoming an American icon. Kraly was the ace of the staff, going 15-10 and posting a 3.28 ERA. He became friends with Mantle even though he was not overly impressed with Mantle's season, as he explained to reporter John W. Fox in 1969: "My opinion of him was so-so. He was a skinny kid, maybe 165, who couldn't pull the ball, bunted his way to .300 and couldn't catch fly balls at shortstop."

In 1950 Kraly moved up to the Western Association and played for the Joplin Miners in Class C ball. Mantle also followed him there, hitting .386 with 26 home runs. Kraly once again was the ace of the staff and went 18-6 that year with a 2.79 ERA! Scouts were pointing to Whitey Ford and Steve Kraly as the top two southpaw prospects in the organization, while Mantle was targeted as the prized everyday prospect. Mantle impressed Kraly far more during this season as he had put on thirty pounds of muscle and almost quadrupled his homer output from the seven he hit at Independence.

While Mantle was impressing Kraly, little Steve was impressing the scouts. Harry Craft, a 6-year veteran of the major leagues, wrote of Kraly in 1950: "Has a live fastball, better than average curve and a fair change. Good control. Pitched six shutouts this season, a fine competitor." Another scout, E.H. Awilling, echoed Craft's opinion, and labeled Kraly as a prospect to keep an eye on: "Has potent fast ball—control good enough, improving rapidly. Not excitable. Always doing better than expected. Seems capable of meeting any and all situations. Watch."

During these early years in professional ball Kraly had one of his most memorable moments. On a night that he had command of his fastball he felt the home plate umpire was missing a lot of strikes. Kraly knew he was painting the low outside corner of the plate but consistently the umpire was calling it a ball. After the game he and Mantle went to a local watering hole and had a few refreshments with the umpiring crew from that night. Steve got up enough courage to converse with the plate umpire during the evening.

"You know, you were not giving me anything on the corner today. Were you seeing everything ok?"

The umpire looked at him and said, "You know, you're right, I can't see those pitches on the corner!"

Kraly's dumbfounded look begged for an explanation.

"You see, I only have a glass eye in my right socket so I can't see those corner pitches too well," the umpire explained. With a smile on his face he moved his hand up to his eye while all eyes at the table were on him—but not for long....

Kraly and Mantle were soon looking at each other in horror.

The umpire stuck his fingers in his socket and pulled out his glass eye. "There, have a look!"

Kraly could not get another sip of his refreshment soon enough.

Two mentors Kraly had coming up through the minor leagues were Phil Page, his manger at Binghamton in 1953, and Hall of Famer Charles Albert "Chief "Bender, one of his minor league pitching coaches. Page taught Kraly how to throw a screwball, which would fade away from righty hitters. Bender taught him how to command his curveball by making every bullpen session have a purpose. Bender required his pitchers to throw twenty curves during a session and the pitchers could not shower until they threw 12 curveballs for strikes.

In 1953 Kraly returned from two years of military service and reclaimed his status as an elite prospect, going 19-2 with the 1953 Triplets. He was called up to the Yankees on July 31st and made his major league debut on August 9th, in front of 42,504 fans at Yankee Stadium, pitching 3 innings of one-run baseball in a 5-0 loss to Billy Pierce and the Chicago White Sox. Kraly was the most surprised person in the stadium when he got the call to come into the game, as he was told by Stengel before the game that he would be throwing in the bullpen just to get his work in.

When it was time to get into the game, Kraly thought he had his nervous energy under control as he walked toward the bullpen gate and then stopped. And waited. And waited some more.

Finally, Ralph Houk, then the Yankees third-string catcher, interrupted Kraly's trance— "Steve, we don't open the gate here. You have to jump over it to get onto the field."

Kraly played the role of the rube expertly, never questioning Houk's advice. He looked at the gate and thought, "No problem, I can hop over that." As Kraly was at the peak of his jump, however, his spikes caught on the top of the fence and he went crashing to the ground, making his first steps onto a major league field a stumble while providing his bullpen mates with a good laugh!

Kraly spent the rest of the season with the big club, going 0-2 with a 3.24 ERA, while also getting involved in a couple more shutouts. On September 15th he lost a 1-0 pitching duel to future Hall of Famer Bob Lemon of the Cleveland Indians. Kraly threw 8 innings, allowing one run on 4 hits while Lemon won his 20th game that day, throwing a 7-hit shutout. Ironically, Lemon had earlier won his 18th game against Kraly with another shutout on August 29th, beating the Yankees 6-0!

Kraly has fond memories of the way baseball was played in his prime. He enjoyed the train travel where they had a club car, sleeping car, and dining car. "The team was like a family, you really got to know each other," he explained.

He is all against the designated hitter and still can't believe today's players charge money for autographs. "If they want money for signing an autograph, they should ask the fans to send money to their favorite charity instead!"

He still gets fan mail and estimates he must have signed 1100 pictures during the last year through the mail. He never accepts money for his signature; if people want to show their appreciation he tells them they can write a check to his favorite cause, the *Children's Home of Wyoming Conference* in Hillcrest, New York.

Thurman Munson to Ron Guidry: "Trust Me"

Thurman Munson came straight from being the fourth player picked in the 1968 amateur draft to the Triplets in June of 1968. The Mets had the first pick in the draft that year and chose Tim Foli from Notre Dame High School in Sherman Oaks, CA. Though Foli had a solid 16-year career playing shortstop in the majors, New York City baseball fans can be forgiven if they find themselves contemplating the effect on both Yankee and Met history if the Mets had not passed on Munson in the summer of '68.

Curiously, the pick right after Munson turned out to be Bobby Valentine, making the 1968 draft the only one ever to produce back-to-back picks that had such a dramatic effect on the baseball history of a city.

When Munson first arrived in Binghamton, he was cocky, self-absorbed and carried a chip on his shoulder that he practically dared someone to knock off. When his teammates first introduced themselves to him to welcome him to the team, they gave him their name and position. Dallas Jones, a 28th round pick in the 1966 draft out of Belhaven College in Jackson, Mississippi, extended his hand to Munson with an innocuous conversation starter.

"Hello, Thurman, my name is Dallas and I play catcher."

Munson looked him straight in the eye and succinctly stated. "Not anymore. I'm the catcher."

No question that Thurman was right—HE WAS THE CATCHER, as even though he joined the team in the middle of the season he caught 67 games and led the team in hitting with a .301 batting average. Though Munson's introductory comment did not sit well with his teammates, his play between the lines and his all-consuming desire to win counter-balanced his misplaced intensity.

Munson joined the Yankees for good in 1969, after a season in Syracuse. By 1974 Munson had matured and had turned his self-absorption into an obsession for fulfilling the team's promise and was elected the first captain of the New York Yankees since Lou Gehrig. By the mid 70's Munson was also letting his sense of humor come out more, using laughter as a tool for motivation. Lou Howell, a former Binghamton Triplet, and Munson's roommate in spring training in '69 knew first hand that Munson always had a sense of humor as well as a miscreant side to him. "I was fast asleep and one night Munson makes a loud noise coming into the room after curfew. I looked up and he was waving his arms in the air," Howell recounted. "All of a sudden he yells 'Look, money's falling from the sky,' and sure enough, bills were falling on me. Apparently he won big at poker that night and he wanted to make sure we got a laugh out of it."

The keys to Munson's learning to lead were his ability to let his playing between the lines do his bragging, and to focus on bringing the best out of his teammates rather than just the best out of himself. When Ron Guidry was making his first start for the Yankees in 1975, Munson came out to the mound to chat with Guidry. He opened the conversation by telling Guidry "Throw a fastball down the middle. Only I'm going to tell the batter you're throwing a fastball down the middle."

Guidry looked at him with a contorted face. In his Louisiana drawl he asked, "Why in hell would you do that?"

Munson replied, "Trust me."

As Munson crouches behind the plate, Guidry goes into his motion and tries to block out the confusion in his mind as he wonders why Munson would tell the hitter what was coming. The hitter is dead set on a fast ball and swings mightily, only to miss! Munson repeats this scenario during the game.

It sinks in with Guidry. Heck, if he can get them out with them knowing what's coming, his stuff must be good enough! After a while, Munson mutes himself behind the plate and Guidry is missing bats with fastballs and sliders, pitching with complete confidence. Munson's confidence has given Guidry a fast path toward believing in himself.

What Guidry didn't know is that this wasn't the first time Munson had used this motivational tactic. Rob Gardner recalled having total faith in Munson as his catcher. "When we were together in Syracuse in '69, I threw a changeup and the batter just corkscrewed himself into the ground, trying to hit that pitch, swinging from the heels," Gardner explains as he sets up his story. "The batter then turns to Munson and says 'What a $%$$ pitch, I dare you to throw that again!' So Thurman comes out and tells me hell, even if he knows it's coming, he won't be able to hit it! So we have a chuckle and we throw the same pitch and sure enough we get another swing and miss!" Gardner is smiling now as he recounts the pleasure of pitching to Munson, "I didn't have to do a whole lot of thinking with Munson behind the plate, he really studied the hitters."

Munson won the American league Rookie of the Year award in 1970 (.302, 6 HR, 53 RBI) and the MVP award in 1976, when he hit .302 with 17 HRs and 105 RBIs. Over an 11-year career, he hit .292 and won three gold gloves as well as two World Championships. Munson's success did not surprise Howell. "The amount of improvement I saw in his game from '68 to '69 was tremendous. It seemed as if he got better every day," declared Howell, who served as Munson's backup catcher in Syracuse in '69. Howell marveled at Munson's ability to hit that whole season. "He would come back from military reserve duty, where he wasn't doing any baseball activity, and pick up without missing a beat," Howell explained.

Despite Munson's accomplishments on the field, because his life ended in its prime and because he was beloved by his fans and teammates, Munson today is most remembered for his untimely death. As has been well documented, he died on August 2, 1979, while practicing takeoffs and landings in his new jet at the Canton-Akron airport. As a tribute to him, the Yankees left his locker untouched in Yankee Stadium from 1979 until the final game there in 2008. Today the locker is in the New Yankee Stadium museum.

Munson's last spoken words were to his two friends who were his companions while he practiced his takeoffs and landings, Jerry Anderson and Dave Hall. After the plane had come to a standstill on the ground, minus its nose and a wing, Munson, pinned in his seat and losing consciousness asked:

"Hey are you guys OK?"

Hall and Anderson were shaken but OK. When Munson lost consciousness, they raced to free him, but Munson's legs were pinned and the door on his side was jammed shut. When fire and smoke engulfed the cabin, they had to jump out of the plane, receiving second and third degree burns. An autopsy showed Munson died from the results of the fire and had suffered a broken neck in the crash as well.

John H. Johnson: From Johnson Field to Kuhn's Right-Hand Man

When John H. Johnson was inducted into the Shrine in 1998, he became the third Johnson elected – George F. was the first and Deron, the slugger, was the second. John H. was the secretary to George Weiss, the general manager of the Yankees, when Weiss asked him to take over the business manager (today called general manager) position for the Binghamton Triplets in 1951.

The opening came about because the current business manager, Chet Lane, had resigned in order to take another job opportunity in California; while Lane moved his wife and two children west, Weiss looked no further than his secretary's adjacent office for Lane's replacement. One of the first moves that Johnson made as the head of the Triplets was to hire Jerry Toman as his assistant, who had started working for the Triplets as a teenager in the concession stands, gone off to war, and had returned to Johnson Field for employment while pursuing a college degree from 1947 to 1951.

Johnson presided over a very successful period in Triplets history, as well as a time of prosperity for the community. The fans came out to support post World War II baseball while the economy of the area also thrived. Many houses were springing up in Johnson City and Endicott as part of the Endicott Johnson housing assistance program and area employees were grateful to the employers in the area, as evidenced by this letter that was printed in the *Binghamton Sun* in 1950:

Mr. Charles F Johnson, Jr.
Endicott Johnson Corporation
Endicott, NY

Dear Mr. Johnson;
Having recently been a patient at the Wilson Memorial Hospital, I wish
to extend my sincere thank you, especially to you, Dr. Steenburg and
special nurses for the splendid medical and surgical care I received
while there.

Thanks also to the nurses of EW2 and Annex 5, as well as to my
relatives, friends, and co-workers for their expressions of get well
wishes extended me.

I wish to express my heartfelt appreciation to you, Mr. Charlie, and to
Mr. George W, for making this wonderful care possible. Within the past
nine months, I have been hospitalized three times and each time
received a bill, marked 'paid in full."

May God Bless you All
John A. Tralovic and Family

Johnson had the privilege of overseeing arguably the greatest two-year stretch in
Binghamton baseball history, as the 1953 team finished with a 96-55 record, scoring 700
runs and only allowing 538 runs. The 96 wins followed a 77-60 record the year before,
and stars of that 1953 team included fellow Shrine inductees Wally Burnette, winner of
21 games (and he won two more in the playoffs), and Steve Kraly, who went 19-2.

During Johnson's relatively short tenure in the front office of the Triplets, over two dozen
players went on to play in the major leagues. The most prominent players during this time
included Johnny Blanchard, Bob Grim, Bill "Moose" Skowron, and Bill Virdon. Also,
Marv Throneberry, later to be known to New York Mets fans as 'Marvelous Marv," when
he became an original New York Met in 1962, had a cup of coffee with the '53 Triplets,
getting 24 at bats. He was one of the first players to have played for the Yankees and the
Mets, joining Shrine mates Rob Gardner, Ralph Terry, and Cory Lidle in accomplishing
this feat.

Johnson used his experience at Binghamton as a springboard to a remarkable
administrative career in baseball. From 1960 to 1970, he served in a variety of roles in the
front office for the New York Yankees, including being farm director from 1961 to 1964
and then serving as Vice President for Minor League Operations in 1965. He only left the
Yankees when he got an offer he could not refuse—from 1970 to 1978, Jonson served as
Commissioner Bowie Kuhn's primary assistant, also serving as Chairman of the Rules
Committee. During his tenure on the rules committee, baseball adopted use of the
designated hitter by the American League. Johnson's tenure in Kuhn's office also saw the
first World Series played at night as well.

Today, the *John H. Johnson President's Award*, established in 1974, is presented
annually to honor the best minor league franchise—taking into account such things as
franchise stability, contributions to baseball in the community and promotion of the

baseball industry. One team from each league in affiliated baseball is nominated for the award, keeping John H. Johnson's contributions to professional baseball in the forefront of minor league administrators.

Lee Thomas: "Carter's Bat Was Like a Hammer"

Lee Thomas, member of the 1998 Shrine Class, was signed out of Beaumont High School in St. Louis, MO., by the New York Yankees in 1954 and began his professional career in Owensboro, Kentucky, where he hit .304 and was a teammate of Tony Kubek, shortstop for the Yankees from 1957-1965. Thomas was elected both for his performance as a Triplet and his accomplishments after he left Binghamton. He had a solid eight-year career as a power-hitting outfielder and first baseman in the majors, hitting 106 HRs and finishing with a career batting average of .255. After retiring as a player, he worked in the player development arena, rising through the ranks to become a general manager.

Thomas played for the Triplets from 1956 through 1959, appearing in 430 games, with the highlight of his Triplets career coming in 1959, when he hit .304 with 22 home runs and 122 RBIs. He was also a mainstay on the 1957 team, which was one of the most successful teams in Triplets history, as it compiled a record of 85-55 for a .607 regular season winning percentage. Joining Thomas on that team were Shrine mates Clete Boyer and Deron Johnson.

The spring of '57 saw Thomas battling with Tom McDonald for the third outfield spot, as Deron Johnson was a lock for the left field job and cleanup hitter while Fred Carpenter was targeted for center field. Thomas made the opening day lineup, hitting 7th and playing right field; he played in 109 games in 1957 and hit .262 with 8 home runs in 321 at bats.

Being an outfielder and first baseman for the Yankees organization in the late 1950's was not a fast way to make it to the big leagues; not with names like Mantle, Maris, Tresh, Pepitone and Skowron forming an impenetrable queue. The professional break for Thomas came in the form of a trade, as on May 8th, 1961, he went to the Los Angeles Angels, along with Ryne Duren and ex-Triplet Johnny James, for Tex Clevenger and Bob Cerv. As a member of the Angels, Thomas had a chance to play regularly and in 1962, he was selected to both All Star squads for the American League, as he hit .290 with 26 HRs and 104 RBIs.

As successful a career as Thomas had inside the lines, it can be argued that he had even more success as a front office executive. He was the general manager of the 1993 Philadelphia Phillies team that lost the World Series to the Toronto Blue Jays on Joe Carter's 3-run home run in Game 6. Before Carter hit his walk-off homer, Thomas had a premonition. He turned to his wife and asked her to leave the stadium with him. Before they got out of the stadium, the game had ended with Carter's homer. "It was like somebody hit me over the head with a hammer," Thomas said.

Though he lost the World Series, Thomas took solace in the fact that he was instrumental in building a National League Championship team. After being fired from the Phillies after the 1997 season, he became a special assistant to General Manager Dan Duquette with the Red Sox and helped lay the groundwork for the championship 2004 team, helping to sign Manny Ramirez and Johnny Damon, among others. Thomas was not there to see Boston's World Series drought end in 2004, though, as he resigned after the 2002 season.

Theo Epstein had replaced Duquette and emphasized the statistical side of the game. Thomas valued scouting over statistics and computers and felt it best to move on. He became a scout for the Brewers, then was out of baseball until Dan Duquette became the general manager of the Orioles in 2011. One of the first calls he made was to Thomas, and Thomas joined forces with his colleague once again, becoming his special assistant.

Bill Virdon: "Will It Mean Something to You?"

Bill Virdon was the everyday center fielder for the 1952 championship Triplets team and established himself as a solid prospect with his superlative defensive play. His outstanding glove, excellent speed, and superior work ethic overshadowed his .262 batting average and power totals of 2 homers and 43 runs batted in.

His potential was evident and he fulfilled it in his inaugural big league season with the St. Louis Cardinals in 1955. Virdon holds the distinction of being one of only two ex-Binghamton players to become NL Rookie of the Year (Jason Bay, who played for the Binghamton Mets in 2002 was the other). In '55 Virdon hit .284, with 17 homers and 68 RBIs in his freshman season, rising to the top of a rookie class that included teammate and third baseman, Ken Boyer, Brooklyn Dodger pitchers Don Bessent, Sandy Koufax, and Karl Spooner, and right fielder Roberto Clemente of the Pittsburgh Pirates.

The Yankees traded Virdon to the Cardinal organization in the spring of 1954 for future Hall-of-Famer Enos Slaughter. At the time, the Yanks saw Slaughter as insurance for their run at a sixth consecutive championship; by year's end, however, the Yanks had no championship and Slaughter had hit only .248. Meanwhile Virdon's promise increased on a day-by-day basis during the '54 season as he hit .333 for the Cardinal's Rochester team, earning him a promotion to the big leagues in 1955. After his outstanding big league rookie season, he was traded to the Pirates early in the '56 season, where his speed and defense enabled him to cover the wide expanses of center field in Forbes Field for the next decade and even garnered him a gold glove award in 1962, which was no small feat, given competition from the likes of Willie Mays and Curt Flood. Virdon's career offensive numbers were solid: .267, 91 homers, 81 triples, and 502 RBI.

In 2007, Virdon recalled his stay in Binghamton as being essential for his big league success. "Binghamton was one of the steps I needed to make it to the majors," he explained. During the '52 season, Virdon learned to play within himself, providing a steady presence in the seventh spot in the lineup as well as outstanding defense day in and day out. Jack Slattery, then sports editor of the *Binghamton Sunday Press*, sounded like a poet as he recalled the most pleasant aspect of that '52 season. "The work of Billy Virdon in center field gave us the most pleasure from an esthetic viewpoint. He is grace personified…his almost careless lope after a routine fly…his daring dashes to the confining center field wall….this seemingly effortless ease with which he goes either to his left or right to scoop and fire, in one fluid motion, tremendously strong and accurate."

For Virdon, Binghamton wasn't only a place to develop professional skills. That year was also the first one of married life for Virdon, and it also marked one of the happiest moments of his life. On September 3rd his wife gave birth to their first child back in his hometown of Pine Bluffs, MO. Commenting on the birth of Deborah Ann Virdon, who entered the world at eight pounds, two ounces, Virdon, alluding to the challenge he had in adjusting to lefty pitching, jokingly said, " I hope she's a righthander." That night Virdon celebrated on the field, hitting in his usual seventh spot, going 2-4 with one RBI as the Triplets beat Albany. Today Virdon has nothing but fond memories of his stay in Binghamton. "The city was beautiful, the people could not have been kinder."

1952 was Virdon's third season in pro ball and his success here solidified his role as a trading chip in the Yankee farm system, as a man named Mantle was running down fly balls in the cavernous center field of Yankee Stadium and providing big-league thunder with his bat, hitting .301 with 23 home runs and 87 runs batted in 1952.

Virdon gives a lot of credit to his Binghamton manager, Jim Gleeson, for his development, both as a player and big-league manager. Virdon proudly states, "He probably helped my career as much as anyone." The lessons Virdon learned from Gleeson stayed with him--defense, speed, timely hitting, respect for the opposition, and confidence were the rules for success that Virdon practiced as a player and later preached as a manager during his 13 years managing in the majors. Ironically, as a manager, Virdon is best remembered not for leading the Pirates and Astros to first place finishes in 1972 and 1980, respectively, but for managing the Yankees in 1974 and 1975, only to never win a game at Yankee Stadium! During '74 and '75 the Yankees played home games at Shea Stadium while Yankee Stadium was being renovated.

Throughout that 1952 season Gleeson managed to the skills of his ball club. Realizing one weakness on his team was a lack of power, Gleeson took advantage of the team's youth and speed, encouraging use of the hit and run and waving runners home from first when balls were hit into the outfield gaps. Gleeson's role as a strategist and leader was evident in his post game address after having lost Game 3 of the Eastern League Championship Series to Reading, 5-1. Gleeson demanded his players not lose focus and made it clear he was disappointed in their play. "I want you out here tomorrow night playing the way you can play. You won the first two games, but these guys aren't going to lie down and quit."

Gleeson warned that the pitcher they would face the next night was even better than the one who had just shut them down. "I understand they're throwing the other left hander (Dick Tomanek) at us tomorrow. Well, let me tell you something. He's got better stuff than this guy who beat us tonight (Roberto Vargas)." After the stern warning, Gleeson pumped up the team, letting them know he knew they were good enough to win. "We've beaten Vargas on nights when he looked a lot better than he did tonight." The Triplets went on to win the Series, four games to one.

Gleeson had already been where Virdon yearned to go and, as an impressionable 20-year-old youngster, Virdon yearned to follow in Gleeson's footsteps and have a productive big league career. Gleeson was an outfielder in the big leagues from 1938 to 1942 for Cincinnati and Cleveland. In 1940, Gleeson's lone year as a regular, he hit .313.

If one play in 1952 summed up Virdon's work ethic and personality, it was his inside-the-park home run against Reading in a 12-5 win for the Triplets. Virdon was a model player, working hard, and following the suggestions of his managers and coaches along the journey to the big leagues. In 1953 his manager for the Kansas City Blues in the American Association recommended he start wearing his reading glasses when he played baseball as well. 1954, his first full year wearing glasses in the field, proved to be his best hitting year as he hit .333.

In 2008 when Virdon received the phone call telling him he had been inducted into the Binghamton Shrine, he asked his caller, "Will it mean something to you if I come back for the ceremony?" When Virdon was told the Shrine committee would greatly appreciate seeing him after more than a half century had passed since he roamed the outfield of Johnson Field, Virdon's reply was filled with humility and gratitude. "I'd be happy to come back if it means something to you. Thank you for the honor."

James Whitney: A Grasshopper Hails From Conklin, N.Y.

James "Grasshopper" Whitney holds the distinction of being the only major league baseball player born in Conklin, New York; he was a star National League pitcher in the 1880's, winning 194 games while playing for the Boston Beaneaters, Kansas City Cowboys, Washington Nationals, and Indianapolis Hoosiers.

As was often the custom in the nascent days of professional baseball, Whitney both pitched and played the field. In 10 years as an outfielder and first baseman he hit .261. Bill James, in *The New Bill James Historical Abstract* ranked Whitney as the tenth best player in the history of the game who was a pitcher and everyday player. The first two members of this top ten were Babe Ruth, and John Montgomery Ward.

Whitney played for the Binghamton Crickets in 1878, when Binghamton played in the International Association, with teams ranging from Manchester, NH in the East to Buffalo, NY, in the West and Pittsburgh in the South. Whitney teamed with John Montgomery Ward, who was elected to the Binghamton Shrine in 2003 and the Baseball Hall of Fame in 1964, to form a formidable pitching duo on that 1878 team.

The 1878 Crickets, though hailed as one of the strongest professional teams outside of the National League, disbanded after only a few months into the 1878 season, reflecting the difficulties in getting minor league baseball to gain a foothold in the sporting scene during the last quarter of the nineteenth century. While local town and company teams were popular in their communities, minor league baseball was still searching for its niche between the amateur ranks and the elite play of the National League. Players were often viewed with suspicion as well. Vernona Gomez, in her biography of her father, Lefty Gomez, described the early ballplayers in less than a stellar tone: "Most professional players traveled from town to town, staying in hotels and cutting a swath through both the local liquor supply and the women."

Whitney may have played in the "Dead Ball" era, but his arm was anything but dead. In his rookie season in 1881 in the major leagues, Whitney threw over 550 innings, starting 63 games! He allowed 2.48 earned runs a game and won 31 games that year, but somehow also managed to lose 33 games! His innings pitched totals for his first eight years in the majors were 550.1, 420, 514, 336, 441.1, 393, 404.2, and 325. Pitch counts obviously were not even a glint in anyone's eyes in the 1890's. Amazingly, in those first eight years, his at bats were 301, 275, 434, 286, 307, 276, 219, and 148.

After his release from the Philadelphia Athletics in July of 1890, Whitney returned to live in Binghamton. He had thrown only 40 innings upon his release, a far cry from the days he could be counted on to throw 500 innings. Less than a year later, on May 21st, Whitney succumbed to tuberculosis; he is buried in Spring Forest Cemetery in Binghamton.

Whitney got his nickname due to his pitching delivery of a "hop, skip and a jump," similar to the actions of a grasshopper. In 1883 and '84, he had a strikeout-to-walk ratio of approximately 10 to 1. Almost a quarter century after his untimely death, Whitney was remembered as one of the fastest pitchers in the game by Jim O'Rourke, a 23-year major league veteran and a 1945 inductee into the Baseball Hall of Fame: "There were no restrictions placed on (pitchers) as to delivery, and they could double up like a jack-knife and deliver the ball. That was the way Jim Whitney used to do, and he would let the ball go at terrific speed. It was a wonder that anyone was able to hit him at all. He was the swiftest pitcher I ever saw."

Bud Fowler: "A Dandy in Every Respect"

John "Bud" Fowler's election to the Binghamton Shrine stems from his playing for the Binghamton Bingos in 1887 and his efforts to integrate minor league baseball in the late nineteenth century. Through no fault of his own, his stay with the Bingos was a short one, but one that left an indelible and sad mark on Binghamton's baseball history.

Fowler was the first African American in organized baseball, making his debut by playing for the Lynn/Worcester team in the International Association in 1878. The International Alliance and the League Alliance were the first two defined minor leagues, as their mission was to work in cooperation with the National League, which was the only major league at the time. Before 1877 the non-major league baseball teams largely existed as independent semi-pro teams. By playing for Lynn/Worcester, Fowler held the distinction of being the first African American to integrate a team in minor league history, pre-dating Jackie Robinson's 1946 stint with the Montreal Royals by 69 years.

The diminutive Fowler was skilled at multiple positions, playing catcher, second base, and pitcher in his minor league career. His primary position was second base, where he displayed a good arm, excellent defense and a sound bat. His career was a peripatetic one, though not by choice. Throughout the 1880's his career followed the same cycle. Join a team, perform well, but move on once objections to his color started being bandied about; from 1878 to 1886 he played for eight teams. In November of 1886 he signed with the Binghamton team and the color of his skin was addressed by Binghamton team officials in an article in The Sporting Life:

"Fowler has not, and will not, be released for any consideration. Fowler is a dandy in every respect. Some say that Fowler is a colored man, but we account for his dark complexion by the fact that... in chasing after balls he has become tanned from constant and careless exposure to the sun."

At first glance, the remarks are clearly a public vote of confidence for Fowler. But upon a second reading, either the remarks were meant to poke fun at those who objected to African Americans integrating the diamond or officials were leaving themselves an out by not openly advocating the signing of an African American. Only a few months later the resolve of the Binghamton officials was tested when on June 27th, nine Binghamton players signed a petition saying they would not play if Fowler were to remain on the team.

Fowler, feeling betrayed by his teammates was unwilling to fight; rather he asked for his release on June 30; it was granted provided that he didn't sign with another International League club. Later that season the Boston *Herald* later printed, "The players of the Binghamton club have each been fined $50 by the directors for having refused to go upon the field six weeks ago unless Fowler, the colored second baseman, was removed." The Binghamton club never recovered from the controversy, however, and by the middle of August, less than two months after the controversy started, the club disbanded.

On July 14th, a scant two weeks after Fowler was granted his release, the International League formally banned any additional signings of African American players. On this same day, league officials were reacting to white players' grumblings and derogatory comments by the press suggesting that the International League change its classification to "colored league." On the same day -- the 14th -- Chicago White Stockings team captain Cap Anson refused to take the field in an exhibition game against Newark of the International League unless African American pitcher George Stovey did not play. Stovey backed out of the game feigning illness. In late July, John Montgomery Ward of the New York Giants and a member of the Binghamton Shrine class of 2003, tried to sign Stovey to a National League contract, but Anson allegedly protested again. Rather than formally exclude African American players, organized baseball executives colluded on the topic, ensuring no African Americans played in the minors or majors.

60 years later, several Brooklyn Dodgers circulated a petition about not playing alongside Jackie Robinson. But when news of the petition reached Dodgers' general manager Branch Rickey and manager Leo Durocher, they quickly stomped it out, fully supporting Robinson. In 1887, there was no similar support for Fowler. Binghamton officials accepted Fowler's resignation and the National League gave credibility to Anson. Organized baseball, by not standing up to its protesting players, would wait until Jackie Robinson played for the Montreal Royals in 1946.

An ironic postscript to this story is that in 1999, before the ceremony inducting Al Downing to the Binghamton Shrine, Downing was strolling the concourse and paused longer than expected at the plaque of Bud Fowler. With a bemused look on his face, he stated.

"That's not Bud Fowler."

In looking at the plaque for John W. "Bud" Fowler, Downing pointed out that the picture they had on the plaque was that of Moses "Fleetwood" Walker, who was actually the first African American to play in the major leagues when he briefly played for the Toledo Blue Stockings franchise in 1883. Jackie Robinson gets credit for integrating baseball because with his play, African Americans were officially welcomed to major league baseball, breaking the unwritten ban against African Americans that existed since Fowler's day.

If you look closely at Fowler's Shrine plaque today, you can see the picture portion of the plaque is thicker than the rest of the plaques adorning the concourse. This is because the Mets laid the correct picture of Fowler over the Walker picture. This correction was made on the urging of local baseball historian and current Shrine committee member, Joe McCann.

Vic Raschi: From the Cellar to the Penthouse

In 1941 the Yankees signed Vic Raschi off the William and Mary campus, which he had been attending after being a standout high school athlete in his hometown of Springfield, Massachusetts. As part of his agreement with the Yankees to leave college early, Raschi got the Yankees to pay for his studies at William and Mary during the offseason so he could get his degree. Raschi would put this degree to use after his playing days were over as he taught and coached at the State University of New York at Geneseo for a number of years.

It took Raschi five years before he reached Binghamton, as he lost the 1943-1945 seasons to World War II. Raschi was one of the few bright spots for the '46 Triplets, as that '46 team was one of the worst in Binghamton history, finishing 45 and one-half games behind the first place Scranton Red Sox and only getting 51 wins the entire season.

Raschi posted a 10-10 record and earned a promotion to the Newark Bears, the AAA farm team of the Yankees in late summer. On September 23rd he made his debut for the Yanks, pitching a complete game and beating the Philadelphia Athletics, 9-6.

In his lone Triplet season, Raschi pitched better than his record indicated, as the Triplets did not give him much run support. While he pitched to a .500 record, the '46 Triplets produced only a .364 winning percentage. Raschi's 10 wins put him in the top twenty pitchers for games won in the Eastern League that year, and other pitchers of note in the Eastern League included future Red Sox hurlers Mel Parnell and Mickey McDermott.

In 1947 Raschi won the first of his six World Championships with the Yankees, joining a staff that included Allie Reynolds, Bill Bevens, Spec Shea, and Spud Chandler. It was Raschi's tenure with the Yankees that got him elected to the Binghamton Shrine, as Raschi was the ace of the Yankee Staff from 1949-1953 when the Yanks won the World Series five years in a row. During that five-year span Raschi won 92 games, winning 21 games in each season from 1949 to 1951.

Raschi was known as a no-nonsense, hard-throwing right hander, with an intimidating mound presence and an ability to come through when the pressure was highest. On the final day of the 1949 season the Red Sox and Yankees were tied for first and Raschi got the starting nod that day. He shut out the Red Sox for eight innings, protecting a 1-0 lead against a lineup that included Hall of Famers Bobby Doerr and Ted Williams and perennial all stars Vern Stephens and Dom DiMaggio. Only after the Yankees scored four in the top of the ninth did Raschi yield any runs as the Yankees beat the Red Sox, 5-3.

Six years later, in the 1952 World Series, Raschi beat the Dodgers in Game 6, forcing the seventh game where the Yankees clinched their fourth consecutive championship. In 11 World Series games, Raschi was 5-3 with a sparkling 2.24 ERA. From 1948 through 1953, Raschi teamed with Allie Reynolds and Eddie Lopat to form a formidable 1-2-3 starting pitching punch; the three pitchers became close friends as did their wives. During the baseball season the families of the three pitchers all lived within a mile of one another in New Jersey and the six of them were the best of friends during the season and remained lifelong friends off the field. The pitchers became known as "The Big Three" and were established clubhouse leaders as well.

Phil Rizzuto succinctly summed up their friendship—"Vic and Sally Raschi, Earlene and Allie Reynolds, Ed and Libby Lopat. Those six were like a family. A happy family."

For most of his adult life, Raschi was a beloved member of the small town of Groveland, outside of Geneseo. His memory is kept alive with various sites and organizations with his surname. Today, the women's softball diamond at SUNY Geneseo is named Raschi Field, in honor of his years serving as baseball coach for Geneseo (currently the college only has a club baseball team). The *Geneseo Rotary-Vic Raschi Little League* organization celebrated its thirtieth anniversary in June of 2013.

Raschi may have been a celebrated Yankee, but he was never too big for Groveland. The following tribute was left by baseball fan Tom Nichols at the Find a Grave web site for Vic Raschi many years after his passing; it shows the everyday elegance of the life that Raschi lived.

```
Dear Vic, I will always remember you as the father of my
friend "Willie" and the marvelous times I had at your house
when your wife was my Cub Scout Den mother. I also remember
you once owned a liquor store in Geneseo, New York.
You were always very nice and interested in us as scouts
and helping out. I remember you fondly as the warm person
you were.
RIP
- Tom Nichols
```

Steve Swisher: Father Knows Best

The 1999 Shrine class included Bud Fowler, Vic Raschi, Al Downing, and Steve Swisher, who became the first inductee associated with the Binghamton Mets. Swisher was the manager of the Mets in the inaugural 1992 season and led the team to the Eastern League Championship in his first year at the helm.

Swisher enjoyed his stay in Binghamton and the community came out in record numbers to support his team. The 1992 team drew over a quarter million fans to what was then called Binghamton Municipal Stadium.

Swisher's management style focused on doing the little things, the things that don't show up in the box score to win games. Before he managed in Binghamton he managed the Tidewater Tides and told the *Newport News Daily Press* that "I believe in going from first to third on a single, throwing to the right base, hitting the cutoff man and taking out the second baseman on the double play, to me that's what wins you games."

Swisher was not hesitant to lash out at the media if he had a problem with the coverage of his team. John Fox, noted Binghamton sportswriter and a member of the Shrine Class of 2011, recalls being on the receiving end of Swisher's rants on more than one occasion. "In one game story I had quoted pitching coach Randy Neimann and Swisher didn't like what was said. He let me have it,' Fox explained, remembering Swisher's tirade as if it were yesterday. "He screamed, 'If you want a quote about something, you come to me. I am the manager of this team and what I say is what counts.' "

In 1992 the B-Mets finished a game behind Canton-Akron in the regular season with a record of 79-59, but won both playoff matchups to garner the championship. Catcher Brook Fordyce, who hit .258 in a 10-year major league career, was a mainstay on that championship team, providing excellent defense and hitting .278 with 11 home runs and

78 RBIs. First baseman Alan Zinter led the team with 16 home runs while center fielder Rob Katzaroff led the team with a .282 batting average and 24 stolen bases.

The strength of the team was its pitching, however, with Bobby Jones leading the way with a 12-4 record and a stunning 1.84 ERA. Future big leaguers Joe Vitko, John Johnstone, and Pete Walker rounded out the rotation. The primary closer was Julian Vasquez, who saved 17 games before he was promoted to Triple A; Chris Dorn picked up the closer's role after Vasquez left.

Swisher not only enjoyed being the manager of a championship team that summer, but he also delighted in the fact that Nick, his 12-year old son, spent the summer with him as well. The always exuberant Nick Swisher, who hit 107 homers for the Yankees during his 4-year sojourn (2009-2012) in the Big Apple, regularly worked out on the Binghamton diamond, getting an early education in baseball both between and outside the white lines.

Before pursuing his managerial career, Steve Swisher served as a backup catcher for the Cubs, Cardinals, and Padres from 1974 to 1982, hitting .216 with 20 home runs and 124 RBIs in his career. Swisher was a graduate of South High School in Parkenburg, West Virginia, and was drafted by the Chicago White Sox with the 21st overall pick of the 1973 amateur baseball draft.

In Swisher's second and final year with the B-Mets in '93, the team finished a disappointing 68-72, but he impressed front office personnel enough so that he was added to the New York Mets coaching staff from 1994 through 1996, serving as the bullpen coach.

While coaching with the Mets, Swisher worked closely with Todd Hundley, who hit 41 home runs in 1996. In 1995 Hundley was still trying to establish himself as a major league catcher and in April of that year, Swisher commented on getting Hundley mentally ready. "Everyone gets to a point in their career where they try to force things. You can't make things happen. You have to get to a comfortable point, a relaxed point. I wanted to get him to the point where he wasn't worried about failing."

Hundley had a 14-year career in the big leagues, finishing with 202 lifetime home runs. No doubt Swisher's experience with Todd, whose father Randy was a catcher in the major leagues for 14 years, helped him in preparing Nick for the pressure of following in the footsteps of a father who played in the big leagues.

Spud Chandler: 'I'll Be Pitching in this Lot!"

While the nation was contemplating transitioning from Herbert Hoover to Franklin Delano Roosevelt and trying to find its way out of its deep depression, Spurgeon Ferdinand Chandler was transitioning from being a baseball and football star for the University of Georgia to a twenty-four-year old professional baseball player in Greater Binghamton, New York.

In 1932 Chandler was signed by the Yankees after he was graduated from the University of Georgia, where he starred in both football and baseball. He waited to sign a professional contract until after he finished college, as he enjoyed studying agriculture and playing both big time sports. Also playing into his decision was that he was offered contracts by the Cardinals and Giants in 1929, but Chandler was a diehard Yankee fan and was willing to wait until his favorite team offered him a contract. When Chandler played football against NYU in November of 1931 at Yankee Stadium, after the game he went to the pitcher's mound and threw footballs through the goalposts. A confident Chandler explained to his teammates "Before long, I'll be pitching in this lot!"

The summer after he graduated from Georgia, Chandler made the transition from amateur to pro a smooth one, as he won 8 of 9 decisions for the Triplets before being promoted to Springfield, where he won all four of his starts. Chandler's rookie campaign proved to be a foreshadowing of his major league career— he had a winning percentage of .833.

Despite a successful year at every step of his minor league career, Chandler did not join Joe McCarthy's Yankees until 1937. Once he arrived on the big league scene, Chandler never looked back, winning three World Championships during his 11-year stay in the big leagues, all with the Yankees. Chandler's success is even more impressive when you realize he lost most of 1944 and 1945 to military service, appearing in only one game in 1944 and 4 games in 1945. Chandler's lifetime winning percentage was .717 (109-43), placing him second behind only Al Spalding on the all-time winning percentage list for pitchers with over 100 wins (Spalding had a .795 percentage). Another distinction that Chandler holds is that he is the only Yankee pitcher to have won the MVP award, due to his 20-3 record and 1.64 ERA in 1943.

While Chandler pitched for the Triplets in 1932 his manager was Billy Meyer, who would go on to manage the Pittsburgh Pirates from 1948 through 1952 and win the National League Manager of the Year Award in 1948. Chandler's teammates on that 1932 team included first baseman George McQuinn, who went on to play for 12 years in the majors, and Henie Groh, who became a 16-year veteran of the big leagues and had a career batting average of .292. Chandler also pitched for Meyer in 1933 for the Triplets, winning another 10 games before being promoted to the Newark Bears, then a Double-A team in the International League.

Chandler loved sharing his pitching knowledge with others; Paul Fung Jr., who followed in his father's footsteps and became a noted newspaper cartoonist, would often attend games at Yankee Stadium in the 1930's as a guest of Lefty Gomez. Gomez was good friends with Fung's dad and Gomez considered the younger Fung a good luck charm, sort of like an unofficial mascot of the team. Years later, Fung Jr. reflected on his time spent with the players. "I pitched for my high school team. I had great teachers…Lefty, Spud Chandler and Red Ruffing. They showed me how to throw a slider and helped me with my curveball and changeup. Then they'd tell me to practice what they preached, and called over Bill Dickey or Joe Glenn to go behind the plate and catch me."

After Chandler finished playing, he also spent time as a minor league manager and scout. While being employed as a scout with the Yankees, Chandler would often work with minor leaguers. In 1950, Marvin Behr, sports editor for the *Binghamton Sun*, noted "Manager George Selkirk is making good use of Spud Chandler's stay with the Trips. The Yankee scout took over the first part of today's practices, working with the pitchers on how to cover first and how to field their position generally."

Al Downing: "I Never Say 7:15 Anymore, I Say It's a Quarter After Seven"

On April 8th, 1974 Al Downing threw a fastball down the middle of the plate to Henry Aaron and Aaron deposited it over the left field fence in Atlanta's Fulton County Stadium, breaking Babe Ruth's career home run record that had endured since 1935. (Ironically, another Shrine member, Vic Raschi, gave up Aaron's first home run in the big leagues in 1954 while pitching for the St. Louis Cardinals.) Years later, after Downing had answered over a thousand questions a thousand times over about what it felt like to give up Aaron's record homer, he had a quick retort:

"I never say 7:15 any more; I say it's a quarter after seven."

Downing won twenty games in 1974, was an American League All Star in 1967 and won 123 games during his career, yet he is mostly remembered for giving up Aaron's record-breaking homer. The fact that Barry Bonds broke Aaron's record does not erase Downing from memory, for Bond's record is tainted with steroid implications and no one remembers who gave up homer # 716 to Bonds anyway. (For the record, it was journeyman Mike Bacsik.)

Downing's election to the Shrine is recognition of both his performance for the Triplets and his work in the majors. In 1961 Downing started 12 games for the Triplets, and went 9-1 with a 1.84 ERA over 98 innings. Despite having just turned 20, Downing was called up to the Yankees on July 19th of that year, and though he only got into five games, he had a ringside seat for the Yankees' championship season. He also pitched in the World Series in 1963, 1964 and 1974..

Downing was born on June 28, 1941, in Trenton, New Jersey and grew up idolizing Willie Mays, Jackie Robinson, and Larry Doby. The Yankees signed him in 1961 off the Rider University campus and assigned the 19-year-old hard throwing lefty to the Triplets for his start of professional baseball. By June, Downing was being recommended for a call up to help the Yankees in what had become an annual pennant drive in the early 1960's.

Downing had little trouble adjusting to life in Binghamton. "There was a lot of talent in that league, but I also knew I could pitch with anyone," Downing explained years later. Some of Downing's pitching colleagues from the Eastern League that year who went on to solid major league careers included Sonny Siebert, Wilbur Wood, and Ray Culp. Future Yankee teammates from that '61 Triplets team included pitchers Dooley Womack and Pete Mikkelson and second baseman Horace Clarke; with pitcher Bob Meyer and reserve outfielder Elvio Jimenez also serving as Downing's teammates for a cup of coffee in Yankee pinstripes.

Downing is a familiar face to sports fans in the Southern Tier. He returns to Binghamton every year in late summer to participate in Jim "Mudcat" Grant's All Star Golf Tournament, which provides financial support to The Broome County Urban League, The Boys and Girls Clubs of Binghamton, Catholic Charities of Broome County, and the Community Hunger Outreach Warehouse (CHOW).

Grant, like Downing, an ex-twenty game winner in the big leagues explains "Every time I come to Binghamton, I think of the great Harmon Killebrew. He would always say, 'Mudcat, we are only here for a little while, and that is to help someone.' And this charity certainly does that."

In 2006 Downing and Grant were the two star attractions for the Hall of Fame's book signing of Grant's "The Black Aces: Baseball's Only African-American Twenty-Game Winners" and their actions that day provided a glimpse of their character.

Unnoticed, Grant and Downing climbed the grand spiral staircase leading to the Hall's Educational Gallery. At the top of the stairs they notice a teenaged young lady fidgeting with her cell phone, taking pictures of herself and her sister. Alice is the older girl with the phone and she and her 13-year-old sister, Emily, smile and giggle as only teenage girls can do. They are combating boredom as their father has dragged them to Cooperstown on this day. As soon as Alice snaps the shot, she and her sister are looking at the picture to see how it came out. Grant and Downing pause and make eye contact with her as they look over her shoulder with big smiles.

Downing breaks his smile by asking, "What's you got there?"

Mudcat counters with, "Hey, take my picture too?"

The four of them are all smiles as Alice takes the picture. Then the two ex-20-game winners follow the serpentine line to their signing table. An hour later, when Alice hands Grant her book to sign, he draws a picture of a catfish next to his signature, telling her "I don't do that for everyone!"

Downing and Grant engaged in small conversation with their fans during the book signing that day, as they do every year when they return to Binghamton to play in Grant's golf tournament. Downing especially enjoys participating in the event, as it provides him with another small instance of giving back to the community where he started his professional journey, as well as giving him a chance to catch up on recent events with such friends as Steve Kraly, Vida Blue, Mike Norris, JR Richard and Ferguson Jenkins, all regular participants in the golf tournament as well.

Bobby Richardson: The Link From the Best to the Worst

Bobby Richardson's stay at Binghamton in 1954 was instrumental in his development as a player and as a man. It was here where he was reminded of the importance of humility outside the lines and of commitment and dedication between the lines.

In Yankee history Richardson is known as the link at second base for the Yankees from Billy Martin to Horace Clarke, which is another way of saying that his reign at second base was the best of times and worst of times for the Yankees. From the day Martin was traded to Kansas City in 1957, Richardson became the leadoff hitter and slick-fielding second sacker for the Yankee teams that dominated the American League and won World Championships in '58, '61, and '62. Later, as Mickey Mantle and Whitey Ford entered the twilight of their careers, Richardson was the mainstay of the 1965 and 1966 teams that were to become the first of many teams to finish in the second division for the Yanks in the 1960's.

Richardson starred for the 1954 Triplets, where he provided great defense and outstanding offense. Before June was done, he was being labeled a "can't miss" prospect. Manager Merrill "Pinky" May of Reading, who hit .301 for the Triplets in 1934 and played in the majors from 1939-1943, echoed the thoughts of many that season— "We just can't get him out. I told my pitchers to throw all sorts of stuff at him, but he just seems to hit everything."

Richardson's ability to put the bat on the ball stayed with him throughout his career—he just never seemed to strikeout. In 5,386 major league at bats, Richardson only struck out 243 times. This was fewer than even Joe DiMaggio, who in 6,821 at bats only struck out 369 times. In 1962, Richardson led the American League in hits with 209.

Arguably even more impressive than his ability to put the bat on the ball and hit for average were Richardson's defensive skills, where he was especially adept at turning the double play. When the Yankees came to play an exhibition game against Binghamton in the 1950's, Marvin Behr, then sports editor of the *Binghamton Sun*, marveled at Richardson's aplomb around the bag. "Did you notice when the Yankees played here Monday that the big difference between a major league infielder and a minor leaguer is the speed with which the big-leaguer gets the ball away on a throw? Bobby Richardson has that ability in big-league style."

Playing at Binghamton provided Richardson not only with physical challenges, but psychological tests as well. Here he played alongside seasoned players who viewed their situations with jaundiced eyes. "At this level of baseball," Richardson recalled, "I began to run into a different sort of atmosphere among the players. Although there were always the enthusiastic, hard-playing boys, I had found others who had grown cynical and bitter from long years in the minors."

On the field, Richardson admired teammate Johnny Hunton's humility. Though an experienced player, Hunton readily accepted his role as a utility player on that Triplet team, playing behind Richardson and shortstop Buddy Carter. Richardson saw Hunton react to a base hit or a strikeout in the same disciplined manner, never breaking his concentration between the lines.

Richardson took the lessons he learned from Hunton to heart, not only during that '54 season when hit .310 for the Triplets, but throughout his big league career as well. In 12 major league seasons, he was elected to 7 All Star teams and was known as the consummate player and gentleman. Off the field, he was president of the Fellowship of Christian Athletes. He may have only spent the summer between his 18th and 19th years in Binghamton, but thanks to teammate Hunton and his all-star play between the lines, that lone Binghamton summer was a big one for Richardson.

In the summer of 2000 Richardson returned to Binghamton for his enshrinement. Honored to be remembered, Richardson graciously signed autographs and chatted with fans in the left field picnic area after his brief induction speech. It was his first return to Binghamton since that summer of 1954, but his view of life was no different from what it was 46 years before and is summed up in his closing of his 1965 autobiography with his reprinting the 4-stanza poem, "God's Hall of Fame," by Walt Huntley, whose theme is summed up in its final stanza:

> I tell you, friend, I wouldn't trade
> My name, however small,
> That's written there beyond the stars
> In that celestial Hall.
> For all the famous names on earth,
> Or Glory that they share;
> I'd rather be an unknown here,
> And have my name up there

Bob Taylor: Henry Street Hero

Bob Taylor Jr. was inducted into the Shrine in July of 2000, within a year of his passing on May 16, 1999. He holds the distinction of being the only member of the Shrine to have been born on the site where NYSEG Stadium now stands, as he was born on Henry Street on May 25th, 1916. Taylor starred as a four-sport athlete for Binghamton Central High School and owes his induction to the Shrine to his baseball playing days in the Negro Leagues from 1938-1941.

Taylor's obituary in the *Binghamton Evening Press* in 1999 credited him with having played for the Pittsburgh Crawfords, Homestead Grays, and Albany NY Black Sox. Interestingly, the Baseball Reference web site (*Baseball-reference.com*) lists his Negro League career stops as being Indianapolis, New Orleans and St. Louis from 1938 to 1941, as well as getting 3 at bats for the Lousiville Black Caps in 1932, while he was only 16 years old.

Taylor, who worked for the New York State Department of Transportation while living in Binghamton with his wife, Genevieve, and his two sons, was an avid community supporter and could be seen at numerous Binghamton Mets games through the years. He even threw out the first pitch of the 1997 season for the B-Mets! In addition to his Shrine honor, he received numerous other community honors, including the Distinguished Service Award from the Binghamton Kiwanis club and serving as a Master of the Chenango Lodge #39.

Upon learning of the honor for her late husband, Genevieve praised the legacy of the Negro Leagues as well as the athletic skills of her late husband, telling reporter Scott Lauber of the *Binghamton Press & Sun Bulletin* a month before the induction that "Many cities are honoring the Negro Leagues, and I'm pleased Binghamton has decided to join that group."

Taylor's colleagues in the Shrine Class of 2000 included Spud Chandler, Eddie Farrell, and Bobby Richardson, making it one of the stronger classes in Shrine history, as well as being the only class to have two inductees who were born in the area, as Eddie "Doc" Farrell was born in Lestershire, which later became Johnson City.

The Shrine class was not the only strong component of that 2000 season, as the 2000 Binghamton Mets set a record with its 15-game winning streak that stretched from the last week in July to August 8th. Before embarking on the winning streak, the team was only two games over .500, but the morning after the streak ended, the team's record was 64-48, and the team never looked back, finishing in first place with a record of 82-58.

Players of note on that Northern Division Championship team included Ty Wigginton, who led the team with 20 home runs; Alex Escobar, the Mets' # 1 prospect at the time, who played center field and hit .288 with 16 homers; pitching ace Tyler Walker, who played in the big leagues for eight years as a middle-inning reliever; and Dicky Gonzales, who led the team with 13 wins.

The winning streak was broken when the team lost to the Trenton Thunder, 11-9. After the game it was evident that general manager R.C. Reutemann had a great deal of pride and respect for his team. He exhorted to *Binghamton Press & Sun-Bulletin* reporter Mike Manigan, "This club has been busting it since day 1." His team wasn't the only thing that Reutemann was vocal about in 2000, as he was the loudest voice on the Shrine committee in discussing Bob Taylor's election to the Shrine. Reuteman was delighted to see Taylor recognized for his contributions to the community and his athletic prowess on the diamond and was happy to lobby for his induction.

Clete Boyer: "Brooks Beat Me Out of About 7 Gold Gloves"

The 1957 season saw Clete Boyer play 93 games for the Triplets AFTER he had already played parts of two seasons for the Kansas City Athletics, who signed him in 1955 after he completed high school in Alba Missouri. Clete's parents, Chester and Mabel, gave birth to 14 children, 7 boys and 7 girls. All of Clete's brothers played professional baseball, with two of his older brothers, Cloyd and Ken, also playing in the big leagues. During parts of five big-league seasons Cloyd won twenty games for the Cardinals and Athletics, while Ken became an All-Star third baseman for the Cardinals, winning the 1964 National League MVP Award. Cloyd also managed the Triplets in 1968 and brother Ron played third base for the Triplets in '68 as well, hitting .183

The Kansas City Athletics signed Clete to a $35,000 bonus in 1955 and while this was good for his pocket book, it wasn't too good for his development. Instead of playing every day in the minor leagues, Clete got only 226 at bats in '55 and '56 with the Athletics, hitting .221. A few years after Clete signed his bonus, Ken Boyer expounded on the mixed consequences of the high signing bonus. "Financially the bonus he got was great, but because of it he's had to do most of his learning in the big leagues. He hit 14 homers last year and when you hit that many you can hit more. Nobody doubts his offensive ability."

In late March of '57 while the Academy of Motion Pictures was selecting Ingrid Bergman for "Best Actress" for her role in *Anastasia* and Yul Brynner for "Best Actor" for *The King and I*, Clete Boyer was hoping to stick with the Athletics, as his two-year guarantee of being on the roster because of his signing bonus had expired. Though he made the team out of spring training, Clete saw little playing time as Joe DeMaestri was ahead of him at short and Hector Lopez blocked him at third. Consequently, in late spring the 20-year old Boyer found himself starting at shortstop for Binghamton, where he hit .242 with 12 home runs. He enjoyed a few post game meals with his teammates at such popular places as "Red's Kettle Inn," "Frankie's" (later "Zopps II," but currently closed), and "Mickey's" (now Giblin's), all within walking distance of Johnson Field. Notable teammates that year included fellow Shrine inductees Deron Johnson and Lee Thomas and the manager was another Shrine inductee, Stephen "Bud" Souchock.

Boyer's 16-year major league career is what got him elected to the Shrine, as he was the starting third baseman for the Yankees from 1960 to 1964, when the Yanks were winning five consecutive AL crowns and two World Championships. In addition to the Yankees, Clete also played for the Kansas City Athletics and Atlanta Braves, finishing his major league career with 162 home runs, 654 RBIs and a .242 batting average. Known as an outstanding fielding third baseman, he won his only gold glove with the Braves in 1969, and would have won a few more except for the presence of Brooks Robinson as the third baseman for the Orioles throughout the 1960's.

"Brooks beat me out of about seven Gold Gloves," Boyer once said. "But God gave me a lot of ability. I felt like Houdini out there. I loved defense and I had a great arm and I was quick with it. I had a lot of ability and I won't deny that. I used to tell people I was Ted Williams at third base. Defense is reflexes and instinct and I had it."

Ralph Houk loved having Boyer manning third base for those Yankee teams of the early 1960's: "Defense wins ballgames, that's why Clete was so important to us," noted Houk in discussing his reign as Yankee manager from 1961-1963.

After finishing his major league playing career with the Atlanta Braves in 1971, Boyer played ball in Japan for a few years. Upon returning to the U.S, Boyer was a major league coach and a minor league instructor. He worked closely with Drew Henson, teaching him the fundamentals of playing third base, after the Yankees signed Henson in the third round of the 1998 draft. Henson only got 9 at bats in the big leagues and left baseball in 2003 to play in the NFL as a backup quarterback.

In his later years, Boyer was often a visitor to Cooperstown, NY, where he would meet and greet fans in many of the shops along Main Street. He also ran "Clete Boyer's Hamburger Hall of Fame" restaurant for many years, which was just outside Cooperstown, on Route 28. He decorated the walls with pictures of his Yankee days and would talk baseball with his customers. Boyer may have had a pivotal role on those great Yankee teams of the 1960's, but his success on the field never interfered with his everyday demeanor off the field.

Fred Norman: "I Didn't Think it Would Go Past 5, but it Did"

Fred Norman played for Binghamton in 1962 and 1963, the only two years the Triplets were affiliated with the Kansas City Athletics. The 1962 team was one of the most intriguing teams in the history of Binghamton, despite its lackluster 60-80 record. Fellow shrine inductees Bert Campaneris and Ken Harrelson were on that team and Hall of Fame manager Tony LaRussa also played 12 games as a 17-year old second baseman. But the most intriguing element of the team started with its manager, Granny Hamner, who had already logged 16 seasons in the major leagues, primarily as a shortstop, when he became the player-manager of that 1962 team.

Amazingly, Hamner performed triple duty for the Triplets that year. Besides playing middle infield and managing the Triplets, Hamner also started 14 games that year as a pitcher, finishing with a 10-4 record—not bad for a team that finished 20 games under .500! Hamner's mound exploits got him promoted to Kansas City as a pitcher at the end of the year, though the results signified that it was time to retire, as he gave up 10 hits and 4 runs in only four innings of work for the Athletics. Hamner's exploits for the '62 Triplets showed what perseverance can bring, as he re-invented himself as a pitcher in the minor leagues from 1960-1962 so he could make it back for his cup of coffee in 1962.

"Little Fredie Norman," as he became known in his major league career, learned his lesson of perseverance well from his Binghamton manager. Despite his success for the Triplets in 1962 and 1963, with Norman winning 16 games and striking out 339 batters in 268 innings, he was not able to stick in the big leagues until 1972, a full ten years after his Binghamton debut. One of the reasons for Norman's long tenure in the minors was his high number of walks, as he averaged almost 5 walks per 9 innings during his ten year minor league career. Control, or lack of, was an annoyance throughout his big league career, perhaps preventing him from greatness, as he finished in the top ten in walks four times ('72, '73, '77, '78).

Also, his small size was a bit of an obstacle for him to overcome, as his stamina seemed to always be in question. In 1978, when managers still looked to pitchers to throw complete games, he set a record which has since been broken, of going 31 starts without a complete game. Of course, many would say Sparky "Captain Hook"Anderson (who was notorious for not staying with his starters for too long) owns that record as well! Norman wound up with 56 complete games in his career in 268 starts, which actually was an outstanding total for someone who toiled so long for Anderson.

Norman thought Anderson was an outstanding manager and he enjoyed playing for him, as well as his pitching coach, Larry Shepherd. Norman recognized that at times Anderson could seem abrasive and he and his pitching colleagues did not appreciate the "quick hook" that Anderson had, but Norman was able to see the complete picture. "Larry and Sparky loved us, but the way Sparky went about it some guys didn't like," explained Norman. "But Sparky did a great job, at times he got hot and heavy in the clubhouse. He knew he needed pitching, that is why he was on us."

From 1973 through 1979 Norman won 96 games, never winning fewer than 11 in a season, teaming with such pitchers as Don Gullett, Gary Nolan, and Jack Billingham to form a solid starting pitching group for the Reds in the 1970's. The highlight of Norman's career spanned the 1975 and 1976 seasons, when the Reds won two World Championships, defeating the Red Sox in the classic '75 series and sweeping the Yankees in 1976. Norman started a game in each of those World Series, though he did not get a win.

In the 1975 World Series Norman, after starting the Game 4 loss to the Sox, came in relief in Game 6, which Carlton Fisk won in the 12th inning with a walk-off home run and which is considered by many to be the greatest World Series game ever played. Norman relieved starter Gary Nolan in the 3rd inning and faced 5 batters, walking two, giving up one hit and retiring two hitters. Billingham came in to get the last out of the inning as Anderson used eight pitchers, trying to clinch the series in six games. (Game 6 had been postponed three days because of rain, so Anderson had a rested staff available.)

Game 7 of that Series was another classic, with the Reds coming back from a 3-run deficit to beat the Red Sox, 4-3. Anderson, staying true to his nickname of "Captain Hook," used 4 pitchers in the game, with starter Dong Gullett giving up all three runs in his four innings. Though the series was about as evenly matched as it could be, Norman never felt the outcome was in doubt, as he explained years later.

"Boston had a very good club, but I think we were just destined. In retrospect, they could just as easily won too, but I never thought about that. I don't think any one of us thought that. I didn't think it would go past 5, but it did."

Pat Darcy, who was a roommate of Norman's in that 1975 season and gave up the game-winning homer to Fisk in Game 6, summed up what pitching for Sparky Anderson was like in the 70's:

"I was pitching against the Cubs. I was getting hammered but I still had some good stuff and we were in the game. Sparky came out to the mound and was walking, which meant he was taking me out. We weren't supposed to say anything to him when he came to take us out of the game, none of the pitchers were. But he came out to the mound and I said, 'I still feel good' and Sparky just looked at me and said, "You'll feel better in the shower."

Though the 1975 World Champion Reds won its division by twenty games and played in a great Fall Classic, Norman feels the '76 version of the "Big Red Machine" was better than the '75 version. "We won our last ten games that season," Norman exhorted. "We won the last three during the regular season and then swept the Pirates in the League Championship Series and swept the Yankees in the World Series as well."

Eddie Farrell's Journey From Dentistry to the Diamond

The July 2000 Shrine induction ceremonies included a large crowd at what was then called Binghamton Municipal Stadium, and over 15 rows of those fans were in attendance to witness the induction of Eddie 'Doc' Farrell into the Shrine. Farrell's local roots played a huge part in the large turnout of fans, as Farrell was born on December 26th, 1901, in the town of Lestershire, which became Johnson City in 1916. Many of his descendants still call Broome County their home and were thrilled to witness their patriarch's tribute.

Eddie 'Doc' Farrell joined the New York Giants in 1925, seventy-five years before he was elected to the Binghamton's Shrine. He joined the Giants fresh off the campus of the University of Pennsylvania, as his contract stipulated that he be allowed to finish his dental studies before playing baseball. Playing in a part-time role, Farrell spent most of his time at third base, hitting .214 in 56 at bats for Hall of Fame manager John McGraw. Given Farrell's erudite background, the nickname of 'Doc' was bestowed on him almost immediately.

It was no disgrace to sit on the bench for that 1925 Giants team as the lineup included future Hall of Famers at more than half the positions—established veteran Bill Terry manned first base and Frankie Frisch was the second baseman while Travis Jackson and Freddie Lindstrom patrolled the left side of the infield at shortstop and third base, respectively. Ross Youngs and Hack Wilson occupied two of the outfield positions. Much to the chagrin of McGraw, that 1925 team had to be one of the best teams ever to NOT play in the post season.

As a light hitting, excellent fielding infielder, Farrell's big-league career was one of short stays in big league towns, as he played for the Giants, Braves, Cardinals, Cubs, Yankees, and Red Sox during his nine-year career. He was a regular player in 1928 and 1929 and had his best year in 1928, when he hit .316 with 4 home runs and 92 RBIs while he split time between the Giants and Boston Braves. In 1928, Farrell again played regularly, but his .215 batting average and 42 RBIs in 483 at bats for the Braves sealed his fate as a backup infielder for the rest of his career.

Farrell played a key role in providing Broome County with one of its proudest baseball moments. Farrell played the first part of the 1930 season for the St. Louis Cardinals and got into 23 games with that World Championship team. One of his teammates was "Wild" Bill Hallahan, who was a lifelong resident of Binghamton and the ace of the staff. Farrell and Hallahan have the distinction of being the only two native sons of Broome County who were teammates on a World Championship team!

Farrell was also in the right place at the right time in 1932, when he spent the entire year on the New York Yankees roster and, although he only hit .175 in 63 at bats, he backed up Frank Crossetti and second baseman Tony Lazzeri. He was in the Yankee dugout when legend has it that Babe Ruth hit his "called shot" home run off of Charlie Root in the third game of the Series. Farrell roomed with Crosetti that year, which was the start of a lifelong friendship between Farrell and Crosetti. In his post-playing days, Farrell was a regular visitor to spring training to visit with Crosetti.

Throughout his career, Farrell was valued as a great glove man and a professional clubhouse presence. In 1933, *New York Sun* columnist Frank Graham explained how enamored Yankee manager Joe McCarthy was of his utility man.

"He's the best all around infielder in the American League. He has everything it takes: speed, agility, big, strong hands, a powerful throwing arm, sturdy legs, a keen eye and a world of—call it intestinal fortitude, if you want to. But you know what I mean, even if it isn't a polite word."

Besides earning his World Championship ring, perhaps the two biggest highlights of Farrell's Yankee career were when he replaced Lou Gehrig twice early in games to help Gehrig preserve his career consecutive games streak and visiting his Johnson City hometown in 1933 as a member of the Yankees when the big league team came to Johnson Field to play an exhibition game. Despite the presence of such stars as Babe Ruth and Lou Gehrig, Farrell was hailed as a hero in his own right during his exhibition stay.

In Farrell's career as a utility infielder he hit .260 with 10 home runs and 213 runs batted in and had the honor of being a teammate of thirty-four players who went on to be inducted into the Baseball Hall of Fame in Cooperstown, NY.

Ralph Terry and the Hall-of-Fame Heart of the Order

In the history of the World Series, there has arguably been only one player who has gone from goat of one World Series to hero of another for the same team and that distinction goes to right-handed pitcher Ralph Terry, who made his debut with the Binghamton Triplets in 1954 and became an integral part of the pitching staff of the AL Championship Yankee teams from 1960-1964.

He won 107 games in his 12-year major league career while notching exactly 1000 strikeouts. His best year was 1962, when he went 23-12, leading the American League in victories; his 298 innings pitched also led the league. He will forever be remembered, however, for giving up Bill Mazeroski's walk off home run in the seventh game of the 1960 World Series, sending the Yanks to a 10-9 defeat in one of the epic games of the World Series. Two years later, Terry demonstrated that life is not determined by what happens to you, but by how you respond to what happens, as he was voted the MVP of the World Series, recording the final out of the seventh game as the Yanks defeated the Giants, 2-1, to give the Yankees their 20th World Series title in 1962.

38 years after his debut at Johnson Field, Terry returned to the Binghamton area to be inducted into Binghamton's Shrine. Before the start of the game that evening he stopped to read the plaques in the concourse and he grew animated as he recognized the names of many of his colleagues and reflected on his career. The gratefulness for being inducted was evident in Terry's voice that evening; during his acceptance speech modesty was his theme as he exhorted on the privilege of playing alongside the likes of Mickey Mantle, Yogi Berra, and Whitey Ford.

As he signed autographs alongside the right field picnic area, Terry genuinely enjoyed taking a few moments to chat with the fans, growing animated with those few fans who were old enough to recall his time pitching for the Triplets. When handed a baseball to sign, without being asked, he followed his name with the inscription "1962 World Series MVP." During that 1962 Series he pitched 25 innings, compiling a 1.80 ERA and throwing two complete game victories. He was on the mound in the seventh inning of Game 7 when, with a runner on first, and needing one more out to wrap up his second win, only future Hall of Famers Willie Mays, Willie McCovey, and Orlando Cepeda stood in his way! Mays brought the Candlestick crowd to its feet with a double to put runners on second and third as McCovey strode to the plate. Yankee fans did not need to be reminded that only two years earlier Terry was on the mound in the bottom of the ninth of Game 7 of the World Series, only to give up the Series winning home run to Bill Mazeroski.

At Candlestick though, it was Terry's time to be the hero, if only by a matter of a couple of feet. McCovey hit a bullet, but it was a line drive right at Bobby Richardson, who caught it for the final out. While McCovey slowly walked back to the dugout, wishing he had hit the ball a couple of feet to either side of Richardson or a foot higher, Terry walked toward Richardson, throwing his glove in the air in utter joy and then he threw his hat in the air as well. Immediately Terry was engulfed in a wave of swarming Yankee jerseys, all topped with visages of victory-filled joy.

Richardson recalled his catch in a matter-of-fact manner. "With Willie McCovey to bat, Houk stepped out to the mound to confer with Ralph Terry about walking or pitching to McCovey. Willie had already hit 2 ground balls to me in the Series and I had bobbled both, just barely nipping him at first in each case. 'Don't fumble the ball,' Kubek said to me, grinning, 'or it will cost us $125,000.00.' A moment or two later McCovey hit one of Terry's fast balls for what looked like a base hit and victory for the Giants. But the ball sank and I caught it chest high, a couple of feet to my left. It was right at me all the way, hard hit, but an easy play."

In 2002, almost forty years after his debut, Terry narrowed his fondest memories of playing for the Triplets to two games. "Beating the Yankees in an exhibition and a 1-0 shutout at Schenectady over Dick 'Turk' Farrell. Bobby Richardson tripled and Buddy Carter scored him on a sacrifice fly. Pitched a one-hitter – Bob Donkersky singled over Bobby's head in the fourth."

Ah, to be a teenager and to beat the Yankees! 1954 marked the final time the parent Yankee club visited Johnson Field to play the Triplets in an exhibition and Terry pitched 3 innings in that game, getting the win, 5-2. He relieved in the fifth inning and held his own against such Yankee stars as Jerry Coleman, Mickey Mantle, Yogi Berra, Hank Bauer, and Moose Skowron. Terry the teenager pitched three innings of relief, pitching in and out of trouble, giving up 3 hits, issuing 3 walks and striking out two. Also on display this day was his penchant for giving up the home run ball, as Mickey Mantle accounted for the Yankee runs with a two-run homer in the top of the seventh. 4,867 fans watched the Yankees lose, a harbinger of their 5-year championship run ending that fall.

Interestingly, 8 days later, Terry would pitch the best game of his season beating the Schenectady Blue Jays, 1-0. Terry went the distance for the win in a game that took only an hour and 57 minutes to complete. However, his recollection of that day was not quite as good as his performance— in actuality, he allowed three hits. Besides the single by Jays' second baseman Donkersky, he also allowed a bunt single by, Dick "Turk" Farrell in the sixth, and a pinch-hit single by outfielder Carden Gillenwater in the eighth. And it was Buddy Carter who hit the triple that scored shortstop George Prigge from first. But Terry can be excused in thinking Richardson knocked in the winning run, for throughout the season Richardson had many game-winning hits on his way to hitting .310.

Terry and Richardson were two of the biggest stars of that '54 team and despite the names of Mantle and Maris, Ford and Berra, those Yankee teams in the early '60's would not have had the same success without the two Triplet imports of Terry and Richardson.

Pete Suder: On Second There Stands the Man with the Hands

Pete Suder is another Shrine Inductee whose stay at Johnson Field spanned multiple years before he went on to a solid major league career. During his Triplet three-year stint from 1938 to 1940 he had 1,368 at bats and hit 30 home runs while stroking the ball for a .282 batting average. He spent his entire 13-year major league career playing for the Athletics, with the last year coming in Kansas City, after the franchise moved from Philadelphia.

He was inducted into the Shrine in 2003, along with Fred Norman and John Montgomery Ward. It disappointed him that he could not make the trip back to Binghamton for his induction, but his age and the health of his wife worked against him. His wife was in a nursing home and he took her lunch every day. When informed of his induction, Suder remarked, "I wish you had called five years earlier, I would have loved to attend the ceremony." Suder had fond memories of Binghamton and once told Connie Mack, "If you ever want to get rid of me, send me back to Binghamton, I loved it there!"

Suder's big league career spanned from 1941 through 1955, with the years 1944 and 1945 being lost to World War II. He primarily played second base in the big leagues, but also saw a lot of time at third as well as short. He was signed by the Yankees in 1935, after graduating from Aliquippa High School in Pennsylvania and was a resident of Aliquippa his entire life, dying there at the age of 90 in 2006. One of his high school teammates was Press Maravich, who went on to become a well-known college basketball coach and also was the father of basketball Hall of Famer and legend "Pistol" Pete Maravich.

Suder was an outstanding fielder and teamed with shortstop Eddie Joost to form an excellent double play (DP) combination for the Philadelphia Athletics in the late 1940's and early 1950's. In 1949 the Philadelphia A's set a single-season double play record of 217 that still stands, and Joost gave much of the credit to Suder, stating "Pete's a great guy to work with, he's always at the right place at the right time. A good second baseman like Pete makes it easy for a shortstop."

From 1949-1952, that A's team turned 629 double plays, which still stands as a record for most DPs over a three-year period. Joost and Suder were the keystone partners during the majority of those double plays and Richard Stoll Armstrong, the Philadelphia A's public relations director in 1952 and now an ordained minister, had some fun with this record-setting keystone combination when he wrote the following poem, which is a takeoff of "Baseball's Sad Lexicon," the celebrated poem by Franklin Pierce Adams, which praised the Chicago Cubs double play trio of "Tinker to Evers to Chance." (This poem is reprinted here, courtesy of Armstrong's blog, *Minding What Matters*.)

      JOOST TO SUDER TO FAIN

Voluminous prose has been written by those
who have this one thought to advance:

that the greatest combine in the double play line
was Tinker to Evers to Chance.

Those three famous Cubs were surely not duds.
Their fielding was something sublime.
They were far and away the class of their day,
the double play kings of their time.

But they've since been dethroned and partly disowned.
No longer as kings do they reign.
For a new DP team is ruling supreme,
known as Joost to Suder to Fain.

These sensational A's have perfected their ways
to the point where they lead all the rest.
As twin killings go, three years in a row
they've ranked as the major leagues' best.

There's never a worry; they'll comply in a hurry,
when a quick double play is desired.
A roller or liner just couldn't be finer,
you can bet that two men are retired.

You may already know what the record books show,
three years they've continued to shine,
all others surpassing this record amassing:
a total of six twenty-nine!

Eddie Joost rings the bell as a shortstop as well
as a mighty good man with the stick.
To select someone who has an arm that's as true,
it would be an impossible pick.

On second there stands "the man with the hands."
If a ball's hit to Pete there's no doubt.
You never need look, jot it down in the book,
it's a cinch that the batter is out.

A hitter's accursed with Ferris on first.
There's no one as clever as he,
in spearing a bounder or sizzling grounder
and completing that tough three-six-three.

A long time from now, when they're telling of how
so and so could get two with no strain,
we'll think of the days of Connie Mack's A's,

and of Joost and Suder and Fain.

During Suder's summer of '38 in the Southern Tier, local sportswriter Al Lamb's "Spinning the Sports Top" column often took delight in the success of that Triplets team. On September 3rd, the day the Triplets clinched the Eastern League title, Lamb noted with pride that Suder and six of his Triplets teammates were named to the Eastern League All Star team, but he also voiced some disappointment. "Perhaps there was some thought that the Johnson City habitués could not have all the positions. What hurts our feelings is that Bruno Betzel was not honored with the managership."

Betzel was the popular manager of the Triplets from 1938 to 1940 and it turned out that being Eastern League Manager of the Year might have been the only award Betzel did not get that year. On July 25th, 2,700 people turned out for "Bruno Betzel Night" at Johnson Field, with Betzel receiving a hat, two floral arrangements, and other tokens of appreciation. Perhaps what was most amazing about Bruno Betzel Night is that the nine-inning game was over in one hour and 43 minutes!!!!

Betzel had a modest big league playing career as a utility man for the St. Louis Cardinals from 1914-1918, but he was revered in the Binghamton area for his outstanding work with that 1938 Triplets team, which some amateur historians argue is the best team in the history of the Triplets franchise. Betzel was honored with another "night" of tribute on September 8th, when he received $350.00 in a collection from the fans, as a sign of appreciation and good luck for him and the team in the Eastern League Semifinal Playoffs. Betzel was touched by the appreciation shown by the town for the team's first place finish. In his thank you to the fans, Betzel said that he had been in baseball many years but never before had he been in city where the manager and the team seemed to be appreciated as much as in the Triple Cities.

Betzel managed 11 players that year who reached the major leagues and Suder was one of his two star players, as Suder tied Tommy Holmes for the club lead in games played with 135 and hit a solid .278 while providing stellar defense at third base.

John Montgomery Ward: A Baseball Pioneer

Since baseball started its run in the Big Apple, various players have paired up with thespians, from Lefty Gomez and Broadway actress June O'Dea in 1932, to Leo Durocher and Hollywood star Laraine Day, who served as an unofficial "first couple" of baseball after being married in 1947, to Joe DiMaggio and Marilyn Monroe, who wed in 1954 to become the nation's biggest celebrity couple of the day. In more modern times, such stars as Alex Rodriguez and Derek Jeter have been linked to various Hollywood starlets as well, though no wedding bells have tolled for them as yet.

But John Montgomery Ward, Shrine Class of 2003, was New York City's trailblazer in this ball player/actress coupling, as he was the first ballplayer of fame to marry an actress of equal fame. In the 1880's, while Ward dominated the diamond and was captain of the

New York Giants, Miss Helen Dauvray was queen of Broadway with her lead roles in such plays as "One of Our Girls," "Walda," and "The Love Chase."

Ward and Dauvray "set the stage" for all the other pairings to follow through their marriage in 1887. Besides her notoriety, Dauvray was wealthy, talented, attractive and an avid fan as well. In the summer of 1887 she spent her own money to come up with a trophy that would be awarded to the winning team between the National League and the American Association, the two major leagues at the time. It became known as "The Dauvray Cup" and if a team won three consecutive championships, the victorious team would permanently keep the trophy. The Dauvray Cup was short lived, however, as the American Association disbanded shortly after the creation of the cup, but the spirit of the Dauvray Cup lives on today with the awarding of a trophy to the winning team of the World Series.

In marrying Ward, Dauvray fully recognized the disdain her choice would draw from the public. Ball players were neither respected in the big city nor the nation in the 1880's. When the story broke that Dauvray was marrying Ward, she made sure everyone knew he was not the prototypical player of the day. "I did not meet Mr. Ward on the ball field or through my connection that I may have had with the national game. I met him socially, and I assure you that he is a most charming and cultured man. He speaks five or six languages fluently, and is otherwise well informed and well bred."

Ward was indeed well educated, having graduated from Columbia Law School in 1885, completing his studies while he played baseball. As busy as Ward was off the diamond, he was just as busy between the lines, as he both pitched and played the field, hitting .275 in 7,656 at bats over a 17-year major league career while winning 164 games during his seven years as a pitcher.

Breaking into the big leagues with the Providence Grays as an 18-year-old in 1878, Ward started and completed 37 games, winning 22 and finishing with an ERA of 1.51. His win totals the next two years were 47 and 39, respectively, with 117 complete games over the two years! Though his pitching career lasted only seven years, it not only got him a plaque in the Binghamton Shrine, but also in Baseball's Hall of Fame class of 1964, as he amassed 164 wins and posted a 2.10 ERA. In 1885 he became a full-time shortstop and went on to play ten more years as a star infielder, for the New York Gothams, New York Giants, Brooklyn Wizards and Brooklyn Grooms.

Ward started the 1878 season with the Binghamton Crickets, which according to his biographer, Bryan Di Salvatore, "was one of the best known and most financially successful teams outside of the National League." Despite its solid reputation, the Binghamton Crickets team was not able to finish the season, as it disbanded in the middle of the summer, and when it did, the Providence Grays of the National League were delighted to pick up the contract of Ward. The folding of the Crickets turned out to be Ward's break, enabling him to pitch in the National League while still a teenager.

Ward is credited with establishing the *Brotherhood of Professional BaseBall Players,* which was formed in 1885. Though unsuccessful in gaining increased rights and payments for players, the Brotherhood laid the foundation for the formation of the *Major League Player's Association* in 1953. The Brotherhood even formed its own league in 1890, called the Player's League, to compete with the National League and the American Association. Ward did his part in trying to build momentum for the Player's League as he played shortstop and managed the Brooklyn Ward's Wizards in the new league, leading them to a second place finish with a record of 76-56. The Player's League only lasted that one season, however, as three leagues and 29 games proved too much baseball for the public to support.

Ward's marriage to Helen Dauvray lasted 6 years, from 1887 to 1893. As with Joe DiMaggio and Marilyn Monroe, Ward's desire for his wife to give up her thespian ways proved to be one of the many obstacles the couple could not overcome. After retiring as an active player, Ward practiced law and played a lot of golf, winning many amateur tournaments; while on a golf course, he met 26-year-old Katherine Waas, whom he married in 1903. Katherine was at his side when he died in 1925. In 1964 Ward was posthumously elected to the Baseball Hall of Fame.

Johnny Blanchard: Raconteur Extraordinaire

The 1961 season is forever coupled with the M & M boys, Roger Maris and Mickey Mantle, who took aim at breaking Babe Ruth's then record of 60 home runs in a season. But what few people remember is that the three-headed catching machine for the Yankees that year hit 64 homers, as Elston Howard, Johnny Blanchard, and Yogi Berra all hit over twenty.

By 1961 Blanchard was a backup catcher to Howard while Berra saw spot duty as a catcher and played left field. Berra hit 22 home runs in 395 at bats; Howard hit 21 HRs with 446 at bats; and Blanchard, in only 243 ABs, matched Howard's 21! Blanchard complimented his HR total with the best batting average of his career, hitting .302. Blanchard had a solid 8-year major league career, winning two World Championships and being the primary pinch hitter for the Yankees of the early 60's.

Blanchard got 93 at bats for the Triplets in 1951, but his .183 batting average gave no indication of what his future held. In 1952 he was sent back to Class C ball, with the Joplin Miners, where he hit over .300 and slammed 30 HRs. Uncle Sam and the Korean Conflict beckoned for the next two years, but when he rejoined the Triplets in 1955, he was the star, hitting 34 home runs and batting .281 for that 75-62 team. Another player of note in the Eastern League this season was a right fielder who hit 24 home runs for the Reading Indians—Roger Maris.

If the Yankee team of 1961 was remembered for the M & M boys, Blanchard's career can be recalled as "H & H," for homers and hilarity always dominated the scene when Blanchard was present, not to mention happy hours too! During his playing days, Johnny liked to imbibe the brews and tell a story or two; he was one of the great raconteurs of the game.

Blanchard's self-deprecating humor had him wondering what would have happened if only he could catch (pun intended)! Because he sure could hit, as evidenced by his setting the then all-time Triplets home run record with his 30th home run on August 23rd against the Williamsport Grays in 1955.

Marvin Behr, the sports editor for the *Binghamton Sun* and owner of a regular sports column in the 50's for the *Sun*, touched on Blanchard's defensive shortcomings as part of a larger article where he criticized the work of manager George "Snuffy" Stirnweiss in handling the Triplets pitching staff:

His handling of the pitching staff appears his most flagrant shortcoming, followed closely by poor direction of base runners. To be sure, the pitching has been hurt by a poor defense—the principal ingredients of which are catcher John Blanchard's inadequate throwing, second baseman Bobby Meisner's inability to pivot on a double play and recurring injuries to shortstop Fritz Brickell. Good throwing is also absent in the outfield.

Behr explained that Stirnweiss' biggest fault was leaving pitchers in too long. When they should have been showering, he left them throwing on the mound. Behr, the next day, did not let up, tenacious in his criticism, as he moved on to base running:

"The biggest base-running rock of the year, we believe, was the one in Allentown when Jack Reed and Bob Meisner were on second and first, respectively, in the ninth inning with two out. The batter was John Blanchard, the league's leading home-run hitter and RBI man at the time, and the score was 5-3 against the Trips. Thus an extra base hit by Blanchard probably would have tied the score and a home run boosted the Trips into the lead. But Big John never got a chance to swing. He took the first pitch, a strike, and Reed and Meisner set out for a double steal. Reed, one of the fastest runners in the Yankee organization, was out at third base and the game over.

Behr went on to explain that Stirnweiss defended the move, saying the wind was blowing in and Blanchard would have had a tough time hitting one out. Behr pointed out that Stirnweiss had no answer regarding the wind's effect on a potential game tying double.

Binghamton was on its way to a third place finish in the eight-team Eastern League in 1955, and Behr's columns reflected his frustration in watching what he felt should have been a first place team. Behr's comments were typical of the sports writing of the time in the *Binghamton Sun* and *Binghamton Evening Press*. The writers for the dueling papers were far more critical than they are in today's *Binghamton Press & Sun-Bulletin.*

One of the most painful games of Blanchard's major league career was arguably the greatest game ever played, the Pirates' 10-9 victory over the New York Yankees in Game 7 of the 1960 World Series. Blanchard was the catcher when Bill Mazerowski stepped to the plate to lead off the bottom of the ninth, with the score tied 9-9. Mazerowski in the batter's box was a familiar site for Blanchard, as Mazerowski was an 18-year-old infielder for the Williamsport Grays during Blanchard's 1955 Eastern League season.

Blanchard knew that Mazerowski liked the ball high so he signaled for a low fastball but Ralph Terry shook him off and threw a slider. It was high. Mazeroski took the pitch for a ball.

Blanchard recalls, "I should have called for Eddie Lopat to come in after that first pitch and talk to Terry. Ralph's slider was not working." (Lopat was the Yankees pitching coach.)

But Blanchard crouched behind the plate, and gave another sign for a fastball. Once again Terry shook his head from side to side.

Another slider was coming.

Another high slider.

Mazerowski swung and all of Pittsburgh exhaled late in the afternoon of October 8th, 1960, as the ball sailed over Berra's head and over the left field wall. The Pirates were World Champions!

Blanchard hit .455 in that World Series and he had a single in the 8th inning of that game to knock in a run and extend the Yankees lead to 7-4 going into the bottom of the inning. But a five-run rally by the Pirates in the eighth forced the Yankees to score two runs in the ninth just to stay alive and Mazerowski's homer turned the game into a bitter memory for Blanchard. "You can't imagine how many times I have gone through every pitch in my mind, and I still can't explain to people how we lost, not only that game but the other three in that series," recalled Blanchard years later.

Blanchard and his teammates gained some satisfaction by winning the World Series in 1962 and Ralph Terry rebounded to be MVP of the 1962 Series. But Blanchard was never able to replicate the success he had in the '61 regular season and was traded to the Kansas City Athletics in May of 1965. John was a Yankee at heart and was depressed over the news of the trade. He was crying in the clubhouse when Mickey Mantle came over to comfort him.

"Don't take it so hard, John. Just think, in Kansas City you're going to get a chance to play."

"Hell, I can't play Mick, that's why I'm crying," Blanchard responded.

The guffaws from Mantle and Blanchard helped dissipate the tears creeping over Blanchard's cheeks.

Frank Verdi: Another "Moonlight" Graham

If you look up Frank Verdi's major league stats on the web site, *baseball-reference.com*, you will see that he played in one major league baseball game, but never got an at bat, putting him in the same category as Burt Lancaster's character of Archie "Moonlight" Graham in the revered baseball film "Field of Dreams," which stars Kevin Costner, James Earl Jones, and Lancaster. Verdi's similarity with Lancaster's character does not end with this baseball oddity, however—ironically both Verdi and Graham played baseball in the Binghamton area, Verdi for the Triplets from 1949-52 and Graham for the Bingos in 1905.

Fans of "Field of Dreams" will recall that Lancaster gives up his chance to get an at bat in the Iowa cornfield when he goes outside the foul lines to dislodge a piece of hot dog from the throat of Ray Kinsella's (played by Costner) daughter to save her life in the final moments of the movie. Though he gives up his chance to get a big league at bat, the character of "Moonlight" Graham secures his role as a man most valuable to the Kinsella family.

As fine a job of acting that Lancaster did portraying Graham, his feat pales in comparison to the real-life role Frank Verdi played when visiting some of his Yankee friends in the 1970's when the Yankees trained in Fort Lauderdale, Florida, and Whitey Ford was serving as a spring training instructor for the Yankees.

One night Ford and his wife, Joan, invited Yogi Berra, Mickey Mantle, and Mike Ferraro and their spouses over to their residence for a dinner of chili and some laughs. Ford had known Verdi since his minor league days and enjoyed catching up with his old pal. The evening became full of drama shortly into dinner. As Whitey tells it:

"We were eating chili, and Mickey started telling a funny story about his experiences in the minor leagues. I had some chili in my mouth and I started laughing. We were in the dining room and I knew I couldn't swallow the chili, so I jumped up to run into the kitchen and spit the chili out in the sink. When I got to the kitchen, I passed out. My sons Eddie and Tommy were there, and they found me lying on the kitchen floor. According to them I started to get purple. Mickey got hysterical. Yogi didn't know what to do. Eddie was going to start giving me mouth-to-mouth resuscitation."

Assessing the situation, Frank Verdi lowered himself to the floor, looked at Whitey's face and then gave him a hard tap in the chest. Almost instantaneously, a chili bean popped out of Ford's mouth and almost immediately he regained consciousness. Though Verdi never pitched a day in his life, on that night he got perhaps the biggest save in Yankee history! To this day, Ford credits Verdi with saving his life.

Verdi was born in Brooklyn, N.Y., and first played for the Triplets in 1949 where he roomed with Queens, N.Y. native Whitey Ford. Verdi played for the Triplets from 1949 to 1952, getting 1,597 at bats and hitting .287 over his Binghamton career. In 1953 he got called up to the Yankees from the Syracuse farm club, appearing in one game as a replacement for Phil Rizzuto in a game against the Red Sox on May 10th.

Years later, in September of 1970, while managing the AAA Syracuse Chiefs, Verdi recounted his big league career to Hugh Delano of the *Syracuse Evening News* as he asks Delano if he has 10 seconds to spare. When Delano nods in acquiescence, Verdi is off and running with his story, the ensuing years embellishing the tale a bit.

"It was in Fenway Park in Boston. We're losing 3-1, and I'm sitting in the dugout enjoying nice weather, watching the game and wondering if I should get a man I know to kidnap Phil Rizzuto. The old master—that's Casey Stengel, crossed himself up by pinch hitting Johnny Mize for Rizzuto and when the inning is over, he gets mad because now he needs a shortstop. Stengel looks down the dugout and tells me 'get off your butt' and play SS—and if you make a mistake I'll kick your butt when you come back to the dugout!"

Verdi takes the field in the bottom of the sixth with the Yanks losing, 3-2. The Red Sox go out in 1-2-3 fashion, without Verdi touching the ball. In the top of the seventh, the Yanks rally, scoring 3 runs to take a 5-3 lead.

"There's two outs and the bases loaded. I was swinging the bat and getting ready to step in," Verdi explains. "But Boston changed pitchers and Stengel decided to have Bill Renna pinch hit for me."

Let the record show that Renna (an ex-Triplet) ended the inning with a groundout and Jim Brideweser (another ex-Triplet) finished the game at short.

Verdi finishes his story. "That was my career—one inning, one game, no at bats, they sent me out after that back to Syracuse and never called me up again,".

Verdi finished his 18-year minor league playing career with a .270 average and 48 home runs and 295 RBIs. His love for the game is evidenced by the fact that he went on to manage twenty-two seasons in the minor leagues, retiring in 1993 after accumulating 1,492 wins.

The highlight of his minor league career was leading the Syracuse Chiefs to back-to-back Governor's Cup Championships in 1969 and 1970. After leading the Chiefs to its second title, Verdi's work even got the attention of the often irascible *New York Daily News* baseball columnist Dick Young, who wrote "If some club in the majors is looking for a man with a Vince Lombardi style of discipline that players seem to appreciate, Frank Verdi's their man. He did an outstanding job with Syracuse in the International League."

Vince Lombardi style or not, Verdi never did get the call to manage in the big leagues. Verdi was living in Port Richey, Florida, when he passed away in 2010. His wife, Pauline, a Binghamton native (maiden name of Pasquale), passed away in 2013.

Ken Harrelson, "The Hawk," and the "Wild Thing"

In 1962, 20-year-old slugging first baseman Ken Harrelson was hitting home runs and knocking in runs on a record pace for the Triplets. Front office executives of the Kansas City Athletics were watching his exploits with enthusiasm and hoping that in a year or two he could be their Mickey Mantle: a colorful, handsome, power-hitting player who could pack the fans in and bring some wins home as well.

His popularity in the Binghamton area soared with each home run and this summer proved to be a foreshadowing of the summer of '68, when he would lead the American League in RBIs as the first baseman for the Boston Red Sox. In the summer of '68, he became a national sensation, as his talent, bravado, sartorial splendor, and high profile personality combined to create a baseball frenzy that became known as the "Hawk." One look at his nose is all you needed to do to understand his nickname.

1962 was Harrelson's first season as a star in the baseball world, albeit the minor leagues, and more than 40 years later he remembered his time in Binghamton as he chatted with a Binghamton resident after he was a guest speaker at Baseball's Hall of Fame in September 2006. "I set the league record for RBIs there that year," Harrelson tells a fan with a grin on his face, and "but Boog Powell broke that record, I think. I also set the team record for home runs with 38 and I think that record still stands!"

Harrelson easily recalled his fondest moment of the 1962 season. "You remember that pump house out beyond the left-field fence? Well I hit a home run over that pump house off of Steve Dalkowsky."

The pump house is still there today, under the Route 17 highway, serving as a sentinel of sorts for marking where Johnson Field once stood.

"Wasn't Dalkowsky that really hard thrower who could top 100 mph?" the fan asks. Harrelson's smile is so wide that only his ears stop it as his eyes also get wide. "Oh yeah, he could bring it. Some say he was the hardest thrower ever."

In 1962, Dalkowsky was having his best season, working under the tutelage of Hall-of-Fame manager Earl Weaver. Weaver took a personal interest in Dalkowsky, trying to simplify the game for him by telling him to just focus on throwing his fastball down the middle of the plate and let his talent do the rest. In 2005, Dalkowsky told reporter Peter Handrinos of Weaver's simplistic pieces of advice:

"Weaver would bang on a water bucket, the water cooler, when he thought I wasn't concentrating enough! He banged on it loud, even during warm-ups. He was a loud guy, anyway. [Umpire Doug] Harvey didn't like it, so he'd whistle after that. The other thing was, he worked on my motion. He drew a line on the mound, and said not to step in front of that line. The idea was to shorten [the motion]. That helped my control 100%."

Screenwriter and film director Ron Shelton played in the minor leagues alongside Dalkowski. His 1988 film "Bull Durham" features a character named "Nuke" LaLoosh (played by Tim Robbins) who is based loosely on Dalkowski. Also in the film "The Scout," Brendan Frasier's character, Steve Nebraska, reminds baseball veterans of Dalkowski, as does Charlie Sheen's "Wild Thing" character in the movie "Major League."

Two of Harrelson's teammates that year, albeit of very short duration, were Tony LaRussa and Bert Campaneris, who played 12 and 13 games, respectively, for the Triplets. LaRussa recalls his short stay in Binghamton with fondness. "When I arrived, I was 17 and the Hawk was having a tremendous year. We used to go to *Red's Kettle Inn* after the games, and I remember Hawk at the head of the table, big as King Kong."

Red's Kettle Inn is still open today, proudly calling itself the longest family-owned restaurant in the area, having been established in 1942 by Anthony "Red" Sobiech, and his wife Lottie. Over a half-century after Hawk ruled the nest at Red's, it is not hard to imagine Harrelson conducting court at one of the dinner tables. Many of the booths still have vintage juke box selection boxes attached to the wall, and though they don't work, you can still read the titles, which include "But You Know I Love You," by the First Edition, Tammy Wynette's "Stand by Your Man," and "Georgy Girl," by The Seekers.

It is a friendly neighborhood bar and restaurant, and its menu calls attention to how Red and Lottie were like a second set of parents to the likes of Tom Tresh, Joe Pepitone, Bill "Moose" Skowron, and the Hawk. There are over fifty pictures of former Triplets that adorn the walls and you are reminded that you are in Yankee country as the photos include such Bronx bombers as Mantle, Maris, Munson, and Mattingly. There is even a picture of Billy Martin and then best friend Bill Reedy, with Martin's jacket prominently displaying a "Racoon Sportsmen's Association" patch. Look further down the wall and you see a photo collage of Whitey Ford's return visit to the place in 1988, complete with a picture of Whitey sitting at the bar, with a dollar bill signed by Ford inserted where another picture should be. Jack Shay, in his book, *Bygone Binghamton*, explains that Ford was handed a twenty dollar bill to sign, but he refused to sign such a large bill, so a one-dollar bill sufficed.

Red's is a half mile from where Johnson Field once stood and when you walk through the doors you enter a time warp and can almost hear the Hawk holding court during the warm summer nights. But you won't hear him ordering a pizza, they still only serve "hot pies" at Red's.

Jerry Toman: Leader in the Best and the Worst of Times

Jerry Toman entered the Shrine in 2004, along with three former players who toiled the Johnson Field diamond for him while he was the general manager of the Triplets— Frank Verdi, Johnny Blanchard, and Ken Harrelson.

While a teenager in the 1940's, Toman was a concession worker at Johnson Field. He served in the Navy from 1944-46 and upon returning to the area in 1947 he worked at Johnson Field and studied at Triple Cities College, which was then an arm of Syracuse University and later was to become Binghamton University. Toman was hired as an assistant to business manager John H. Johnson in 1951, which was the same year he received his degree; he became the business manager of the Triplets in 1956, replacing Herm Krattenmaker, who resigned to take a similar position with the Yankees' Richmond farm team.

Toman held the front office leadership position the longest in the history of the franchise, and also had the distinction of being the franchise leader during the best of times and worst of times. Attendance was at its peak in the decade following World War II and the Triplets teams of the late 1950's contributed a number of players who would become members of the five consecutive American League pennant-winning teams for the Yankees from 1960-1964. But just as the New York Yankees had a rapid decline in the late 1960's, the Triplets did too, as the late 1960's saw attendance suffer a steep drop for a variety of factors, including the popularity of television and the decaying condition of Johnson Field. Binghamton lost its franchise in 1968, when New York State's Route 17 Highway ran through what had been the Johnson Field outfield.

During Toman's reign, the Triplets won two Eastern League titles (1958 and 1967); Toman also had the distinction of being the only Binghamton general manager to work for three different major league affiliations: The Yankees, the Kansas City Athletics ('62 and '63) and the Milwaukee Braves (1964).

After Binghamton lost its baseball franchise, Toman remained in the area, working as a stock broker and remaining heavily involved in the community, serving as an active member of Saint James Roman Catholic Church in Johnson City, and as a member of the board of directors of the Johnson City Senior Citizens Center. Ironically, the senior citizen center stands on the site once occupied by Johnson Field.

Jerry's wife, Eleanor, ran the Loft's Candy Shop at 239 Main Street in Johnson City for a number of years and during the off seasons, Jerry could be found behind the counter at the gift shop, using it as an off season base of informal operations for the Triplets as well, as customers could come in to talk baseball and buy tickets, etc.

Toman loved his work as a minor league executive and would often talk about the link between the community and the minor leagues. By being in charge of the Triplets, Toman combined his love of baseball with his desire to see the local economy prosper. "I think any sporting activity means a lot to any community—economy wise. Everybody benefits because you're doing business with local businesses—cleaners, laundry, restaurants, the whole bit." Though he was bitterly disappointed with the loss of the AA franchise, Toman kept his love for baseball throughout his life and his induction to the Shrine was one of his cherished memories. He was a resident of Binghamton when he passed away on August 30th, 2012 at the age of 86.

His obituary noted that "His love of baseball and the New York Yankee organization were superseded only by the love for his wife and family."

Rob Gardner: 15 Innings of Fame Instead of 15 Minutes

Rob Gardner grew up on Binghamton's West Side on Chapin Street and graduated from Binghamton Central High School. He signed his first contract with the Minnesota Twins but was selected by the New York Mets from the Minnesota Twins in the first-year player draft in 1963.

After winning 37 games in his first three years in the minor leagues, Rob broke into the majors with the NY Mets on September 1, 1965. Most young players can recall their major league debut as if it were yesterday and usually call it one of the greatest days of their professional career. Though Rob remembers his debut, not all of the memories are soothing. He took the mound at Shea Stadium, against Turk Farrell and the Astros and he lasted only three innings, though he struck out six Astros, including Rusty Staub and Joe Morgan. The first inning was brutal, however, as he gave up five runs on only three hits, with two errors being made by his teammates. His final pitching line read three innings, six hits, seven runs, one walk and six strikeouts, as the Mets lost to the Astros, 8-5.

A key error in that first inning was a dropped fly ball by outfielder Ron Swoboda. What really added fuel to the fire is that Gardner and Swoboda were roommates at the time. It's probably safe to say they discussed more than whose turn it was to do dishes or take out the garbage when they returned home that night. One person attending the game that night was Binghamton native and former voice of the Binghamton Triplets, Ken Gilchrist. Kenny was so upset with Swoboda's fielding that he got up from his seat in the middle of the game, yelled at Swoboda and called him a bum. Gilchrist was met with a friendly ovation from the surrounding spectators as he made an early exit from the stadium.

One of the highlights to Rob's career was a game he pitched for the Mets on Saturday, October 2, 1965, in the nightcap of a doubleheader against the Phillies. The game turned out to be one of the more memorable games in baseball history. The Mets and Phillies were closing the season by playing a doubleheader on Saturday afternoon before finishing the season the following day. In the second game that Saturday afternoon, the Phillies batters were interested in having a quick game as they needed to rest up for the next day. "It seemed as if, after the first three innings, I had thrown only nine pitches, those Phillies batters were all swinging at the first pitch," recently recalled Gardner.

Gardner threw 15 shutout innings in this game, only allowing five hits. Dick Allen just missed a home run with a long fly ball that Cleon Jones caught against the fence— Allen may have been swinging early in the count, but he was connecting, as besides his long fly he also had two of the Phillies' five hits off Gardner. The fifteen innings that Gardner completed still stand as a franchise record and probably will never be broken as pitch counts practically guarantee that no Mets pitcher will ever throw 15 innings in a game again.

Chris Short, who won 135 games during his major league career, was Gardner's mound opponent that day and when manager Gene Mauch tried to take him out of the scoreless duel, Short retorted, "I'm not coming out if that S.O.B. on the other side isn't coming out!" Indeed, Short matched Gardner inning for inning, departing after the fifteenth. After 18 innings the game was called, with neither team having scored. Some people get 15 minutes of fame in their lives, but Gardner got 15 innings of fame on this day!

After brief stints with the Cubs and Indians, Rob was traded to the Yankees prior to the start of the 1969 season. He would play the next 2 seasons at their Triple A club in Syracuse, just an hour up the road from his family. In a total of five years with the Syracuse Chiefs, he compiled a record of 37 wins and 18 losses. His best year was 1970 when he went 16-5 in helping the Chiefs to the Governor's Cup Title, the championship of AAA. He was also named the minor league pitcher of the year in 1970.

His success at the Triple-A level led to another promotion to the big leagues. His finest season in the majors came with the NY Yankees in 1972 when he was 8-5 with a 3.08 E.R.A in 20 games. In November of 1972 he was traded with Rich McKinney for Moises Alou. He pitched in 3 games for the Oakland A's before the Milwaukee Brewers purchased his contract. Arm and elbow injuries limited him to pitching in 13 major league games in 1973. He tried pitching for two more years in the minors, but his arm did not cooperate and he only appeared in 14 games in '74 and '75 and never made it back to the majors.

In reflecting on his career, Gardner stated the most important thing he learned in the minors was simply "to never give up." His minor league career was outstanding as he won 88 games over 12 years and had an E.R.A. of 3.21. That success in the minors gave him the opportunity to win 14 games and pitch over 300 innings in the big leagues from 1965 to 1973.

After he retired from baseball, Rob returned to Binghamton, where he worked for 26 years as a firefighter and paramedic for the Binghamton Fire Department. His self-deprecating wit is evident when he responds to a question about his stardom by having pitched for both the Yankees and the Mets— "I refer to it as 'Bubble Stardom'—the bubble burst real fast!"

Gardner currently splits his time between Florida and Binghamton and can often be found on a golf course!

Bob Grim: Hometown Hero

Along with Jake Pitler and Rob Gardner, Bob Grim joined the Shrine in 2005, his induction largely based on two outstanding seasons, one in the majors and one in the Class A Eastern League. He went 24-6 for the Yankees in 1954, winning the American League Rookie-of-The-Year Award. Three years earlier, he was the ace of the Binghamton staff, going 16-5 with a 2.39 E.R.A.

Grim was a literal hometown hero, as the Yankees signed Grim to a professional contract after his graduation from Franklin K. Lane High School in Brooklyn in 1948. In his first three years as a professional, Grim steadily progressed, winning 24 games and finishing the 1950 season with Norfolk in the Class B Piedmont League, where he was a 10-game winner.

Grim started the 1951 season pitching for Beaumont in the Double-A Texas League for manager Harry Craft, but not being able to crack the starting rotation, he pitched out of the bullpen, appearing in 4 games with a 7.71 E.R.A. He was sent down to Binghamton in May to pitch in the starting rotation and was immediately impressive, throwing a complete game in a 4-3 loss to the Wilkes-Barre Indians in 11 innings.

 By early June, *Binghamton Sun* columnist Marvin Behr recognized Grim's pitching prowess was going to be a season-long story as he gushed about Grim while acknowledging the skill the Triplets had for maximizing run production in a 4-1 win over Schenectady. "But of equal importance with the Triplets' penchant for squeezing the most runs out of their hits is the emergence of Grim as a standout pitcher. The slender right hander, who boosted his record to 4-1 with last night's victory, has completed all five games that he's started since joining the club."
.

Despite the pitching of Grim and the presence of two other Shrine members, Johnny Blanchard and Bill "Moose" Skowron, who got 93 and 57 at bats respectively, the '51 Triplets only finished 69-69, good for sixth place in the Eastern League.

After Grim's outstanding season in Binghamton in 1951, his fastball and slider were gaining him recognition by the Yankees, but Uncle Sam's Marines signed him up for two years of military service in 1952 and 1953, delaying the start of his big league career until 1954. Grim won his 24 games in his rookie year by only throwing 199 innings, as he doubled as a starter and reliever. It took until 1985, when Tom Browning won 20 games for the Cincinnati Reds, for another rookie pitcher to win twenty; ironically, as with Grim, Browning's rookie season was also the only year he would win twenty games.

That 1954 team won 103 games and was led by the pitching of Grim and Whitey Ford (16-8), with Johnny Sain gaining 22 saves. Mickey Mantle (.307-27-100) and Yogi Berra (.325-22-125) led the way offensively, but somehow the team finished 8 games behind the Cleveland Indians! The Indians were led by the hitting of Larry Doby (.272-32-126) and Al Rosen (.300-24-102) while Early Wynn and Bob Lemon both won 23 games.

Arm problems prevented Grim from ever replicating his success from 1954. "After my rookie year, my arm began hurting. X-rays showed nothing, but there were calcium deposits on my elbow. That was bad: I was a thrower, not a finesse pitcher." Grim traced his problems to throwing his slider so often. Years after his retirement, he gave the following advice to young pitchers. "Stay away from the slider. It's a great pitch, but it's awfully hard on your arm."

The only other year that Grim won more than 7 games was in 1957 when he won 12 games and saved 19 others, serving as a "closer" before the term came into vogue, as he finished 36 games. The 1957 season provided Grim with both a career highlight and a lowlight. The highlight was Grim's selection to the American League All Star team. The lowlight was his performance in the World Series against the Milwaukee Braves.

After throwing two scoreless innings in a 4-2 home loss to the Braves in the second game of the series, Game 4 saw Grim relieving Tommy Byrne in the bottom of the tenth with the Yanks holding a 5-4 lead. Byrne had walked the first batter and the 45,804 fans at County Stadium were noisily cheering for the Braves to get a win and tie the series. Future Hall of Famer Red Schoendienst sacrificed the runner to second. Now Johnny Logan and Eddie Mathews were coming up with only one out.

Logan got the game even with a double to left. Mathews now stepped in the batter's box.

And Mathews sent everyone home happy, hitting a two-run homer to give the Braves a 7-5 win. The Braves went on to win two of the next three games and became World Champions, as Lew Burdette beat the Yankees three times in the series. While Burdette won the World Series MVP, Grim and the Yanks went home. The next year, after appearing in 11 games, Grim and Harry Simpson were traded to the Kansas City Athletics for Virgil Trucks and Duke Maas.

Known as a hard-nosed player who would brush back a player in his playing days, Grim also had a great sense of humor. His nephew, Bob Grim, who now works for the Chicago White Sox, recalls "He grew up in what was Brooklyn Dodger territory in New York and in 1955 after the Dodgers beat him and the Yankees in the World Series, the neighborhood got together and had a victory parade right in front of my uncle's house! They actually hung him in effigy, a dummy in a Yankee uniform. We actually have film that they took of that and we still break it out every so often just to watch it. He really enjoyed that."

Bob and his wife, Marilynn, lived in Shawnee, Kansas after his playing days. Grim suffered a fatal heart attack on October 23rd, 1996, in Shawnee.

Jake Pitler: Binghamton was "Home Sweet Home"

Born Jacob Albert Pitler in New York City, "Jake," as he would become known, was the son of Russian-Jewish immigrants. Having six younger siblings, Jake found himself having to work at a young age.

One of his jobs as a youth was selling newspapers near Pittsburgh's Forbes Field. Oddly enough, one of his fellow "newsies" was future Pittsburgh Steelers owner, Art Rooney. Jake began his professional baseball career in 1912, mainly as a way of making money. It seemed to be the best way of earning a living without a formal education.

His first stop was in Connellsville of the Class D Ohio-Pennsylvania League; however, the team disbanded in June of 1913. He then signed with the Jackson Convicts of the Class D Southern Michigan Association league, where he played second base and hit .301 in 1914. The team was named for the state prison located in the city.

Pitler then spent the majority of the next two years playing for the Chattanooga Lookouts of the Southern Association (A ball). Following an impressive start of the season for Chattanooga in 1917, where he hit .364 in 42 games, Pitler made his major league debut at Forbes Field for the Pirates on May 30, 1917, starting both games of a doubleheader against the Chicago Cubs. He went 1-for-4 in a 6-5 loss to the Cubs in the first game and picked up another hit in the 2nd game as the Pirates rebounded to beat the Cubs, 2-1.

Pitler soon found himself as the everyday second baseman, sharing the infield with the great Honus Wagner, not bad for a guy only five-foot-eight and 150 pounds.
On August 22, 1917, Pitler set a major league record for putouts in a single game by a second baseman with 15. This is still a record almost a hundred years later! On this day the Pirates battled Brooklyn in a 22-inning marathon, with the Pirates losing to the Brooklyn Robins, 6-5. Pitler had a pretty good game at the plate, going 3 for 9.

Pitler's big-league career was short, as he only played parts of two seasons in the majors, where he hit .232 and knocked in 23 runs. At 5' 8" and 150 lbs., Pitler made his mark with his glove, leading the NL in fielding percentage for second baseman in 1917, with a .966 mark.

In 1918, the Pirates traded pitchers Burleigh Grimes and Al Mamaux, and utility infielder Chuck Ward to the Robins for outfielder Casey Stengel and veteran second baseman George Cutshaw. The arrival of Cutshaw essentially meant the end of Pitler's major league career, as Pitler played in only two major league games in 1918.

Jake decided to play in independent baseball leagues for the next several years and finally made it back to organized baseball with a stop in Binghamton with the Triplets in 1928. According to his son Larry, it was while playing for Binghamton that he decided to make the city his year-round residence as he had made several friends and liked the area. Jake became a player-manager at Elmira in 1929 which he enjoyed because it was only an hour from his newly adopted home.

From 1930 through 1938, Jake had managing stints all around the Northeast in cities like Hazelton, Elmira, Scranton, Springfield, Portsmouth, Wilkes-Barre and Jeannette. In 1938, he began a job as the director of the Atlantic Baseball Schools, which was located in Binghamton. It was a league of amateur baseball teams that was sponsored by the Atlantic Refinery, later known as ARCO.

In 1939, the Brooklyn Dodgers had entered a team in the brand new Pony League (Class D), which had teams in Pennsylvania, Ontario, and New York. The newly formed Olean Oilers were in need of a manager and Jake was recommended for the job by the Elmira Pioneers manager. Jake took the helm in Olean in 1939 and won two straight league championships. While managing in the minors for Brooklyn, Jake was credited with pointing out future Dodgers Duke Snider, Clem Labine and Ralph Branca; his biggest scouting find in Olean was during an open tryout where he discovered Gil Hodges.

Finally, in 1947, Jake was promoted to be the first base coach with the Brooklyn Dodgers. He spent 11years as Brooklyn's coach and gained the utmost respect of all the players, not to mention members of the fine arts community as well. Poet, diehard Brooklyn Dodgers fan, and Brooklyn resident Marianne Moore affectionately referred to Jake Pitler in her 1956 poem "Hometown Piece to Messrs. Alston and Reese, " where she urged on her Dodgers to win it all again as they did in 1955. In her poem, she recognizes Pitler's popularity and his charitable endeavors by referring to "Jake Pitler Night," which was held on August 23, 1956, as well as his fondness for September callup Don Demeter, who patrolled the second base bag in hawkish fashion:

Jake Pitler and his Playground "Get a Night"—

Jake, that hearty man, made heartier by a harrier
who can bat as well as field—Don Demeter.

Pitler was such a fan favorite while in Brooklyn that he was honored with not one, but two "Jake Pitler Nights." Jake requested that in lieu of gifts, money be collected for the Beth-El Hospital in Brooklyn. The $8000.00 collected went to establish the "Jake Pitler Pediatric Play Therapy Room."

Pitler was known throughout his career for working well with young players, both amateur and professional. Johnny Logan, 4-time NL All Star and a member of the Shrine's 1993 class, remembered Pitler's interest in him as a star high school athlete when Pitler got him invited to the Dodgers spring training site at Bear Mountain, NY:
"I happened to be invited by Jake Pitler to get the feel of professional baseball .They weren't going to sign me. They just wanted to have one of the super scouts look me over. They took young kids they thought might be successful. I worked out there, and then went back to high school. I remember Jake Pitler being a great influence with the Brooklyn Dodgers. I went to one session where one of our speakers was Branch Rickey, and what an outstanding speaker he was. He had a baseball in his hand, and he talked about it for an hour and a half."

During spring training in 1947, newspapers conjectured whether Jackie Robinson would get a promotion to the Dodgers. *The Sporting News* pointed out that of the top ten hitters in the International League in 1946, only Robinson had not received a callup to the big leagues. Pitler was one of Robinson's biggest advocates this spring, tackling the issue of race head on, telling the press, "It would be a crime not to let this boy come up because of his color. Wait till you see him in action….He's terrific." In 1950, Pitler was even more effusive in referring to Robinson's talent and his importance to Brooklyn's pennant hopes, "He's the indispensable man. When he hits we win. When he doesn't we just don't look the same."

Pitler earned his stripes in the Shrine for hitting .285 for the 1928 Triplets (543 at bats) and for his tenure as the long time first base coach for the Brooklyn Dodgers. He had a front row seat for the glory years of New York City baseball, where the Yankees, Dodgers and Giants dominated talk of the summer. He was there when Jackie Robinson broke the color barrier in 1947 and he was there when Johnny Podres shut out the Yankees in Game 7 of the 1955 World Series. He wasn't there, however, for the move to Los Angeles after the 1957 season. Pitler did not want to leave his Binghamton home, so he retired from his uniformed job and became a scout for the Dodgers, focusing on watching young amateur players in the Northeast.

Every year that Pitler left for Vero Beach to attend spring training as the Dodger's first base coach, the area's Jewish Community Center would throw a send-off party in his honor. Pitler's name is still mentioned every year on the Binghamton University campus in Vestal, NY, as the university still awards the "Jake Pitler Award" annually to a senior athlete for career achievement and leadership.

Jake passed away at Binghamton City Hospital (now Binghamton General Hospital) in 1968 at the age of 73.

Bert Campaneris: "His Nickname Was Dagoberto but His Real Name is Campy"

If Bert Campaneris ever gets an introduction like the title of this short profile, he will no doubt have achieved his dream of being elected to the Baseball Hall of Fame. For years, George Grande, as master of ceremonies for the Cooperstown inductions, was known for flipping a player's real name with his nickname. Dodger fans can still hear Grande say "His nickname was Harold, but his real name was 'Pee Wee,' " as he introduced Harold "Pee Wee" Reese to the Cooperstown crowd every year.

Bert "Campy" Campaneris began his professional baseball career at age 20 with Daytona Beach of the Florida State League. It was with Daytona that Campy, according to the *1963 Sporting News Annual Baseball Guide*, performed one of baseball's most amazing pitching feats on August 13, 1962, when he pitched both right-handed and left-handed in a game. At the time, he was playing right field when his manager, Bill Robertson, called on him to assist the lackluster pitching staff that day.

In his first inning of work, while pitching right-handed, he faced three batters, striking out two. The next inning, he flipped his glove over to the other side and pitched that inning left-handed, striking out two more. During his two innings of work, he yielded only one run on one hit, and had four strikeouts, but his team still fell to Fort Lauderdale, 11 to 4. In another game with Daytona Beach that season Campaneris played all nine positions, a task he would repeat as a major leaguer on September 8, 1965, on what would be deemed "Campy Campaneris Night."

His ambidextrous pitching display would also be repeated during his first season in Binghamton in 1962. He did not have as much success this time, as in his two innings of work he walked four, did not strike out anyone and gave up 5 runs, though only one of them was earned. Campaneris appeared in 13 games for the Triplets in 1962, when the team was a Single-A affiliate of the Kansas City Athletics. He also played in 35 games for the Triplets in 1963. His overall batting average as a Triplet during those two partial seasons was .290 and he also had 13 stolen bases.

Off the field Campaneris was mild mannered and reserved, but between the lines, his competitive spirit brought out the best in him, as he got on base any way he could and, once he did, his primary objective was to see how fast he could advance around the bases. He prided himself in being a sparkplug for the Oakland A's dynasty from 1972-1974.

In the 1972 American League Championship Series against the Tigers, Campy's fiery nature got the best of him. In the second game of the series, he led off the game with a single, stole second and third, and then scored. He had gotten two more hits and scored another run by the time he led off the bottom of the seventh with the A's holding a 5-0 lead and about to take a 2-0 lead in the series. Almost immediately, upon his stepping into the batter's box, Tiger reliever Lerrin LaGrow threw his first pitch hard and straight at Campy's legs, hitting him with the pitch.

Campy retaliated with fury, hurling his bat at LaGrow, with the bat spinning like a propeller as it passed near the mound. The benches immediately cleared for both teams, but umpire Nestor Chylak (who was elected to the Baseball Hall of Fame in 1999) quickly restored order and prevented Campy from charging the mound. When the dust settled, both LaGrow and Campaneris were ejected from the game. Campaneris would be suspended for the rest of the series and conspiracy theorists wondered if Billy Martin, manager of the Tigers, had ordered LaGrow to throw at Campaneris, in the hopes of not only unnerving Campaneris, but also to light a fire under Martin's dormant lineup. (Although the Tigers came back to win the next two games, the A's won Game 5 to advance to the World Series against the Cincinnati Reds.)

In his 19 years in the big leagues, Campy led the league in various categories. In 1968, he was tops in plate appearances (707) at bats (642), hits (177), and stolen bases (62). 1972 was another banner year for him, again leading the American League in plate appearances and at bats, while also leading the league with 52 stolen bases; this year also was the first of three consecutive World Series titles for the Athletics. During his career, Campaneris was selected to the All-Star team six times and also led the American League in stolen bases in six years as well.

His lifetime stolen base total of 649 ranks him fourteenth all-time. Of the 13 players ahead of him, eight are in the Baseball Hall of Fame. When Campy was called by the Shrine committee for his induction, he genuinely felt honored and humbled by his selection. He said he looked forward to seeing his old stomping grounds in upstate New York. He also stated whenever he played with or against someone from his Triplets days, they would always meet up at some point and make mention of Binghamton.

While in town for his induction, he enjoyed a day trip to Cooperstown where he walked the streets of the famed town, toured the museum and eventually met up with an old friend, Clete Boyer, who happened to be sitting outside a restaurant, signing autographs for passerbys.

Maybe it was because he was in Cooperstown that made Campy feel like a kid again. He had some fun sneaking up on Clete and asking if he would pose for a picture with him. When Clete looked up, a huge smile came to his face and the two baseball greats spent the next hour or so reminiscing about the old days.

While Campy's career is long over, many baseball experts question if maybe someday, Cooperstown will come calling for him. His lifetime numbers compare favorably with Hall of Fame shortstops Luis Aparicio and Ozzie Smith. While Smith beats out Campy in career on-base percentage by a mere .026, Campy's on base percentage is identical to Aparicio's, at .311; and while Smith and Aparicio compiled identical lifetime batting averages of .262, Campaneris finished only points behind, with an average of .259. Finally, using the modern "Wins above Replacement" (i.e., "WAR," a statistic that shows how many wins a player is credited with when compared against an average replacement player) statistic, Campaneris posts a respectable 53.2, though it trails Aparicio's 55.7 and Smith's whopping 76.5. No doubt Smith dominates the WAR category due to his defensive prowess at shortstop.

Though the credentials of Campaneris for Cooperstown can be debated, his credentials for the Binghamton Shrine transcend discussion; he was a great addition to the Shrine class of 2006, which also included the ex-Yankee great and Triplets manager, Lefty Gomez; outfielder William Kay (Bingos); and ace of the 1992 Binghamton Mets, Bobby Jones.

Lefty Gomez and the Night He Screamed, "Turn off the Water!"

Lefty Gomez is the only member of the Shrine whose primary Binghamton connection was being a manager of the Triplets. (Though technically he was also a player, as he started one game in each season he managed.) Lefty managed both the 1946 and '47 Triplets, though it wasn't his managing ability that got him inducted into the Shrine, as he led the Triplets to last place finishes in both his years at the helm. His managing career stood in stark contrast to his major league pitching career, where he finished with 189 wins against 102 losses, and won twenty games four times. Gomez started five All-Star games, including the first one in 1933 when his mound opponent was Binghamton's own

"Wild" Bill Hallahan, and Lefty was widely regarded as the best pitcher in the American League from 1931-1938.

Gomez won five World Series with the Yankees and he excelled in the post season, as he was undefeated in 7 World Series starts, going 6-0 with a 2.86 E.R.A. Gomez was inducted into Baseball's Hall of Fame in 1972 while Binghamton's Shrine came calling for him in 2006.

As great a pitcher as Gomez was, he might have been an even better story teller. After he retired from the game, he went to work in public relations for the Wilson Sporting Goods Company and he was in great demand as an after-dinner speaker. Of his stay managing in Binghamton, Lefty summed up his experiences by stating "When we were rained out, we had a victory dinner."

One of his favorite Binghamton stories was when he was coaching third base with a runner at second and a Triplets hitter stepping into the batter's box. Suddenly Gomez called time and called the bat boy over, as he saw a boy of about 4 climbing the net behind home plate. Gomez told the bat boy, "There's a little kid climbing the screen behind the catcher. Tell his parents to get him to come down right now or leave the park!"

The bat boy looked at Gomez quizzically and said "Well, we'll get that kid down, but we won't be talking to the parents."

"Why not?' asked Gomez.

"Because he's your son, Mr. Gomez!"

Lefty then took a closer look and when play resumed he was so busy watching his son, Gery, that the runner from second got picked off because Gomez did not see the infielders sneaking behind his player.

Gomez played in a fantastic era for the Yankees—while the country battled unemployment and depression at the beginning of the decade and pre-war jitters at its close, Gomez and the Yankees were winning championship after championship. Gomez was the bridge from the "larger than life" exploits of Babe Ruth to the elegant style of Joe DiMaggio. Lefty was close friends to both the Babe and DiMaggio, and he had a special relationship with DiMaggio.

The friendship with DiMaggio started when the Yankees assigned DiMaggio to room with Lefty in 1936 and the friendship lasted a lifetime. About the only thing they initially had in common was that they were both from the San Francisco area and were now playing baseball in New York. Gomez was garrulous, DiMaggio was taciturn. Gomez was married to a beautiful Broadway actress and DiMaggio was an introverted bachelor.

But in a short time they bonded and a deep trust grew between them. Indeed, if Joe DiMaggio ever confided to anyone about his relationship with Marilyn Monroe, Lefty would have been the man. Just as DiMaggio had hoped Marilyn would give up her acting and focus on being his wife, when Lefty was courting his wife, June, he too had asked her to give up her career as a Broadway musical-comedy actress. One evening, he brought up the topic one too many times.

He was in full exhortation mode as he told June, "You can leave the show and relax at home with what the Yankees are paying me."

June O'Dea, Broadway musical-comedy star of such works as "Here's Howe," "Billie," and "Of Thee I Sing," then gave her best performance. She excused herself, went to the bathroom, opened the door, lifted the toilet seat and dropped her Tiffany's engagement ring in the toilet. Looking at Lefty, she then flushed!

Lefty immediately left the room and got the building superintendent to turn off the water and had some plumbers check the pipes and drains. Remarkably, Lefty got his ring back, apologized to June, went back to Tiffany's to get the ring cleaned, and wound up marrying June in 1933. No doubt that story helped DiMaggio get through difficult times when he commiserated about having to share Marilyn Monroe with the world.

After his two-year stint managing the Triplets, Gomez took a job as a roving minor league pitching coach with the Yankees for a year before going to work for Wilson in October of 1948. At the request of then Binghamton general manager Jerry Toman, he returned to the Binghamton area in January of 1956 to speak at a hot stove event in late January. Gomez formed one half of the greatest duo ever to speak at a hot stove dinner in Greater Binghamton, as the other player on the dais that evening was Whitey Ford. Baseball fans had an unparalleled evening as they listened to the two greatest lefthanders in Yankee history!

Gomez' Hall of Fame class was one of the greatest classes ever, as Yogi Berra, Sandy Koufax, Buck Leonard, and Early Wynn were his induction teammates. An insight into Gomez's humble nature can be seen in his answer to a letter from Clifford Rachline from the Baseball Hall of Fame on February 7, 1972. Rachline was questioning the year Gomez was born--all the records agreed on the date of November 26th, but some records showed he was born in 1909 and others said 1910. Lefty's response was –

Dear Clifford:

None of the dates are correct. I was born on November 26, 1908 in Rodeo, California. Still can't believe I've been elected to the Hall of Fame.

Regards to all,
Lefty Gomez

Bill "WB" Kay: Binghamton's All-Time Hit King

"WB" (Walter Brockton) Kay joined the Binghamton Bingos in 1914 as a 36-year-old outfielder seven years AFTER making his debut for the Washington Senators. Curiously, Kay made his major league debut on August 12th, ten days after the legendary Walter Johnson made his debut with the same team. While Johnson went on to win 417 games over a twenty-two year career with the Senators, Kay got 60 at bats in his 29-game career, all of which came in 1907. Though he hit .333, Kay never got another call to the majors, finishing his career by playing 15 more years in the minors.

Kay was a mainstay of the Bingos from 1914-1919, when he played in 559 games, amassing 2007 at bats. His batting averages during his Binghamton sojourn ranged from .308 to .378, and he still holds the record for the most at bats by any player who donned the uniform of a Binghamton team, beating out shortstop Jose Coronado, who garnered over 1700 at bats for the Binghamton Mets from 2007 to 2011.

The reign of "WB" Kay in the Greater Binghamton Area was one of growth. European immigrants would arrive in the area and ask "Which way EJ?" as the shoe manufacturer was becoming a prized employer, producing 54,000 pairs of shoes every day. By 1914 the town of Lestershire had increased is population by 39% from only four years earlier and The International Time Recording Company (ITR, later to be renamed IBM) was experiencing tremendous growth as well, as its move from Binghamton to Endicott gave it space for much needed expansion.

Johnson Field had opened its gates in 1913 and was drawing record crowds for its Sunday games, which were free. An overflow crowd greeted the Bingos on the first Sunday of the season in 1914, as The *Binghamton Evening Press* told its readers "Ground rules were necessary, owing to the territory skirting the outfield being thickly populated by hundreds of fans unable to obtain seats in the stands from which to view the contest."

As well as the area was doing, its prosperity took a back seat to the happenings during Kay's debut game for the Bingos in 1914, as Kay and his teammates played in one of the greatest games ever played at Johnson Field. The Bingos opened the season at home on April 30th against the Utica Utes, with Kay manning right field and batting fifth. On this day the Bingos managed only one hit off of Utica's Frank Oberlin, but won the game 1-0, as they scratched a run across the plate in the bottom of the ninth. First baseman Jim Calhoun started the inning with a walk and when pitcher Festus Higgins laid down a bunt, the throw from catcher Ed McDonough got past first, putting runners on second and third. Then Binghamton outfielder Pete Curtis knocked in the run with a sacrifice fly.

What made the game so unique is that while Oberlin only gave up one hit to the Bingos (catcher Bob Peterson had a single), Higgins not only shut out the Utes that day, but he did not allow a hit—Opening Day and there was one hit between the two teams and the home team had a win and a no hitter!

"The most remarkable game of baseball I ever witnessed," concluded John H. Farrell, president of the New York State Baseball League. Almost as amazing as the pitching performances is that the game only took one hour and twenty minutes to complete!

Heading into the 1914 season, Kay was expected to be a key man in the Binghamton lineup as he had hit over .300 in each of the previous four years in the minors. His broad shoulders and 6' 2" frame added to his presence at the plate. Even after he got off to a slow start, only hitting .210 by May 21st, *Binghamton Evening Press* sportswriters were telling their readers that while the success of the Bingos was open to debate, the performances of Bill Kay and second baseman Bill Cranston were not.

"It is too early in the season to venture a prediction as to the position the Bingos will occupy on September 13th. Kay and Cranston may now be well down the list as hitters, but well posted baseball fans are quite positive in their assertions that these two men will show a reversal of their present form before long and start spurts of the ladder, hitting around .300 'ere the season is half gone."

Indeed, by the middle of the summer, Kay's name was prominent in the box scores and in the daily baseball stories, though sometimes it seemed as if the writers were not using English to describe the events. Witness the following description taken from the reporting of a 6-run third inning that gave the Bingos an 8-4 win in the middle of June:

"The third inning must have been a nightmare for manager Phelps. Binghamton chalked up six runs before the third man was out. A single by Cranston started the row. Hartley followed with a two-ply clout, sending Cranston to third. Two runs were scored on Peterson's triple. Not to be outdone, Kay smashed for three hassocks, bringing in Peterson."

A two-ply clout? That must be a double. Three hassocks? One can only be thankful that term for a triple never caught on. But with Kay looking to score from third, the sportswriter could not refrain from another verbose description→ "There was Kay waiting to ring the home bell as soon as someone could pole a hit."

By season's end Kay had apparently "poled" a lot of hits, as he finished as the team's leading hitter with a .322 mark.

During his lengthy stay a Johnson Field, Kay hit safely 687 times, giving him the all-time area hit record. His lifetime average as a Bingo was .342.

Bobby Jones: September 12th–Prelude to a Pennant

The outstanding pitchers who have worn the uniform of the New York Mets have been numerous and the names roll off the tongues of longtime Mets fans—Tom Seaver, Nolan Ryan, Pedro Martinez, Doc Gooden and David Cone form a formidable starting five, and then there's Jerry Koosman, Ron Darling, Al Leiter, Johan Santana and Jon Matlack forming another queue of five. And Met fans know that any hope the Mets of today have of playing meaningful games in September anytime soon rests on the development of today's top pitching prospects—Matt Harvey, Zack Wheeler, Noah Syndergaard, Rafael Montero, and Cory Mazzoni—all of whom have called Binghamton their home in the past few years.

But ask those same longtime Mets fans who turned in the best post-season pitching performance of any Met and only a few know the answer—ex-Binghamton Met Bobby Jones! This righty pitcher hailed from Fresno High School in California, the same school that produced star big league pitchers as Dutch Leonard, Jim Maloney, Dick Ellsworth, and Tom Seaver. Jones called Binghamton his home in the summer of 1992 and led the Mets to the Eastern League Championship that year.

Dawn broke on Sunday, October 8th, 2000 with the Mets holding a 2-1 lead in games over the San Francisco Giants in the National League Division Series. That afternoon, in Game 4, Jones opposed Mark Gardner and faced a lineup that included future all-time home run leader Barry Bonds and that season's NL MVP, Jeff Kent. In the top of the fifth inning, with the Mets holding a 2-0 lead, Kent led off with a double and Ellis Burks moved him to third with a fly to right field. Jones then pitched around JT Snow, walking him before getting Rich Aurilia to fly to left. Up next was catcher Doug Mirabelli, and Jones, sensing opposing pitcher Mark Gardner would hit for himself, walked Mirabelli as well. Jones then got Gardner to pop out to second to end the inning.

Then Jones didn't just shut the door. He SLAMMED it, retiring the Giants in order in each of the next four innings, completing a 1-hit shutout, sending the Mets to the National League Championship Series against the Cardinals and ultimately to New York City's first Subway World Series since 1956. (Jones's masterpiece held the record for a complete game with the fewest number of hits allowed in division post-season play until Roy Halladay broke the record with his no-hitter against the Reds in Game 1 of the 2010 National League Division Series.)

Jones made Bobby Valentine, the Mets' manager, look like a genius for starting him. Though Jones had won 11 games for the Mets in 2000, his E.R.A. was over five runs a game and there was much debate in the media over who should get the start. "I'm so happy for Bobby Jones," Mets pitcher Al Leiter said after the game. "I'm so proud of him. To go out and pitch the best game of his life and dismiss all the critics who thought this was a bad decision. He went out and nailed it."

Jones did not come close to replicating his feat in the next two starts he had that post season, as he gave up nine runs in nine innings. But his success against the Giants did not come as a surprise for those fans that came out to see him pitch for Binghamton in 1992. He was phenomenal that year, going 12-4 with an E.R.A. of 1.88, while striking out 143 hitters and walking 43 in 158 innings. In recognition of his great numbers at Binghamton, Jones was rated by *Baseball America* as the 28th best prospect in all of baseball going into the 1993 season. Though he had only an average fastball, Jones was able to command both sides of the plate with it and also had excellent command of an outstanding curveball. The Binghamton fans who had watched him pitch in '92 knew he was something special; in a post-game jersey auction that year, Jones's jersey went for the highest price by far, well over $600 dollars.

On Saturday night, September 12, 1992, Jones had given Binghamtonians a sneak preview of what he could accomplish in a series-clinching performance. On that Saturday evening before a standing room only crowd of 6,255, Jones and the B-Mets beat the Canton-Akron Indians, 5-2, to win the Eastern League Championship Series, 3 games to 2. Jones threw a complete game 4-hitter, giving up two unearned runs, while striking out nine and not issuing a walk. He did not retire the final 13 batters as he would against the Giants 8 years later; instead he retired the final 16 hitters! If not for the three errors the Mets made behind him, leading to unearned runs in each of the first two innings, Jones would have hurled a shutout.

Jones pitched ten years in the majors, compiling an 89-83 record with an E.R.A. of 4.36 in over 1500 innings. He has the most major league wins of any pitcher going up to the big leagues who has worn the blue and orange of the Binghamton Mets, leading second place finisher Cory Lidle by seven.

Injuries and a troublesome back caused Jones to retire at the age of 32 after the 2002 season. He pitched the final two seasons of his career for the San Diego Padres, as he signed with them as a free agent before the 2001 season.

Brook Fordyce: A Roll of the "Dyce" Pays Off

Some people see the glass as half empty while others see it as half full. Brook Fordyce always sees the glass the same as he does life, always completely full. Brook has suffered some serious injuries in his life but he never let them prevent him from moving forward. In 2007, Brook was inducted into the Binghamton Baseball Shrine, both for his play during the inaugural season of the Binghamton Mets as well as his accomplishments at the big league level.

When Brook was in high school at St. Bernard in Uncasville, Connecticut, he suffered a serious injury playing football. The upper left side of his body became paralyzed from a hit in a football game. Brook did not miss any school during his two-month recovery time. In fact, when he is asked about the injury, he says "It was just one side. Just my arm and stuff."

As a reporter looks at him with raised eyebrows, Fordyce elaborates. "It wasn't negative at all. It's positive. It's something I had to go through and I'm sure I came out of it better. Hey, it could've been worse, right?"

The bout of temporary paralysis was a non-event compared to what Fordyce experienced in the early morning hours of January 24th in 2002 when he woke up with a horrible feeling in his stomach. After stumbling into his bathroom, he began vomiting. His wife, Jaci, was awakened by the commotion and saw a scary scene unfold, as a dark liquid was coming out of Brook's mouth and he was losing strength by the minute. Jaci called for an ambulance and the nervousness of the night turned to outright fear when they were told Brook was vomiting blood. "It didn't look like blood, there wasn't anything bright red. It was black, like tar," Brook recalls. At the hospital doctors quickly discovered Fordyce had ruptured an artery and they saved his life by cauterizing the artery and giving him blood infusions. "The doctors called it a freak of nature. It was like a dream or an out-of-body experience. I was lucky," explains Fordyce, who fully recovered to take the field in 2002, hitting .231 for the Baltimore Orioles.

The New York Mets drafted Fordyce in the third round of the 1989 amateur baseball draft and his selection proved fortuitous. Of the 54 players the Mets drafted that year, Fordyce was one of only two players who debuted with the Mets and played in over 600 major league games—Butch Huskey, a seventh-round pick, was the other. Fordyce followed the normal career path through the minors, starting in rookie ball and moving up the farm system ladder on a level-by-level basis. He arrived at high Class A ball in St. Lucie in 1991 and in 1992 he landed in Binghamton, ready to handle the young pitching staff for the first season of baseball in the Triple Cities in 23 years. Fordyce did such a good job with the pitching staff that Binghamton captured the Eastern League Championship, finishing with a 79-59 record and an outstanding 3.12 E.R.A. Fellow Shrine mate Bobby Jones was the ace of the staff, posting a 12-4 record with a 1.88 E.R.A.

Besides providing sound defense with a .996 fielding percentage, Fordyce also excelled with the bat, as he was a middle-of-the-order presence in the lineup. He finished second on the team in batting average with a .278 mark and second in RBIs, with 61. His 11 home runs in 475 at bats were also good enough for third place on the team. Fordyce was remarkably consistent throughout the year, as on June 21st he was hitting .275, with 7 homers and 25 RBIs.

When the Mets visited the New Britain Red Sox in the middle of the season, Fordyce told Don Amore, reporter for the *Hartford Courant*, the importance of being able to relax "I'm very relaxed at the plate right now and the hits are falling for me. I'm having fun this year and that's the important thing. I don't worry about my batting average, if I'm having fun, I feel like it's a good year."

Binghamton Manager Steve Swisher noted that Fordyce was doing everything being asked of him and that his steadiness at the plate was a big plus. "He's showing us the kind of offensive ability we need to see from him, he's using the whole field."

Following two more years at the Triple A level, Brook made his major league debut with the New York Mets in 1995. He would play parts of the next three seasons in the majors; finally, he got a long look with the Chicago White Sox in 1999, which was his first full season in the big leagues. He played in 105 games with the Sox, hitting an impressive .297 with 25 doubles and 49 runs batted in only 362 plate appearances.

On July 29th, 2000 Fordyce was one of four players to be traded to the Orioles for Harold Baines and Charles Johnson. He played parts of four years with the Baltimore Orioles, having his finest season in 2003 when he played in 108 games and hit .273. Fordyce's final year in organized baseball was 2004 with Tampa Bay.

During the 2007 Shrine induction ceremonies, Brook was met by some friends, as well as a former battery mate from the 1992 season, Tom Wegmann, who won 9 games for Binghamton in 1992. After the completion of the ceremonies, Fordyce and his induction mate Charlie Keller III signed autographs along the right field line and then watched the rest of the game from a stadium skybox. Fordyce and Wegmann, once reunited in the skybox, found it easy to fall back into their locker room days with Binghamton.

At one point Wegmann and Fordyce were bantering about one of the empty beverage bottles at the table; both of them needed a beverage, but both were also quite content to remain seated and watch the game. Soon they started commenting on the uniqueness of the empty bottles at their table. Before long, Mike McCann, their host for the evening, took the bait. He offered to get them each a new and full bottle and when he returned with their drinks, they had huge open smiles on their faces and blurted out at McCann, "It works every time! Thanks for being our legs!"

McCann smiled wanly, wondering at first why they just didn't ask him to get them a beverage. But as their conversation wore on, McCann realized they were just reliving their days as young men pursuing a dream and Fordyce, despite his big league success, was just recalling when meal money was limited and fame was the furthest thought from his mind.

Fordyce was selected in the third round of the 1989 amateur baseball draft and finished his 10-year major career appearing in 623 games, compiling a .258 average, with 41 home runs and 188 runs batted in. Brook retired from active playing in 2004 and currently is a private instructor and coach in Florida. His baseball camps go by the name of "Team 4 Dyce," and various videos from his camps can be found on the internet on *Youtube* (http://www.youtube.com/watch?v=fedPCxoJOhY).

Charlie Keller III: A Promising Career Cut Short

Charlie Keller III was destined to become a baseball player. He was the son of the New York Yankee great from the 1940's, Charlie "King Kong" Keller, and in 1961 he had one of the best seasons any Triplet ever had. As a Triplet that season he hit thirty-eight doubles, seventeen triples, nineteen home runs and had 104 RBIs, while leading the Class A Eastern League with a .349 average. His success in '61 is what propelled him into the Shrine, joining Brook Fordyce, Cory Lidle and George McQuinn in the class of 2007.

As a child, he was always a proud Yankee fan, cheering for his father and other teammates like "Old Reliable" Tommy Henrich, Joe Gordon, and Joe DiMaggio. Charlie graduated high school in 1957 and spent six months in the army reserves before following in his father's footsteps and attending the University of Maryland, where he starred in baseball. After one year at Maryland, he signed with the Yankees and went to Fort Lauderdale for spring training.

Keller began his professional career at St. Petersburg (Class D), where he hit a respectable .291. However, he developed back problems and required surgery. In 1960, he was late getting to spring training because of his recuperation from his surgery. He spent his second professional season with Class C Fargo-Moorhead of the Northern League. Even though he got a late start on the season, he still showed a lot of promise, hitting .304 in 119 games.

Keller's next stop would be the finest of his shortened career, as he excelled with the Triplets. He did not suffer from a lack of confidence in that season of '61. During his induction visit back to Binghamton, he recalled his hubris as a Triplets outfielder. "Early in the season I hit a home run that hit the baseball sign above the fence in right center field, so I collected $75.00 worth of merchandise from a local merchant. My wife wanted to spend the money right away, but I had my eyes on a TV set," Keller explained. "The TV was a lot more than $75.00, but I told my wife 'Let's wait, I'll be sure to hit that sign again soon.' "

Well the season continued and though Keller continued to get his share of hits, he had difficulty hitting that sign. As the season's end approached, he and his wife wound up cashing in his $75.00, but not for a TV. Keller's face is filled with a smile as he concludes his story—"About two weeks after cashing in our winnings, I did manage to hit the sign again, getting another $75.00 dollars" He still chuckles about that story when recalling it. He even remembers the name of the merchant—*Babcock's Hardware and Sport Shop.*

Keller played in AA Amarillo and AAA Richmond in 1962, but developed back problems again. After undergoing a second back operation, his career would soon be over. Keller explained, "Back problems were common in my family. My dad's career was cut short by back problems, and so was my brother Don's, who also played minor league ball."

Following his baseball career, Charlie returned to the University of Maryland and earned a degree in accounting. He became a CPA in a large accounting firm and eventually opened his own firm, where he employed over 200 people. He also continued to help run the family business "Yankee Land Farms," which was a standardbred harness racing horse farm that his father started. "Yankee Land Farms" became one of the most successful breeding farms for standardbreds in the nation before closing its doors in 2006.

Charlie fondly recalls his playing days in the Yankee organization whenever he is approached about it. All of his memories are not from the baseball diamond, however. He has played in his share of golf tournaments through the years and still enjoys telling of a charity golf event he decided to play in with his father and a couple of his father's friends. It just so happened that those two friends who rounded out the Keller's Captain and Crew were Yogi Berra and Joe DiMaggio! "Once the word got out that my dad, Berra, and DiMaggio were playing with me, I became a very popular fella," chuckled

Keller. "After our round of golf finished that day, I think we were in the parking lot for an hour or so signing autographs."

Although Keller was known to cover a lot of ground when he played in the outfield, on a personal level he has not covered much distance. Today Keller lives in Frederick, Maryland, the very same town where he grew up, having been born there on August 4th, 1939.

Cory Lidle: An Eerie Echo

Cory Lidle was signed out of high school by the Minnesota Twins as an amateur free agent in 1990, after graduating from South Hills High School in West Covina, which is just outside the "City of Angels." He was a posthumous inductee into the Shrine in 2007; at the time of his induction he would have been 35 years old had he not died in a small plane crash in New York City on October 11, 2006.

Lidle's Shrine selection was based on both his 1996 season with the Binghamton Mets and his nine-year major league career. Cory went 14-10 during his one season with Binghamton, leading the league with 190 innings pitched and finishing second in victories to the 16 registered by Carl Pavano of the Trenton Thunder, which was then a Double-A farm club of the Boston Red Sox. Lidle finished his major league career with a record of 82-72 and had an E.R.A. of 4.57 over 1320 innings.

On April 1, 1993, ten days after he turned 21 and after pitching for two years at the rookie league level, Lidle might have thought the Twins were playing an April Fool's joke on him when he was handed his release. After all, he went 2-1 and had an E.R.A. of 3.71 for the Elizabethon Twins in the Appalachian League in 1992. But it was no joke and Lidle had to pitch in an independent league in 1993 to keep his dream alive. His perseverance was rewarded at the end of the season, as the Milwaukee Brewers purchased his contract. He then pitched in the Brewers' organization for two years before the Brewers traded him to the Mets for catcher Kelly Stinnett in January 1996, opening the way for Lidle to have his banner season with Binghamton, where he was the ace of the staff.

He equaled Bill Pulsipher's franchise mark with 14 wins and led the club with 141 strikeouts and 6 complete games. That complete game record may never be broken, given today's pitch-count limits. Now a pitcher can go through a whole career with only a handful of complete games. Ironically, even with the results Cory had in 1996, he was overlooked for the Eastern League All-Star game—but by 1997 he was at Shea Stadium, winning 7 games and posting an impressive 3.53 E.R.A in 81 innings for the New York Mets.

Following the 1997 season, Cory was chosen by the Arizona Diamondbacks with the 13th pick in the expansion draft. He spent most of the season on the disabled list, however, and was selected off waivers by the Tampa Bay Devil Rays in the off-season of 1998.

After two sub-par seasons with Tampa, he was traded to the Oakland Athletics as part of a seven-player, three-team trade.

Once back in California, his career stabilized and even thrived. His first year in Oakland, 2001, he finished with a 13-6 record and a 3.89 ERA; from 2002 through 2006 Cory won 69 games. The Yankees traded for him on July 30, 2006 and he finished the year in the Yankees' rotation, making 9 starts and getting 4 wins. As the 2006 season drew to a close, Lidle was approaching free agency and he anticipated there would be a lot of interest from various teams in his services, as he was viewed as a reliable, back-of-the-rotation starter, who could be signed at a relatively low price.

However, Cory never got to test the free agent market or listen to an offer from the Yankees to re-sign. After the 2006 season concluded, on October 11, 2006, Lidle, who was a pilot, was aboard a single-engine *Cirrus SR20* plane that was flying over the East River when it crashed into the Belaire apartment complex on 72nd Street in Manhattan's Upper East Side. The flight had originated from Teterboro Aiport in New Jersey and had circled the Statue of Liberty before heading north along the East River. Also with Lidle was his flight instructor, Tyler Stanger.

It has never been determined who piloted the plane when it veered off course and crashed into the Belaire, which is only about 250 feet from the banks of the river. In 2009 the National Transportation Safety Board ruled pilot error caused the crash. It was a windy day and the plane crashed shortly after turning around along the narrow path of the East River. Ironically, a month before the crash, Lidle had stressed his focus on safety when flying by telling a *New York Times* reporter, "The whole plane has a parachute on it. Ninety-nine percent of pilots that go up never have engine failure, and the one percent that do usually land it. But if you're up in the air and something goes wrong, you pull that parachute, and the whole plane goes down slowly."

The news of the plane crash hit all New Yorkers hard, bringing back memories of the commercial airliners that crashed into the World Trade Towers on September 11, 2001. It also gave an eerie echo of the ill-fated plane crash involving the New York Yankees' beloved catcher, Thurman Munson. Munson was killed making touch-and-go landings and takeoffs on August 2, 1979 near the Canton-Akron, Ohio airport, just a short distance from his home.

Lidle's memory lives on not only in the minds of New York baseball fans, but in fans throughout the country as Cory played for seven different teams during his major league career. Today, baseball helps keep the memory of Lidle alive. Over 160 amateur baseball teams participated in the 8th annual Cory Lidle Memorial Baseball Tournament from November 29 through December 1 in Southern California in 2013. This tournament is sponsored by the *Cory Lidle Foundation*, whose mission is to provide a "chance for Cory's family, friends, colleagues, admirers and acquaintances to continue Cory's important mission of charitable giving."

Cory Lidle left behind his wife Melanie and six-year-old son Christopher. One of the baseball diamonds where Cory played as a youth while growing up in West Covina, California, was named "Cory Lidle Field" in his memory. Melanie remarried in 2010 with the blessings of Cory's parents; Melanie met the man she married through baseball, as he was her son Christopher's little league coach in 2007.

George McQuinn: No Depression When He was at Bat

In 1933, the country was in the middle of the Great Depression, San Francisco witnessed construction beginning on the Golden Gate Bridge and baseball's very first All-Star game was played at Chicago's Comiskey Park. The soon-to-be called "mid-season" classic showcased the National League stars versus the greats of the American League. Oddly enough, both starting pitchers, "Wild Bill" Hallahan of the St. Louis Cardinals' "Gas House Gang" and Vernon "Lefty" Gomez of the New York Yankees would later become members of the Binghamton Baseball Shrine.

The Binghamton Triplets were in their 11th year of their existence in the Eastern League, but their first full year as an affiliate of the very powerful New York Yankees. The team was laced with talent that produced several major leaguers, including Spud Chandler and Willard Hershberger.

Perhaps the most prominent player on that '33 team was George Hartlet McQuinn, as he delighted visitors to Johnson Field with his prowess at the plate. The success of Endicott Johnson and IBM also filled the area with unparalleled enthusiasm. McQuinn led the league in batting (.357), slugging percentage (.540), and doubles (48)—his 48 doubles remain a Binghamton franchise record. McQuinn had also played for Binghamton in 1932, hitting .319. Both of his years in Binghamton he played for Billy Meyer, who would go on to manage the Pittsburgh Pirates from 1948-1952.

Besides starring for the Binghamton Triplets for two years, George McQuinn was a major league veteran of 12 years, finishing his career with a batting average of .276 with 135 home runs. Interestingly, his minor league career was almost as long, as he played 11 years, hitting .320 with 77 home runs.

As impressive as McQuinn's stats and those of his teammates were in Binghamton in 1933, the best minor league team he ever played on was probably the 1937 Newark Bears, then a Double-A affiliate of the New York Yankees in the International League. Some of George's teammates included Charley "King Kong" Keller, who hit .353, as well as: Babe Dahlgren (.340), Joe Gordon (.280), Tommy "Old Reliable" Heinrich (.440), Willard Hershberger (.325), Bob Seeds (.305), and Buddy Rosar (.332.)

Besides all that hitting, there was that princely pitching staff that went 110-48. Joe Beggs led the way with an impressive record of 21-4, Atley Donald went 19-2, Steve Sundra 15-4 and Vito Tamulis 18-6. Newark won the pennant by 25 ½ games, captured the playoffs in eight straight games and went on to beat Columbus in the AAA Championship, despite dropping the first three games.

Even though McQuinn was a dominating player wherever he played in the minors, his hopes of being called up to the Yankees were broken every year by the presence of Lou Gehrig playing in the Bronx. McQuinn played in 38 games in the majors in 1936, but it was as a member of the Cincinnati Reds, as the Reds acquired him from the Yanks for the '36 season. After being reacquired by the Yankees for the 1937 season and being stuck in the minors once again, McQuinn finally got a break when he was drafted by the St. Louis Browns in the Rule 5 amateur draft. He became the regular first baseman for the Browns from 1938 through 1945.

George's first year with the Browns was highlighted by his hitting safely in 34 consecutive games. During that span, he hit over .400. His streak began in late May and extended well into June, though it almost came to an end in the 30th game against Washington. By the ninth he still was hitless and he had five batters scheduled to hit ahead of him. The Browns rallied though and he was able to pick up a single to keep the streak alive for a few more games.

Most of McQuinn's major league career was spent with the St. Louis Browns of the American League. In his eight years with the Browns, he compiled a .283 batting average with 254 doubles and 108 home runs. The St. Louis Browns made their only World Series appearance in 1944 and lost to their cross-town rival, the St. Louis Cardinals, 4 games to 2. In the first game of that World Series McQuinn hit a game-winning two-run homer, giving the Browns a 2-1 victory. It was the Browns first and next-to-last World Series victory. McQuinn is the only member of the Browns to hit a home run in a World Series.

George was traded to the Philadelphia Athletics in 1945 for Dick Siebert. A year later, he was released by Philadelphia and the Yankees came calling once more. McQuinn's career was rejuvenated by returning to the Bronx in 1947, as he helped the Yankees capture the World Series over Brooklyn in seven games. He hit .304 that year with 13 home runs and 80 runs batted in. However, father time was gaining on him. After a dismal 1948 season, he was released; his major league career was over.

George passed away in 1978 at the age of 68; he was inducted posthumously into the Shrine in 2007, whose class is the only one thus far to have included two ex-Binghamton Mets in Cory Lidle and Brook Fordyce. Charles Keller III, an ex-Triplet, rounded out the class.

Edgardo Alfonzo: "Fonzie" in His Happy Days

In 1991, Edgardo Antonio Alfonzo was signed by the New York Mets as a free agent at the age of seventeen. He left his hometown of Caracas, Venezuela for the rookie-level Gulf Coast League Mets. Never in his wildest dreams did he think the move would result in a 20-year professional baseball career.

"Fonzie" made the usual trek through the minor leagues going from rookie level in the Gulf Coast League, then on to Class A ball in Pittsfield and St. Lucie. His year at St. Lucie in 1993 was promising, as he finished with a .294 batting average and 86 RBIs. The following year he spent with Double-A Binghamton, where he divided his time between short and second and his numbers once again were encouraging. Fonzie finished with an impressive .293 batting average, 15 HRs and 75 RBIs. The Binghamton Mets captured the Eastern League Championship that year, beating the New Haven Ravens (affiliate of the Colorado Rockies) in the Northern Division Playoffs and the Harrisburg Senators (affiliate of the Montréal Expos) in the championship series.

Alfonzo was "Mr. Clutch" in the playoffs and during the span of one week in September he showed everyone the meaning of "grace under pressure." On Tuesday night, September 6th, in the first game of the Northern Division Playoffs, the B-Mets were trailing the New Haven Ravens, 1-0, going into the bottom of the eighth. As outstanding as Bill Pulsipher was pitching, having only given up one run through 8 innings, the Rockies' Juan Acevedo was even better, throwing a 6-hit shutout entering the bottom of the eighth. At the start of the half inning, the B-Mets caught a break as Acevedo hurt himself running to cover first on Ricky Otero's slow ground ball. Acevedo got the out, but Otero's speed down the line also got Acevedo out of the game with a leg injury. Reliever Mark Volsand came in and promptly gave up a single to shortstop Rey Ordonez. Up next was Alfonzo, batting third in the order. Alfonzo then hit a two-run homer, sending the 2,521 fans into a controlled frenzy. Pulsipher shut down the Ravens in the ninth and the Mets won the first game and went on to win the series.

The following Tuesday, in the pivotal game of the Eastern League Championship Series, with the series tied at 1, Alfonzo provided an encore performance. This time the Mets were trailing, 4-2, entering the bottom of the ninth inning and it looked like Jason Isringhausen would be a tough luck loser on this night. But the dynamic duo were about to strike again. With one out, Ordonez reached first on a single. And amazingly, Alfonzo again hit a two-run home run, this time to tie the game! The 3,047 fans in attendance celebrated wildly, slapping one another on the back, giving hugs to new-found friends and filling Henry and Lewis Streets with cheers. Hardly anyone noticed first baseman Frank Jacobs approaching the plate as the fans basked in Alfonzo's feat. People had barely sat down when Jacobs ignited another celebration with a game-winning, walk-off home run!

When the B-Mets clinched the championship the next night on their home field, Steve Phillips, then the New York Mets' Director of Minor League Operations and future general manager, was in attendance and gave a short speech honoring the team. He had hopes of star players joining New York over the next few months, including Bill Pulsipher, Jason Isringhausen, Robert Person, Rey Ordonez, Ricky Otero and Edgardo Alfonzo. "It will be a long time before you ever see a team with as much talent as this one, if ever," Phillips shouted to the fans as the players watched in champagne soaked jerseys and wide-eyed faces.

After posting his impressive season in Binghamton, Fonzie made the jump straight to the majors. He spent his first eight years of his major league career with the New York Mets. He was a consistent, hard-nosed player and aside from his rookie year, never played fewer than 120 games a year while in New York.

When Fonzie first arrived with the Mets, his manager, Dallas Green, soon compared him to the great Tony Gwynn. In an article in the *Newark Star-Ledger*, Green stated, "He (Alfonzo) knows how to hit. He prepares himself. He knows how to hit certain pitchers. I'm not making this kid into a superstar, but what I see in this kid is his capability. He can eventually become that kind of hitter…He's a thirty-year-old 21-year-old."

After eight years with the Mets, Fonzie's career totals were looking pretty good. He had a lifetime batting average of .292, 1136 hits, 212 doubles, 120 home runs and 538 runs batted in. His final season with the Mets was an excellent one, as he finished with a .308 batting average, good enough for tenth in the National League in 2002. However, the Mets only offered him $5 million per year for two years after that season.

Fonzie felt he deserved more than that and opted not to return. Fonzie didn't have to wait too long for another team to come calling. Several teams expressed interest in him, including the A's, but the San Francisco Giants became the team that ended up signing him. The Giants were at the point of ending their contract with Jeff Kent, so the availability of Alfonzo was perfect timing. The Giants signed Edgardo to a four-year, $26 million contract. He played three of those years with the Giants and the final season, which would be his last in the majors, was split between the Los Angeles Dodgers and Toronto Blue Jays. However, he only played in thirty games that year for both teams. The rest of the year was spent back in the minors.

Overall, Fonzie ended up with a 20-year professional baseball career, with 12 of those years coming in the major leagues. He had ups and downs along the way, but finished with a lifetime average of .284, hitting 146 home runs and knocking in 744 runs over 12 years. Alfonzo excelled in the post season, hitting .299 in 131 at bats.

In 2012 he had the honor of being selected to the all–time Mets team as its second baseman, beating out such players as Ron Hunt, Wally Backman and Felix Millan.
Alfonzo and Mike Piazza led the Mets to the National League Championship in 2000, where they and their teammates had the honor of playing in the subway series against the Yankees. That year marked Alfonzo's best in the major leagues, as he was selected to the All-Star team and hit .324, with 25 home runs and 94 RBIs. Alfonzo also represented Venezuela in the 2006 World Baseball Classic.

In 2008, Fonzie was voted into the Binghamton Baseball Shrine. Though he looked forward to his Shrine induction, he was unable to attend, as his love for the game found him playing with the Long Island Ducks, an independent league team. (Editor's note: Alfonzo signed to play with the Ducks after he was elected to the Shrine.)

Gene Bearden: A Golden Arm and a Purple Heart

Henry Eugene "Gene" Bearden was born in Lexa, Arkansas. His early childhood was spent on the playing fields of Tennessee and like many boys in the 20's and 30's, he idolized the great Lou Gehrig. Like Gehrig, he threw and batted left-handed.

At 19, he signed his first baseball contract with the Philadelphia Phillies and began his pitching career with Moultrie of the Georgia-Florida League. The next two seasons were spent with Miami Beach of the East Coast League and by 1942 he landed in Savannah, Georgia, in the Sally League, going 4-4. As with many ballplayers of his era, his career would then be put on hold due to military service in World War II.

Bearden entered the United States Navy and after basic training, he was assigned to the cruiser *USS Helena* as a machinist mate. The *Helena* was one of the surviving ships of the December 7, 1941 attack on Pearl Harbor, but not before she suffered excessive damage from Japanese torpedoes. She remained out of action until the summer of 1942.

One early June morning of 1942, the *Helena* was part of a task force that battled Japanese destroyers in the South Pacific. During the heavy fighting, the *Helena* was hit by torpedoes and sunk. The entire crew of 900 went overboard; two rescue ships were dispatched to her aid, but were called back into combat to continue the battle. Finally, after two days, the recue ships returned to assist the survivors. Bearden was in one of the lifeboats that housed the crewmen awaiting rescue.

He suffered a severe head and knee injury that would land him in a hospital for the next two years; a metal plate was implanted in his skull and a metal hinge put in his knee. His recovery included having his spirits lifted with the Navy awarding him a Purple Heart.

After his discharge from service, Bearden resumed his career in 1945 and was assigned to Binghamton of the Eastern League. The Triplets finished in 7th place in 1945 with a record of 56 wins and 81 losses. One can only guess how many losses the team would have suffered had Bearden not gone 15 and 5 with 17 complete games, including 2 shutouts! His 15 victories were 26% of the team's total wins. Bearden was an all-around player, and when he wasn't on the mound, he was often pinch hitting and playing in the field, as he complimented his pitching prowess by hitting .274 with three home runs in 146 at bats.

In 1946 Bearden was promoted to the Oakland Oaks of the Pacific Coast League, where he won another 15 games while losing only 4 for manager Casey Stengel. It was under Casey's managing that Bearden developed the pitch that would become his bread and butter–the knuckleball. He grasped the ball in such a way it would sail to the plate with literally no spin and would break down sharply as it reached the hitter.

In December 1946 the Yankees traded Bearden to the Cleveland Indians in a multiple player deal. Cleveland management was so surprised with the success he had with the "knuckler" that they kept him on their roster to begin the 1947 season. Bearden was given a relief appearance in early May, but with little success. He pitched only 1/3 of an inning and gave up several hits and 3 earned runs. That would be his only appearance in 1947. He was returned to Oakland, where he went 16-7 with a 2.86 earned run average.

The 1948 season proved to be a much better story for the ex-Triplet, as Bearden broke into a pitching rotation that included future Hall of Famers Bob Feller, Bob Lemon, and Satchel Paige. The Indians didn't start Gene until early May, when manager Lou Boudreau sent him out to face the Washington Senators. He beat the Senators for his first major league win and then won his next three starts, sending him on his way to the best year in his career. Boudreau was delighted with the rookie's performance; Bearden ended the '48 season with 20 wins against 7 loses and a league-leading 2.43 ERA and completed 15 of 29 starts, with 6 shutouts. Bearden finished second in the Rookie-of-the-Year voting, behind National League shortstop Al Dark, as just one award was given between both leagues.

Cleveland finished the 1948 regular season in a tie with the Boston Red Sox. With a choice between Feller and Lemon, manager Boudreau surprised everyone when he opted to go with Bearden on one day's rest. Boudreau felt that Bearden was the most effective pitcher at that moment. Skeptics scoffed at Boudreau's decision—left-handers were at a disadvantage with the famed "Green Monster" of Fenway only 315 feet away. Bearden responded by throwing a 5-hitter, leading the Tribe to an 8-3 victory, giving the Indians the title and the southpaw a 20-win season.

Bearden started the third game of the 1948 World Series in Cleveland's Municipal Stadium before a crowd of 70,306. He shut out the Braves, 2 to 0, with five hits and gave the Tribe a one-game lead in the series. Using his patented knuckleball, slider and fastball, he not only handcuffed the Braves but got two of Cleveland's five hits and scored a run. Then in Game 6, he came in to relieve Bob Lemon in the sixth inning to protect a 4-3 game for a save and claim the World Championship for the Tribe, the franchise's last World Series title.

Unfortunately, Bearden never came close to duplicating his rookie season. He was placed on waivers by the Indians in 1950 and ended his career with a record of 45 wins and 38 losses. He also pitched for the St. Louis Browns, Detroit Tigers and Chicago White Sox. In 2001, the Indians celebrated their 100th anniversary and Gene Bearden was selected as one of the greatest 100 players in team history.

Gene passed away March 18, 2004 of congestive heart failure at the age of 83. Bearden was inducted posthumously into the Shrine in 2008, forming 25% of one of the stronger Shrine classes, which included Edgardo Alfonzo, Joe Pepitone, and Daniel Casey.

Dan Casey: You Be the Judge—The "Mighty Casey" or Not?

Ernest L. Thayer's famous poem, "Casey at the Bat," first appeared in the June 3, 1888 edition of the *San Francisco Examiner* and ended with the infamous lines –

And somewhere men are laughing, and somewhere children shout,
But there is no joy in Mudville – mighty Casey has struck out.

More than a half century later, in 1939, Daniel Maurice Casey, retired Binghamton trolley conductor, was recognized at the inaugural Hall of Fame Induction ceremony in Cooperstown, NY, as the potential inspiration behind Thayer's poem. As baseball marked its 100th anniversary celebration in 1939, the Hall of Fame and major league baseball officials thought it appropriate to invite Casey to the celebration and today, 125 years after the publication of the poem, the question of "Was he or Wasn't he?" lingers.

Dan Casey was his own biggest promoter, and in 1938, the 50th anniversary of Thayer's poem, his story was gaining attention. He was eager to tell it, even though his strikeout sealed a loss to the Giants on that day. He became an expert narrator in setting the stage for his tale:

"I was a left-handed pitcher for the Phillies. I guess you'd call me the Hubbell of my time. We were playing the Giants in the old Philadelphia ballpark on August 21, 1887. Tim Keefe was pitching against me and he had a lot of stuff, but I was no slowpoke myself. It was the last of the ninth and New York was leading 4 to 3. Two men were out, and there were runners on second and third. A week before, I had busted up a game with a lucky homer and folks thought I could repeat."

The facts of Casey's story are true, right down to his claim that he was the "Hubbell of my time." In 1887 he won 28 games for the Phillies and completed 43 of his starts. In 1938, the Baltimore Orioles of the International league even invited him take an at bat against Rogers Hornsby before its game on May 19th. The *Binghamton Evening Press* ran a story under the following headline the next day →

Mighty Casey Fails to Show Baltimore Fans How He Fanned in Mudville; he hits Single: 4,000 Eyes upon him as former Binghamton Conductor Blasts hit off Hornsby After taking two Vicious Whiffs.

The article led with the following sentence, "Old Dan Casey, former street car conductor in Binghamton, about whose striking out Ernest Thayer reportedly wrote the poem, 'Casey at the Bat,' a half century ago, proved here last night that he doesn't always strike out." Indeed, after taking two swings and missing, the 74-year old Casey singled to left off of the great Rogers Hornsby. Said Casey, "I'll have to admit, that Hornsby didn't have as much on the ball as Tim Keefe did that time!"

Skeptics of Casey's story point out that the Baltimore franchise was no doubt just trying to capitalize on the 50th anniversary of Thayer's work. And a year later, they say, Cooperstown was more interested in promoting a good story rather than facing the facts. And of course, the most important element they are quick to report is that Ernest Thayer always denied his poem was about any one particular player.

But there are those Binghamtonians who no doubt believe Daniel Casey's story. They point out that "If Seneca Falls can claim to be the real Bedford Falls, Why Can't our

Casey be the Real Casey at the Bat?" Indeed, the second weekend of every December, the New York State town of Seneca Falls, located approximately one hour and 45 minutes northwest of Binghamton, celebrates the movie 'It's a Wonderful Life" with a weekend full of events. The town is proud to call out its similarities with Hollywood's Bedford Falls, including both being mill towns, and both having a bridge from which a member of the town leapt in order to save someone who had tried to commit suicide by jumping from the bridge. The town can even prove that Frank Capra, the film's director, passed through Seneca Falls the year before "It's A Wonderful Life" was made.

Daniel Maurice Casey never told his story as strongly as has the town of Seneca Falls and though his being the legendary "Casey" can be debated, there is no disputing Casey's Binghamton past and his success on the mound from 1884-1890. Born in Binghamton in 1862, he went on to win 96 games in the majors, and he is one of three members of the Shrine to have back-to-back twenty-win seasons (1886 and 1887) in the big leagues. (Jim Whitney did it from 1881-1884 and Lefty Gomez accomplished the feat in 1931 and 1932.) After his big league career was over, Casey also pitched for the Binghamton Bingos in the early 1890's, winning 6 games.

The summer of 2014 marks the seventy-fifth anniversary of the Baseball Hall of Fame, but there will be no Daniel Casey parading down Main Street as Thayer's "Casey." Perhaps what Daniel Casey needs now is for his story to capture the attention of the Preservation Association of the Southern Tier (aka, P.A.S.T.), which celebrates Binghamton's history through its annual October performance of "Spirits of Binghamton's Past, A Downtown Walking Tour." This tour is open to the public and includes visits from 13 "ghosts" of prominent Binghamton residents; three of the more prominent 'ghosts" include Willis Kilmer, creator of the Binghamton Press; writer Rod Serling; and architect Isaac Perry. The addition of Daniel Maurice Casey to this tour would give it an even 14 spirits and perhaps rekindle a forgotten debate.

In closing this look at Casey's past, we'd be remiss if we did not mention his batting average, which Casey often overlooked. While he may have been a dominant pitcher for a spell, his batting average was another story, and it may well explain why P.A.S.T. has passed him over. Casey's approaching the plate would instill no fear in any opposing team--he hit .162 and hit only one home run in 710 career at bats!

Joe Pepitone: Playing in His Back Yard

Joe Pepitone was born on October 9, 1940, the same day as John Lennon of *Beatles* fame. While Lennon was unique to the music world, Pepitone was something unique to the baseball world. He was inducted to the Shrine in 2008, along with Edgardo Alfonzo, Gene Bearden, and Daniel Casey.

Joe was signed by the New York Yankees in 1958, fresh out of Manual Training High School in Brooklyn; the Yankees were not scared off by Pepitone being shot in the early spring of his senior year at Manual in a school yard dispute. "The bullet had struck a rib and caromed out my lower back…missing three vital organs by inches. I was on the critical list for six days, in the hospital for twelve," recounted Pepitone years later.

He came to the Triplets in 1960 as an outfielder. Other Triplets teammates who went on to become his teammates with the Yankees included infielders Horace Clarke and Pedro Gonzales, pitchers Hal Reniff and Bob Meyer, and shortstop/outfielder Tom Tresh. Binghamton was a season of adjustment for Pepitone, and not just because he had gotten married in the offseason. He came to the Triplets with an entitled arrogance, having put two successful minor league seasons under his belt.

"I had hit ten home runs in spring training and the minute I saw the Binghamton park with its short fences, I said to myself, I'm gonna hit a ton of home runs this season," recalled Pepitone in his 1975 autobiography, *Joe, You Coulda Made Us Proud*. After the first few weeks of the season, however, Pepitone started seeing more breaking pitches and more inside fast balls, and his hubris declined almost as fast as his batting average. "I was hitting nothing and I couldn't stand it. I got so depressed, I thought I just couldn't do it, that I'd never make it as a ball player," lamented Pepitone. The turning point for Pepitone came when the Yankees sent sixty-five-year old Bill Skiff, ex-manager of the 1951 Triplets and a seasoned baseball coach, to work with Pepitone.

"Bear down, concentrate, and you'll see there's nothing to fear," admonished Skiff. "Another thing, when you go into a slump, you don't stop hustling, you don't give up. You bear down more, you run on every ball. You're fast enough to steal a lot of hits if you flat out (run)." After working with Skiff, Pepitone concentrated on not bailing out and maintaining his balance at the plate; his confidence steadily returned as he stopped feeling sorry for himself. By the end of the season, Pepitone had salvaged his season, hitting .260, with 13 home runs and 75 RBIs.

The next year, 1961, Pepitone solidified his prospect status by having an outstanding season for the Amarillo Gold Sox in the Texas League, where he hit .316 and had 21 home runs. He spent most of his time in center field, but also played 16 games at first, as the Yankees felt he could also be a viable first base option.

Pepitone joined the New York Yankees in 1962, spending his time as a reserve outfielder for all three spots and backup first baseman to fellow Shrine member, Bill "Moose" Skowron. Pepitone started 27 games, impressing the Yankees with his 7 home runs in only 138 at bats. The Yankees showed their confidence in Pepitone when they traded Skowron to the Los Angeles Dodgers in November of 1962 for pitcher Stan Williams. Skowron had had a fine season in '62, batting .270 and knocking in 80 runs while hitting 23 home runs, but the Yankees favored Pepitone's fielding prowess, power, and youth.

Pepitone's first two years as the regular first baseman for the Yankees were filled with performance and promise. He hit .279 in 1963 and led the team in RBIs with 87 and his 27 home runs were second only to Elston Howard's total of 28. In 1964 Pepitone had an even better year, hitting 28 homers and knocking in 100 runs for the Yankees, who were American League Champions both years.

Despite hitting 31 home runs in 1966, Pepitone never lived up to the front office hopes of the Yankees. In eight seasons in New York he batted .252 and hit 166 home runs, with an on base percentage of .294. He was never again selected to an All-Star team after his three consecutive selections from 1963-1965. He did, however, continue to field his position well, as he won gold gloves at first base in 1965, 1966 and 1969.

During his time with the Yankees, Pepitone lived the life in the fast lane. He squandered his money, and became known as anything but a hard-working teammate. In fact teammate Jim Bouton, in his highly controversial book "Ball Four," described Pepitone as vain, always carrying around a plethora of hair products in an attempt to control his balding pate. When Pepitone later joined the Chicago Cubs, he became the first player to use a hair dryer in the clubhouse.

The Yankees traded Pepitone to the Houston Astros in 1969 and in 1970 he was purchased by the Chicago Cubs. The Cubs sent him to the Atlanta Braves in 1973, but he was released a few weeks later.

After retiring from baseball, Pepitone returned to baseball in 1982 as a batting coach for the Yankees but was replaced later in the season by Lou Piniella. In the late 1990s he was hired once again by the New York Yankees as a special consultant.

His career can be best summed up in the brief forward the New York Daily News provided for Pepitone's autobiography in 1975, "Joe Pepitone did it all and now he tells it all. Here is the whole story unashamedly brought to life—the highs, the lows, the big blasts, the strikeouts, the endless nights and the agony on the field that followed, and what it meant to have it all and throw it away piece by piece."

If Pepitone had better remembered what he learned from Bill Skiff during his 1960 stay in Binghamton, his promise might have been fulfilled during his sojourn in the Big Apple.

Dale Long: Lefty Catcher and a Hefty Hitter

Dale Long was inducted into the Shrine in 2009, along with the ex-Dodger Danny McDevitt and ex-Binghamton Met, Quilvio Veras. Long had an outstanding season with the 1950 Triplets, when he led the Triplets to a second place finish, with a record of 81-58. He also went on to a 10-year major league career as a first baseman.

Born February 6, 1926 in Springfield, Missouri, Long later moved to North Adams, Mass, where he became a star baseball player as well as a talented football player. He was issued a contract from the Green Bay Packers for his talents as a punter and place kicker. His mother, however, was not fond of football and fretted over the potential of injury to her son. So instead of signing a contract to play professional football, Long began playing baseball in 1944 with the Milwaukee Brewers of the American Association, where his manager was future Hall-of-Fame skipper Casey Stengel.

According to the late Robert Sauve, high school classmate of Long's, during Dale's early minor league years, Long would not show up at North Adams High School until October, when the baseball season was over. He would stay for about four months, or until spring training started. After doing this for a few years, when he showed up in October to begin classes, school administrators were waiting for him and politely told him his presence in the high school halls would not be necessary— they gladly handed him his diploma and asked him to never come back!

Long's minor league career got off to a slow start, as his high in home runs for a season sat at 8 until 1948, when he hit 18 homers for the Lynn Red Sox, a Class B team of the Boston Red Sox. From 1945 until his big-league debut in 1951, Long played for five different organizations, with his best season coming in 1950, when he arrived in Binghamton to play first base for the Triplets. In 133 games he hit .287 with 27 home runs and 130 runs batted in, which led the Eastern League. The Triplets finished 9.5 games behind the Wilkes-Barre Indians, which was then a farm club of the Cleveland Indians.

In 1951 Long made his major league debut for the Pittsburgh Pirates on April 21st as he pinch hit for pitcher Junior Walsh in an 8-3 loss to the Cincinnati Reds. Long found playing time hard to come by for the Pirates and after only giving him 12 at bats in 10 games, the Pirates put Long on waivers and the St. Louis Browns claimed him on June 1st. He finished the year with the Browns, hitting .238 in 105 at bats only to have the Pirates reacquire him in December. Long spent the next three years in the minor leagues, returning to the majors with the Pirates in 1955. He had a good year in 1955, hitting 16 home runs and driving in 79 runs while hitting .291. Long was a regular first baseman for the next three seasons and was selected to the 1956 All-Star squad, when he hit a career-best 27 home runs.

Though he was selected to the All-Star team in 1956, it was not his biggest thrill that year. From May 19th through May 25th, Long played in eight straight games and hit a home run in all eight games! Up until Long's feat, the most consecutive games for hitting homers stood at 6 and was done by several players.

On May 19[th,] at Forbes Field, Long started his streak by hitting a home run in the eighth inning against left hander Jim Davis. The next day, Long homered in both ends of a Sunday double header against the Milwaukee Braves; Ray Crone was the victim in the first game, Warren Spahn in the night cap. The next day saw the Cardinals visit Pittsburgh for a two-game series and Long connected off of Herman Wehmeier and Lindy McDaniel to make it 5 games and 5 home runs. The Pirates then traveled to Connie Mack Stadium in Philadelphia and the pressure on Long grew.

Bobby Bragan, the manager of the Pirates, moved Long up one place in the batting order, thinking it might give him an extra swing. Long tied the record with his sixth consecutive homer against tough lefty Curt Simmons. The next day, Long waited until the eighth inning again until he connected off of Ben Flowers. Seven games, seven home runs! Long extended his record with a home run off Carl Erskine the next day as the Dodgers visited Forbes Field. Newcombe ended the streak the next day, on May 26th, giving Long an 0-4 collar— but not before Long hit a towering fly to left center that Duke Snider caught approximately 450 feet from home plate!

Thirty years after he performed his feat, Long recalled its significance in 1986. "Each year it seems to get bigger and bigger," he reflected. "Some day somebody will break it and they'll forget all about me. It's there to be broken. They break 'em all the time." Now, over half century later, Long's record still stands, though he has company. Since Long's feat in '56, only two other major leaguers have hit eight home runs in eight consecutive games, both in the American League—Don Mattingly in 1987 and Ken Griffey Jr. 1993. No player in the National League has ever matched Long's feat.

Early in his major league career Long nearly became the first left-handed catcher in modern league history. Pirates GM Branch Rickey, always looking for an edge and willing to try anything, came up with the idea and had Long work with the pitchers in the bullpen and do various drills to improve his ability behind the plate. But Long only caught in one exhibition game before the Pirates gave up the experiment.

In 1957 the Pirates traded Long and Lee Walls to the Chicago Cubs for Gene Baker and Dee Fondy. On August 20, 1958, in a game against the Cincinnati Reds, Long again wrote his name in the record book, this time with an assist from manager Bob Scheffing. In the ninth inning, using his first baseman's glove, Long caught a half inning when catcher and former Triplet Cal Neeman was ejected in the first game of a doubleheader. Long became the first left-handed catcher in the majors since John Donahue caught 22 games for the St Louis Browns in 1902.

In addition to Pittsburgh, Long's 10-year career included stops with the St. Louis Browns, Chicago Cubs, San Francisco Giants, New York Yankees and Washington Senators. He got to play in two World Series with the Yankees, appearing in 5 games, getting 2 hits and driving in a run in eight at bats. According to Yankee teammate and Binghamton Shrine member Clete Boyer, Long was a true Yankee, a great teammate who was a welcome addition to the clubhouse.

Long finished his career as a player in 1963 and served as a Yankee coach before trying his hand as a minor league umpire. On January 17, 1999 at the age of 64 he died in Palm Coast, Florida.

Danny McDevitt: Closing Time Was His Time, and Not Only at Ebbetts Field

Many ball players dream of achieving baseball immortality in one form or another from the first time they play catch with their fathers. Few players actually get to secure their place in the record books—and sometimes those who do so are not aware of what they are accomplishing when they do it! For example, Jim Delsing, on August 19, 1951, never thought he would be remembered for being the answer to the trivia question, "Who was the pinch-runner for the midget Eddie Gaedel?"

So was the case on September 24, 1957, when Danny McDevitt was handed the ball by manager Walter Aston to start against the Pittsburgh Pirates at Ebbetts Field. McDevitt shut out the Pittsburgh Pirates 2-0 that day, striking out nine, and allowing only five hits. Three weeks later Dodgers owner Walter O'Malley announced the team was moving to Los Angeles, thus giving McDevitt the honor of throwing the last pitch at the famed ballpark. One of the saddest parts of that final game was that only 6,702 people witnessed the event. Years later, McDevitt recalled his shutout, "I don't remember anyone making a big deal after the game. I was making $7,500, the minimum, and all I was trying to do was leave a good taste in their mouth for next year." (Interestingly, he was the first of four southpaws to throw the last pitch in a New York ballpark. Johnny Antonelli threw the last pitch at the Polo Grounds in 1957; Oliver Perez threw the last pitch at Shea Stadium in 2009, and Andy Pettitte threw the last pitch at Yankee Stadium in the same year.)

McDevitt was born in New York, NY, but grew up in Hallstead, Pennsylvania, just a chip shot away from Binghamton. Although he never suited up for the Triplets, his hometown's proximity to Binghamton resulted in McDevitt's induction into the Shrine in 2009, along with induction teammates Dale Long and Quilvio Veras. McDevitt is the only graduate of Hallstead High School to play in the big leagues.

The New York Yankees signed McDevitt to a professional contract in 1951, but his career as a Yankee was a short one. After getting off to a rough professional start, going 1-6 with an E.R.A of 7.95, he was released by the Bronx Bombers. Luckily for him, the cross-town Brooklyn Dodgers signed him.

Over the next six years, he spent time with seven minor league clubs for the Dodgers, as well as serve time in the military in 1953 and 1954. He finally got called up to the big leagues in 1957, after going 6-4 with a 1.86 ERA for the St. Paul Saints of the American Association. McDevitt had an excellent rookie season for Brooklyn, throwing 119 innings and finishing 7-4, with a 3.25 E.R.A. He was tied for fourth in starts that year with Sal Maglie, trailing Don Drysdale, Don Newcombe, and Johnny Podres. Roger Craig and Sandy Koufax started 13 games that season.

With all the competition for starting spots, Danny began the 1958 season with the Saint Paul Saints. After an impressive start, going 9-4, he wound up back in the majors with the new Los Angeles Dodgers. Unfortunately, he would soon develop a sore arm and struggled the rest of the year. Also adding to his troubles was being a young man with a little fame in the "City of Angels." The distractions were plenty and so were the parties. Hollywood celebrities were seen nightly at the Los Angeles Coliseum, where the Dodgers played until the new stadium was built at Chavez Ravine. He remembers names like Bing Crosby and Lauren Bacall being around the stadium. When his turn came up in the rotation, he always wanted to hurry up and finish the game as quickly as possible so he could enjoy the nightlife.

During his years with Los Angeles, Danny received his pilot's license. He became good friends with pitching great Sandy Koufax and they would sometimes go flying together. One day during spring training in 1960, McDevitt rented a plane from the Vero Beach airport, which was next to the spring training facility of the Dodgers, and Koufax accompanied him. He decided to have a little fun and zipped by Holman Stadium. When Koufax and McDevitt landed, Danny was told Buzzy Bavasi, general manager of the Dodgers, was looking for him. Bavasi then let McDevitt know where he stood in the pitching plans for the Dodgers when Bavasi told him "I got no problems with you flying planes but don't ever take Koufax up with you again!"

The Dodgers decided that his losing record of 19-22 after 4 years was enough and sold him to the Yankees in December of 1960. In the middle of the '61 season the Yankees traded McDevitt to the Twins for infielder Billy Gardner. McDevitt finished his major league career with the Kansas City Athletics in 1962, going 0-3, with a bloated ERA while pitching primarily in relief. He retired after pitching in two games for the Portland Beavers in the Pacific Coast League in 1963.

He later tried his hand at umpiring and worked alongside Ron Luciano in the minors, but gave it up when he knew there was discussion about his being called up to umpire in the big leagues. "I realized that at that level all the umpires had 'cut stomachs'—ulcers—from the stress, and I didn't want to wake up every day with that."

He later worked for the federal government, running antipoverty programs in Alabama and Mississippi before settling in Georgia. Danny truly enjoyed his trip to Binghamton in 2009 for his shrine induction. Unfortunately he passed away just a little more than a year later at the age of 78 in Georgia.

Quilvio Veras: July Was His Month

The Shrine came calling for Quilvio Veras (Kill-vee-oh Vair-us) in 2009, recognizing his outstanding 1993 season with the Binghamton Mets, when he hit .306 and stole 52 bases, as well as his solid 7-year major league career. His accomplishments in the majors included posting a lifetime .270 batting average and stealing 183 bases. He was an excellent leadoff hitter, retiring with a .372 on base percentage, and he was respected as a fine-fielding second baseman, known for his excellent range.

Veras was 18-years old when he was signed by the New York Mets as an amateur free agent out of the Dominican Republic in November of 1985. After five successful seasons as a minor leaguer, the Mets traded Veras to the Marlins for power-hitting outfielder Carl Everett. It was a classic trade of "speed for power," where two promising players were dealt to fill the respective needs of their big league clubs—the Mets traded a potential leadoff hitter and stolen base threat for an outfielder with middle-of-the-lineup potential.

While Everett showed some promise in 1995, hitting .252 with 12 homers in 289 at bats, he never lived up to expectations with the Mets and was traded after the 1997 season. Once Everett left the Mets, he went on to hit 173 more home runs and knock in over 100 runs two times in his career. Veras, meanwhile, literally hit the ground running for the Marlins, as the speedster led the National League with 56 stolen bases in 1995. As with Everett, Veras's stay with his new team was a short one. After the 1996 season, Veras was traded to the Padres, but he never fully recaptured the magic of his freshman season. Speed was a dominant part of his game and knee and hamstring problems slowed him, both literally and figuratively. Interestingly, part of the reason the Marlins traded Veras was because future Met Luis Castillo had become the organization's choice to man second base.

In his rookie season Veras was clocked as getting to first base in 3.8 seconds, but in spring training of 1997 his time had decreased to 4.4. seconds. Though by April of that year he would get this time down to 4.2 seconds, the decrease in speed could be likened to a pitcher losing eight miles per hour off his fast ball. And just as a pitcher would have to adjust to such a huge change in his pitching repertoire, Veras also had to adjust, picking his spots to steal bases instead of running at will.

On Opening Day in 1997, Veras got a measure of revenge against the Mets' organization for trading him. In what must have seemed like an April Fool's Joke for the Mets, in the bottom of the sixth inning, Veras was part of a Padres trio that hit back-to-back-to-back home runs to highlight an 11-run inning. The Mets' starter, Pete Harnisch, had thrown five shutout innings entering the sixth, only to be driven from the mound after giving up consecutive home runs to Chris Gomez, Ricky Henderson, and the slap-hitting Veras. The Padres went on to beat the Mets that day, 12-5, and Veras would only hit two more home runs the rest of the season.

Veras had a penchant for back-to-back feats in his career. On back-to-back days in July, though four years apart, Veras was again part of baseball history. On Saturday, July 14, 1995, in a game against the Dodgers, Veras came up in the top of the ninth inning with two outs and the bases empty against his friend from the Dominican Republic, Ramon Martinez. The Dodgers held a 7-0 lead against the Marlins and Martinez had been dominant in the game. Veras worked the count to 2-2 and then hit a routine fly to left where Roberto Kelly caught it for the final out. While Kelly settled under the ball, catcher Mike Piazza raced to the mound, as Veras had just made the final out of a no-hitter!

On July 15th in 1999, in the top of the third inning with the Padres and the Mariners in a scoreless game, Veras scored from second on a grounder hit deep into the shortstop hole by Phil Nevin. This was the first run ever scored in Seattle's new stadium, Safeco Field. For the record, the Padres beat the Mariners, 3-2 in that inaugural game.

As significant as his "back-to-back" feats and his outstanding 1995 rookie season were for Veras, the 1998 season was the defining one for Quilvio, as it was the best of times for him as well as the worst of times. The lowest point came when Veras had to leave a game because his brother had been murdered in the Dominican Republic. The high point of the season came against the Yankees in the World Series. Though Veras had a disappointing series, going 3 for 15 as the leadoff hitter, and the Yankees swept the Padres, playing in the World Series was one of the highlights of Quilvio's career.

In keeping with the theme of the month of July providing the home for significant events of Veras's career, Quilvio played his last game on July 13th in 2001. In a 7-1 win against the Orioles he went 1 for 3, raising his season average to .252. A short time later, however, Veras was released by the Braves, as he had difficulty staying healthy.

Since he retired from active playing, Veras has stayed closed to the game, serving as a minor league instructor.

Wally Burnette: "A Good Ol' Boy and a Real Good Pitcher"

The Binghamton Triplets may have seen their greatest season in 1953. They finished atop the Eastern League with a 96-55 record, and won the playoffs at the end of the year. The team included 11 players who reached the major leagues, including Cal Neeman, Jerry Lumpe, Jim Finigan, and Herbie Plews, just to name a few. Although that '53 team had some pretty good hitters, it was its pitching staff that fueled its success.

The staff starters had a combined record of 82-34, and while Ed Cereghino (11-3, with an E.R.A. of 2.59), Mike Schultz (12-7, 2.73), and John Wingo (15-8, 3.00) had outstanding seasons, their seasons paled in comparison to those of staff aces Steve Kraly and Wally Burnette. Kraly, despite missing at least seven starts due to his finishing the season with the Yankees, finished with a record of 19-2 and a 2.08 E.R.A. The pitcher holding the honor of leading the staff in wins was right-hander Wally Burnette, who finished 21-10 with an E.R.A. of 2.10, not counting his two wins in the post season. Burnette's year is arguably the greatest season any pitcher had in a Binghamton uniform, as he threw 249 innings in 31 games, only allowing 192 hits and 58 earned runs; amazingly he only gave up 6 home runs the whole season!

Wally was born and raised in Blairs, Virginia, where he was a star on his high school team at Spring Garden. He was signed by the Yankees in 1948 and ended up splitting the 1948 season between the Roanoke Rapids (Coastal Plain League) and the Blackstone Barristers (Virginia League). In 1949 he continued in Class D with Easton of the Eastern Shore League. It was in Easton where Wally started to hone his practice, finishing the season 13-6 with a 2.77 ERA.

He continued his pitching prowess in 1950 with the Amsterdam Rugmakers of the Can-Am League, going 14-10, which got him a late season promotion to the Norfok Tars (Class B) for 2 games. Wally lost the next two seasons to military service in the Korean War; when he returned, he was assigned to Class A Binghamton where he had his superlative season. Though he won 27 games over the next two seasons, he did not get called up to the Yankees, as the Yankee rotation was filled with the likes of Whitey Ford, Bob Grim, Tommy Byrne, Eddie Lopat, and Bob Turley over 1954 and 1955.

On July 11, 1956, Burnette finally got the break he had been waiting for as he was traded to the Kansas City Athletics. Burnette made his major league debut four days later, beating Chuck Stobbs and the Washington Senators, 8-0, as he allowed only 4 hits and walked one while striking out four. Ironically, it would be the only shutout he would throw in the big leagues. Just as interesting, the player the Yankees received in return for Wally was left-hander Tom Lasorda, who would become a Hall of Fame manager for the Los Angeles Dodgers.

Wally had an impressive rookie season, throwing 121 innings and posting an E.R.A. of 2.89, despite only winning 6 games as the 1956 Kansas City Athletics finished in last place in the American League, with a 52-102 record. No doubt Burnette must have wondered what his record might have been had he pitched for the Yankees, as the Bronx Bombers finished the regular season at 97-57.

Wally's major league career was short lived, though successful, as he had a career E.R.A. of 2.89. He injured his shoulder in 1958 and tried to work his way back to the big leagues by returning to the minors from 1958-1961, but a return to the big leagues was not to be. Following his playing days, Wally moved back to Virginia where he and his wife ran *Burnette Grocery* for 31 years, which was a gas station, restaurant, and convenience store.

He passed away in 2003 due to complications from lung cancer. His daughter, Lisa Cox, mourned his passing by recalling his kind and down-to-earth nature. "He was one of the strongest men I've ever known, but he had one of the biggest hearts too," Cox said in praise. "He was a good ol' country boy."

In 2011, Wally Burnette was inducted into the Binghamton Baseball Shrine posthumously. His wife Katie, son Tony, daughter Lisa, son-in-law Ricky Cox and granddaughter Alisha Cox were proudly on hand to participate in the on-field ceremonies, where they were joined by Wally's former teammate and good friend Steve Kraly.

John W. Fox: His Magic Number was 61!

Ellicottville is a community of about 1,700 or so people located in western New York, just north of Salamanca. It is best known now for its booming skiing and golf resort of Hidden Valley, but for veteran Binghamton area baseball fans, it is also recognized as the hometown of John W. Fox, long-time sports reporter and editor for the *Binghamton Press*, now known as the *Binghamton Press & Sun-Bulletin*.

After graduation from high school, John arrived on the Syracuse University campus in February of 1944. On his very first day there he went to the offices of the school newspaper, *The Daily Orange*, and approached the female editor-in-chief meekly, mentioning his previous sports coverage for the weekly publication, *The Ellicottville Post*. The editor-in-chief smiled at him and excitedly stated, "John, you just became my assistant sports editor!" Fox was shocked but excited about the new task. Being a male heavily tipped the scales in his favor, as he was one of only two males on the staff, with much of America's youth serving in the armed forces.

John spent all of 1944 and one semester of 1945 at Syracuse, but his fourth semester was interrupted by a call from Uncle Sam. At the time he left school for military service, his tuition was $200.00 per semester—a far cry from what it is today!

Fox arrived in Japan during the final four months of his army stint and was destined for infantry duty, but while awaiting assignment, he and one of his army buddies (who had a background in radio) borrowed a jeep, drove to Eighth Army headquarters in Yokohama, and asked if the public relations office needed anyone with civilian experience in either radio or sports writing. As with his first day on the Syracuse campus, John's inquisitiveness paid off—he was given the assignment of covering service athletes in a wide mix of sports, with his writing often appearing in the army's *Stars & Stripes* newspaper.

Following the war Fox returned to Syracuse in 1947 to finish his education. He, as with the many males now walking the campus, was able to use proceeds from the G.I. Bill to pay for his studies. During Easter break of 1949 he was tipped off to a sports writing job being available at the Binghamton Press as the paper was adding a Sunday edition. So he hopped a Greyhound bus to Binghamton for an interview and he was hired, with his first month on the job coming in June.

Right around the time Fox came to Binghamton, a little lefthander by the name of Whitey Ford also came to town. In the summer of '49 many Johnson City residents thought of Johnson Field as "Ford's Field," as Ford was dominant on the mound. Recently Fox recalled that summer—"Ford's cocky mound performances sparked the Triplets from the cellar. Despite the team's last-gasp .500 regular-season record, the team won the post-season championship, with Ford getting three post-season wins following his league-leading 1.91 regular-season E.R.A."

Fox remained with the *Press* from 1949 until his retirement from full-time duties in 1993, not only writing about professional teams but also numerous high school and college teams as well. After his official retirement, he was awarded the title "sports editor emeritus" and still wrote a Sunday column for the paper until June of 2010, which enabled him to celebrate his 61st anniversary of writing for the paper!

One of the first things Fox did while working for the *Binghamton Press* was help to establish the annual award now known as the "Press and Sun-Bulletin Athlete of the Year." The award began in 1949 with future baseball Hall of Famer Whitey Ford being the first recipient. There have been a total of 65 award recipients through 2013, including six other members of the Shrine—Bob Grim (1951 Triplets), Steve Kraly (1953 Triplets), Deron Johnson (1957 Triplets) Ron Luciano (1958--for Syracuse football), Rob Gardner (1970 Syracuse Chiefs), and Bobby Jones (1992 Binghamton Mets). When baseball returned to Binghamton, Fox was also instrumental in developing the Binghamton Baseball Shrine.

In the 1950's and up until 1961, the *Binghamton Press* sent Fox south to cover the Triplets for spring training. He would cover the team from the first day of spring training until the team headed north and was joined by his sports writing colleagues from *The Binghamton Sun* (morning newspaper) and the *Endicott Bulletin* (afternoon paper). These trips helped the reporters gather material for use during the season, as well as keep readers aware of the prospects who were likely to start the season with the Triplets.

Fox used diverse methods for gathering background information. In the early 1950's, he did not own a car so he actually rode the team bus back to Binghamton from Orangeburg, South Carolina, where the team was training. Another time he even shagged balls in short center during batting practice while conducting a mid-morning interview with future Hall of Famer, Whitey Herzog, who was then an 18-year-old Triplets candidate. John also offered to pick players up at either the airport or bus station when they were assigned to the Triplets. Fox recently recalled his first impression of Ralph Terry when he picked up Terry after he arrived from Yankee camp in St. Petersburg for Triplets spring training in 1954. "He had a duffle bag under one arm and a Scrabble™ game under the other."

Shagging flies and serving as a chauffeur weren't the only unorthodox ways Fox got breaking sports news. During the 1965 season Fox would often take a cab to cover the Triplets; as the season drew to a close he engaged in his usual chit-chat with his cab driver. Fox explains, "Frank, my soft-spoken Yellow Cab driver of dozens of trips to the ballpark and return home, said, 'Well, Mr. Fox, last night the young man had another shutout for Buffalo, and is being promoted.' He'd never before mentioned being the father of Binghamton Central grad Rob Gardner, 20, who was going to join the New York Mets in September of '65."

When asked for names of some of the players he most enjoyed covering, one of the first names Fox mentions is Bobby Richardson, whom Fox first met at 1954 camp in Orangeburg, South Carolina, during spring training. Fox elaborated, "He was just a real nice guy, a class human being." Frank Verdi, Triplets infielder from 1949-1953 and manager in 1966 and 1968, was another player Fox remembers fondly. "He was a dear friend of mine for so many years, right up until his death." Though Fox is quick to point out that there were a lot of "good guys" to pass through Binghamton, Richardson and Verdi are at the top of the list, with center fielder Bill Virdon right up there as well. "Bill Virdon is a real gentleman too," Fox reminisced, 'he was just a great young man to be around."

Fox explains that he became a Yankees fan through his covering the exploits of so many Yankee farmhands in the 50's and 60's, and the names roll off his tongue as if it were only yesterday — "Richardson and Terry, Ford and Downing, Skowron and Clarke, Munson and Stafford, Lumpe and Pepitone, Tresh and Coates, et. al." Ironically, he now finds himself rooting for the Boston Red Sox, as he lost interest in rooting for the Yankees during the years when there was no baseball in Binghamton.

These days, John is retired and living in Port Dickinson and loves to spend time with his beloved wife Terry and their children and grandchildren. Onlookers at his 2011 induction

143

included his wife, Terry, and daughters, sons-in-law, and several grandchildren. Fox is proud to be a member of the Shrine he helped create and continues to serve as a voting member of the Shrine committee.

Harry Lumley: Home Run King in the "Dead Ball" Era

Harry Lumley was born on September 29, 1880, in Forest City, PA., about 40 miles south of Binghamton. He moved to Lestershire (later Johnson City) as a child and started his baseball career by playing for Endicott-Johnson's town baseball team. He was one of the early sluggers of the game and was inducted into the Shrine in 2011, along with pitcher Wally Brunette and veteran baseball writer John Fox.

Lumley made his professional debut at age 20, in 1901, for Rome of the New York State League, where he hit .350. The following year he hit a league-leading 8 home runs for Saint Paul of the American Association. Eight home runs do not seem like a lot by any standard, but keep in mind that this was the "Dead Ball Era" and home runs were scarce, so hitting 8 HRs made Lumley one of the top power-hitting prospects in the game. In 1903, Lumley showed everyone that he was an all-around hitter and not just one laden with power, as he led the independent Pacific Coast League in hitting with a .387 average while playing for the Seattle Siwashes. This three-year stretch of outstanding performance led to Lumley's joining the major league Brooklyn Superbas for the 1904 season.

As a rookie in the National League in 1904, Lumley continued his phenomenal performance. He hit .279, with 9 home runs and 78 RBIs, and the *Binghamton Press* praised Lumley's rookie exploits in October while letting the local denizens know of Lumley's value as well, as the paper reported "...today he is known as one of the best batters and base runners in America. It is said that manager Hanlon was offered three pitchers and $5,000.00 for Lumley by Chicago, but Hanlon said he would sell him for no less than $10,000.00."

Lumley's 9 homers led the National League that year and he went on to hit 25 homers in the next three seasons, establishing himself as one of the most feared hitters in the game. (We can only speculate how many millions of dollars Lumley would be worth in today's market!)

Lumley was a true star in the National League for his first five years, with his best year coming in 1906, when he led the league in slugging percentage and hit .327, losing the batting crown to Honus Wagner and his .339 average. While Lumley was making big news in the big leagues, back in his hometown, the International Time Recording Company (ITR, later to become IBM in 1914) was making big news of its own, as it announced expansion plans to move from downtown Binghamton to neighboring Endicott. The new location of ITR became known as the "Magic City" and the "Valley of Opportunity," as ITR and Endicott Johnson were expanding rapidly in the region, providing well-paying and steady jobs for its denizens. Unfortunately, Lumley's career would take an opposite path.

An ankle injury in 1907 limited Lumley to 127 games and although he was named captain of the Superbas in 1908, the next two years saw a rapid decline in his production. Lumley's major league career lasted until early in the 1910 season, when he started the year with Brooklyn, but after hitting only .143 in 21 at bats, he became the player-manager of his hometown Binghamton Bingos. Lumley was on a short leash with Brooklyn in 1910, as in 1909 as a player-manager for the Superbas he brought the team home with a 55-98 record, fifty-five and one-half games out of first! He patrolled the outfield for 6 full years for the Brooklyn Superbas from 1904 to 1909 and finished with a lifetime batting average of .274 in the big leagues, with 38 home runs.

He played for and managed the Bingos from 1910-1912 and finished his career in 1913, playing for two rivals of Binghamton—Troy and Scranton, two of the other franchises in the 8-team Class B New York State League. In six minor league seasons, the 5'10" Lumley hit .333.

After his playing days were over, he opened the Terminal Café, a bar and eating place at 49 Henry Street in Binghamton. The Binghamton Transportation Center now sits where Lumley's Terminal Café once stood. The Café closed in 1937 and Lumley passed away a year later, in 1938, at the age of 57.

Gene Monahan: "It Really Is a Wonderful Life"

Affectionately known as "Geno," Gene Monahan grew up in Fort Lauderdale, Florida, and he just might have been the most excited teenager in town when the Yankees moved into their new spring training facilities in Fort Lauderdale in 1962. While still in high school, Geno was bagging groceries in a local supermarket and attending Yankee spring training games whenever he could. Often he would stand outside the gate and ask if there was any work for him. One day he got an affirmative answer and his career with the Yankees was born.

Geno started as a ball boy for the Yankees that spring and was "wide-eyed" throughout March as he went to work in the same clubhouse that such greats as Mickey Mantle and Roger Maris also called their home. Remember, Maris and Mantle had just come off their record-setting home run campaign where they hit 61 and 56 HRs, respectively. Besides starring on the diamond, Mantle and Maris were also becoming stars on the silver screen too, as they had significant roles in "Safe at Home," the 1962 movie whose key plotline had them saving face for Hutch Lawton, a little leaguer who lies to his teammates about being friends with Mantle and Maris. Monahan could relate to the wishes of Lawton's character as Geno got to interact with the "M & M" boys all spring.

Also present in that locker room were Yogi Berra, Elston Howard, and Tony Kubek—not to mention Geno's fellow Shrine inductees Whitey Ford, Johnny Blanchard, Tom Tresh, Bobby Richardson, Al Downing, Ralph Terry, Clete Boyer, Joe Pepitone, Moose Skowron and Dale Long! The path from Johnson Field to the Bronx was well traveled and fans of the Yankees were plentiful in the Southern Tier. When the big club went to open the season in the Bronx, Monahan was kept on to work for the minor league team that played in the Florida State League. Halfway through the season, the clubhouse attendant quit so Geno assumed those responsibilities as well.

That minor league locker room experience fueled Geno's desire to work in a sports locker room as a career. He sensed that the job as a sports trainer would soon require a college education, so he enrolled into a program at a junior college and eventually transferred to Indiana University. Geno served as the head trainer for the Binghamton Triplets in 1967 and 1968, treating such players as Thurman Munson, Al Downing, Bill Burbach, and Mickey Scott. While at Binghamton he used the offseason months to complete that degree in physical education at Indiana University.

Geno was fortunate enough to work with many great people during his career and he received a lot of guidance along the way, but he credits former Yankee clubhouse attendant, Pete Sheehy, as giving him the best career advice—"Keep your eyes and ears open, and your mouth shut and you will go a long way in this game." That advice held true for Monahan, as his work for the Yankees lasted almost half a century! "Pete was like a father to me," explained Monahan. "He even bought the christening dress for my first child."

When asked what his greatest moment was in baseball, Geno recalled the home run Chris Chambliss hit off Mark Littell in the 1976 American League Championship Series. The Chambliss home run gave Monahan the opportunity to go to his first World Series. He also fondly remembered the 1996 World Series against the Braves, when the Yankees had lost the first two games in their own ballpark. Recalled Monahan, "Steinbrenner was on the team bus, riding to the airport, and complaining in frustration to manager Joe Torre." Torre's response was to show restraint and exhibit a graceful confidence as he told Steinbrenner the Yankees would go down to Atlanta, win all three games, and come back and win the Series at home. Well, the Yanks did just that!

Torre wasn't the only leader who was a calming influence on Steinbrenner regarding events surrounding that '96 Championship team. When the team was invited to the White House to be congratulated by Bill Clinton, Monahan recalled Clinton's admonishment to Steinbrenner during the ceremony, "George, you do realize you're not allowed to tell the president what to do!"

Of all the great things that occurred during Geno's career, he says there are two events that stand above all the rest—the births of his two daughters, Kellie and Amanda.

Monahan was one of the only three people in the Yankee organization to survive the entire length of George Steinbrenner's ownership. Monahan often jokes "the boss probably fired me more times than all the Yankee managers combined, but I never knew about it!"

At the end of the 2009 season, Geno was diagnosed with throat cancer, which caused him to miss his first spring training with the Yankees since that day he stood outside the locker room, looking for work in 1962. After his treatment was over, he resumed his duties, and on Opening Day in 2010 he received an emotional standing ovation during the team's World Series Ring Ceremony (for its 2009 World Championship).

At the start of the 2011 season, the Yankees announced that Geno would retire at the end of the season. On Old Timer's Day on June 26, the Yankees honored their longtime trainer with a tribute that was televised as part of the day's festivities. After he retired from the Yankees, Monahan moved from Hackensack, NJ to Mooresville, NC, to start a second career in NASCAR. He is currently the trainer for Hendrick Motorsports, helping the pit crew and drivers stay in shape for race days. He works with such NASCAR legends as Jeff Gordon, Jimmy Johnson, Dale Earnhardt Jr., and Kasey Kuene.

Gene Monahan was truly humbled and surprised by his selection to the Shrine in 2012. He was thrilled that he was thought of in the same context as such players as Whitey Ford and Thurman Munson. "I've had a wonderful life in baseball, staying in the best hotels and working with fantastic people and seeing some great games, but through it all I have just been a worker," Monahan explained. "And to be treated like royalty during my return to Binghamton to receive this plaque was such a thrill. Binghamton will always hold a special place in my heart."

Curtis Pride: The Pride of the B-Mets

Throughout history, baseball has seen its share of ball players who had to overcome adversity in order to play the game they loved. Pete Gray was a one-armed outfielder for the Saint Louis Browns in 1945; Monty Stratton pitched several years after losing a leg in a hunting accident; Moredecai "Three-Finger" Brown was good enough to pitch his way to the Hall of Fame; and let's not forget Jim Abbott, born with only one hand, who pitched for several teams and tossed a no-hitter for the New York Yankees.

Curtis Pride came into this world on December 17, 1968. Before he was a year old, tests confirmed that he had been born with a profound hearing loss, leaving him with only 5% residual hearing. His hearing loss was attributed to his mother's having rubella while she carried Curtis. By the time Pride was in seventh grade he was attending regular classes at his public school. In addition to a tremendous work ethic, which enabled him to become a fluent lip reader, Curtis was also blessed with an abundance of athletic talent, as he excelled at multiple sports at *John F. Kennedy High School* in Silver Springs, Maryland.

Pride not only excelled in baseball, but he starred in basketball and soccer as well. His basketball playing earned him a scholarship to the College of William and Mary in Williamsburg, Va; his soccer prowess enabled him to be a member of the United States National Team that participated in the Junior World Cup in Beijing in China in 1985; and his baseball skills convinced the New York Mets to draft him in the 10th round of the 1986 baseball amateur draft. (As a result of his performance for the U.S. soccer team, Pride was even selected by *Kick Magazine* as one of the top 15 youth soccer players in the world!)

By the time the baseball draft in 1986 was held, Pride had already accepted his scholarship offer from William and Mary, but the Mets got creative and worked out a deal where Pride would play professional baseball on a part-time basis, essentially during the late spring and mid-summer months, when school was not in session. Interestingly, there are only two people who have attended William and Mary and also played major league baseball—and both are in Binghamton's Baseball Shrine! Besides Pride, the other player is Vic Raschi, star pitcher for the New York Yankees and the 1946 Binghamton Triplets.

Pride's baseball career started in 1986, when he reported to the Kingsport Mets in the Appalachian League (rookie ball). The adjustment to professional baseball was difficult, as he hit only .109, playing in 27 games and getting 46 at bats. Though Pride's part-time status and hearing handicap compounded his difficulty in adjusting to minor league life, Pride never lost sight of his goals. He returned to Kingsport in both 1987 and 1988, and his statistics in 1988 were impressive as he hit .284 and hit 8 homers in 268 at bats. Following stops at Pittsfield (Massachusetts), Columbia (South Carolina) and St. Lucie (Florida), in 1992 Curtis landed in Binghamton, his first stop at Double A. Though Binghamton would finish in second place with a 79-59 record and claim the Eastern League Championship by winning the playoffs, Pride's season with Binghamton would be a difficult one.

It was a season of adjustment for him, as there were numerous big league prospects among his opponents. Over forty of the pitchers who pitched in the Eastern League that year would go on to play in the big leagues, including such solid major league performers as Paul Byrd, Carl Pavano, Dave Mlicki, Sterling Hitchcock, Pete Walker and Alan Embree. Pride spent most of the year joining Bert Hunter and Rob Katzaroff in the outfield, but he ended the season with a disappointing .227 batting average while he struck out 25% of the time (110 strikeouts in only 440 at bats). Other than his initial season with Kingsport, his statistics in Binghamton were the worst of his career, and his output caused the Mets to lower their expectations of him and he became a minor league free agent at the end of the season.

The Montreal Expos signed Pride and assigned him to their AA team in Harrisburg, in the Eastern League. The change of scenery with the Washington organization worked wonders as it didn't take Curtis long to adjust to the league in his second tour of duty -- he hit an impressive .356 in his first 50 games, earning him a promotion to Triple-A Ottawa of the International league. He continued to play so well in Ottawa, hitting .302 in 262 at bats, that the Expos gave him his first taste of the majors when they called him up in the final month of the season.

September 14, 1993 proved to be Pride's debut day in the majors, as he came on as a defensive replacement in left field in the bottom of the eighth and then popped out to center in the top of the ninth, as the Expos defeated the Cards, 12-9, at Busch Stadium. Pride's inning-and-a-half of play gave him the distinction of becoming the first deaf player in the major leagues since outfielder Dick Sipek played his one season for the Cincinnati Reds in 1945, hitting .244 in 170 at bats.

Curtis finished his major league playing career in 2006, having played for 6 teams, including the Expos, Angels, Red Sox, Yankees, Tigers and Braves. His career batting average was .250 and he had his best year playing for the Tigers in 1996, when he hit .300 and had a career best in homers and RBIs, with 10 and 31, respectively.

Today Pride is the head baseball coach at Gallaudet University, a leading college for the deaf and hearing impaired. When Pride was inducted into the Binghamton Baseball Shrine in 2012, a few of his players and one of his assistant coaches came up to watch his special night. They were very easy to spot in the stands—each one of them was wearing game-used jerseys from Pride's career. Pride gave a short speech, thanking the fans and the community for their support.

The 421 games that Pride played in the majors during his 11-year career are the most played by a deaf player since William Hoy ended his major league career in 1902. By the time of his retirement, Hoy had played in 1,797 games during a 14-year career.

Pride was awarded the *Tony Conigliaro Award* by the Boston chapter of the Baseball Writers of America in 1996, and in 2010 he was appointed to the President's Council on Fitness, Sports, and Nutrition by President Barack Obama. He and his wife are actively involved in the *Together with Pride Foundation*, which helps hearing impaired children in numerous ways, including providing hearing aids.

Bill Skowron: A Moose Is On the Loose

Many people know that moose are usually seen roaming around the wilderness of Canada and the northern parts of the United States. However, in 1951 one showed up at Johnson Field. Skowron got 56 at bats for the Triplets in 1951, as he joined the Triplets as a reward for the outstanding season he had playing for the Norfolk Tars, where he led the Piedmont League (Class B) in hitting with a .334 average and also hit 18 home runs.

Bill "Moose" Skowron was originally signed by the New York Yankees in 1950 as an amateur free agent after leaving Purdue University, where he hit .500 as a sophomore, a record that lasted 10 years—not too bad for a kid on a football scholarship! His nickname was not acquired from his football exploits or his beefy build, but rather from a haircut he got from his grandfather when he was eight years old.

"When I was about 8 years old living in Chicago, my grandfather gave all the haircuts to his grandchildren," Skowron explained. "He shaved off all my hair. I was completely bald. When I got outside, all the older fellows around the neighborhood started calling me Mussolini. At that time, he was the dictator of Italy. So after that, in grammar school, high school and college, everybody called me Moose."

He made his long-awaited major league debut on April 13, 1954. When he broke camp with the Yankees in 1954, he had to be wondering what took so long for the Yankees to bring him to the Bronx. In 1952, he had hit .341 with 31 HRs and 134 RBIs for the

Kansas City Blues, the AAA farm club of the Yankees. The problem for Skowron was the same issue that many Yankee farmhands had throughout the 1950's, as the Yankees seemed set at every position. The player in front of Skowron was Joe Collins, who provided the big league team with excellent defense and a solid bat. For the first four years of his stay with the Yankees, Skowron would split his playing time with Collins, finally earning his place as the regular first basemen from 1956 until 1962. During that time, he played in five consecutive All-Star games (1957-1961).

Skowron was a popular and above average player with the power-filled New York Yankee teams that hammered out seven American League pennants and four World Series titles from 1955 to 1962. He also had the pleasure of being a member of the 1963 Los Angeles Dodgers, which swept the Yankees in the World Series that year.

On two separate occasions, he homered twice in the same World Series as he was often at his best in clutch situations. In the eight World Series' in which he played, he hit .293 with 8 HRs and 29 RBIs in 141 at bats. He was on a World Championship team five times, with his most memorable long ball in a World Series game coming in 1958, when he hit a two-out, three-run shot off Lew Burdette in Game 7 in the top of the 8th inning, giving the Yankees a 6-2 lead, which turned out to be the final score.

Ironically, his lowest moment in Series play also came against the Milwaukee Braves. The year before he came up with the bases loaded and two outs in the bottom of the ninth in Game 7 against the very same Lew Burdette—but he grounded into an unassisted force out at third to end the 5-0 loss to the Braves.

After the 1962 season, Skowron was traded to the Los Angeles Dodgers in exchange for pitcher Stan Williams. Although his only season with the Dodgers was less than memorable with a .203 batting average and four home runs, he shocked his former teammates in the World Series, hitting .385 with a home run as the Dodgers swept the Yankees.

Moose was born in Chicago, Illinois on December 18, 1930 of Polish decent and was inducted into the National Polish-American Hall of Fame on June 12, 1980. Moose was a member of the 2012 Shrine class, along with ex-Triplets and long time New York Yankees trainer Gene Monahan and ex-Binghamton Met Curtis Pride. Skowron was inducted into the Shrine posthumously, as he passed away on April 20, 2012 due to complications from lung cancer.

Willard Hershberger: A Heavy Cross to Bear

The front pages of the *Detroit Free Press* on the morning of August 4, 1940 shocked the sports world. Under a picture of a catcher poised to throw a baseball, an article with a dateline of August 3rd stated "Willard Hershberger, 29-years old, catcher for the Cincinnati Reds' baseball club, committed suicide in his hotel room today by cutting his throat with a razor blade, Medical Examiner Timothy Leary announced tonight."

In true journalistic fashion, the lead paragraph had captured the Who, What, Where, and When, but missing was the "Why?"

People cope with stress in their own ways. Some exercise, others take up hobbies, but every now and then, the stress stays with them for a long time until it boils over. For backup catcher and pinch hitter Hershberger, it boiled over in the Copley Plaza Hotel in Boston on a hot Saturday afternoon in the middle of a pennant race that saw his team hold a six-game lead over the second place Chicago Cubs. His suicide fulfilled the prediction he had given his manager, Bill McKechnie, only one day before, "My father killed himself and I will too."

Cincinnati was playing a doubleheader against the Boston Bees that Saturday and when Hershberger did not show up at the ballpark, McKechnie was worried. He had had a long conversation with Hershberger the day before and had taken him to dinner to get Hershberger feeling better; by the time he said good night, McKechnie thought his mission was successful as he saw an upbeat in Hershberger's spirits. But with Hershberger being a no show to the ballpark on Saturday, McKechnie sent the word to the front office to check on his backup catcher. Dan Cohen, a businessman traveling with the Reds and a friend of Hershberger, was asked to go to the hotel and look for Willard. Cohen, with the help of a maid, entered his room and discovered Hershberger's lifeless body lying on towels that lined the bathroom floor, soaked with the blood that flowed from Hershberger's neck.

Willard McKee Hershberger grew up in Fullerton, California where his father worked in the city's oil fields. On November 21, 1928, Hershberger's father Claude, took his own life with a shotgun. It was believed at the time the elder Hershberger had become distraught over financial worries. A teenaged Willard discovered his father's body, a sight that would haunt him the rest of his life. Claude had killed himself with Willard's shotgun, which Willard had casually placed in the hallway after a day of hunting.

Hershberger was an iconic image of the "All American boy" right up until this point, serving as the senior class vice-president and as captain of the basketball and baseball teams. His circle of friends included two other high achievers—future Hall of Fame shortstop Arky Vaughan and future President Richard Nixon.

William Knack, in a 1991 article in *Sports Illustrated*, quoted Florence Designer, a physical education teacher at Fullerton during Hershberger's years—"A very lovable human being, very happy and well-adjusted until...that terrible thing happened with his father."

Hershberger had a fine year for the Binghamton Triplets in 1933. He hit .304 with 105 hits, 18 doubles, 3 triples and 2 home runs while being a teammate of Shrine mates Spud Chandler and George McQuinn. His finest minor league season came in El Paso when he hammered out 154 hits on his way to a .356 batting average. Perhaps the biggest impediment to Hershberger's achieving true fame in his career were the catchers he played behind—while toiling in the Yankee farm system in the 1930's his path to the big leagues was blocked by Hall of Fame catcher Bill Dickey; during his tenure with the Reds, Hershberger backed up another Hall of Famer, Ernie Lombardi.

When you look at his lifetime statistics, one can wonder what he would have accomplished had he played a full career and not had Dickey and Lombardi ahead of him. His major league totals include a lifetime .316 batting average. Ironically, it's the exact same average he had in the minor leagues for his eight seasons.

Throughout his career, Hershberger was fortunate enough to share the field with several outstanding players, including Hall of Famers Ernie Lombardi (with Cincinnati) and Bobby Doerr (in the Pacific Coast League, with the Hollywood Stars). Many fellow Binghamton Triplets also crossed his path during their minor league careers, including Ernie Koy, Jack LaRocca, Merill "Pinky" May, and the aforementioned Spud Chandler and George McQuinn.

The Saturday evening of Hershberger's suicide, manager McKecknie gathered his team at the hotel and told him they were not to blame. He told of Hershberger's troubled memory of his father and of Willard's thoughts of suicide. He also told them of Hershberger's disappointment in his recent play, as his batting average had fallen to .308 from .353 a few weeks earlier. He asked the team to dedicate the rest of the season to the memory of Hershberger.

The Cincinnati Reds went on to win the World Series that year in seven games over the Detroit Tigers. They dedicated the Series win to their fallen teammate and voted a full financial share be given to Hershberger's mother. McKechnie never forgot Hershberger and that tragic day in 1940. "I thought I had talked him completely out of it," McKechnie said. "I thought everything was put back together again. I couldn't keep a bodyguard on him." McKechnie attributed the "WHY?" to a personal issue that troubled Hershberger.

"He told me what his problems were," McKechnie said at the time. "It has nothing to do with anybody on the team. It was something personal. He told it to me in confidence, and I will not utter it to anyone. I will take it with me to my grave."

Take it to his grave McKecknie did, on October 29, 1965, in Bradenton, Florida.

Tom Tresh: Carrying on the Family Business

Thomas Michael Tresh was destined to be a baseball player. He was born September 20, 1938 in Detroit, Michigan, the son of Mike Tresh, a former major league player. The elder Tresh was a catcher from 1938-1948. He played for the Chicago White Sox and Cleveland Indians.

One of the advantages of having a major league ballplayer for a father was that Tom became familiar with the game and its lifestyle. His father exposed him to major league ballparks and dugouts early in life.

Tresh was an all-around athlete at Allen Park High School in Michigan, receiving nine letters in baseball, football and basketball. His athletic background led him to Central Michigan University where he played shortstop. Against his mother's wishes, Tom left college after only one year to sign a $30,000 bonus with the New York Yankees.

Tresh began his professional career in 1958 at St. Petersburg of the Florida State League and worked his way up to the Binghamton Triplets of the Eastern League in 1959. He played 42 games with the '59 Triplets, hitting .243 as a shortstop. He returned to Binghamton in 1960 and, showing his athleticism and versatility, split his time between short and third, batting .246 in 130 games. During his leisure time while with the Triplets, Tresh enjoyed relaxing by playing on local miniature golf courses, as this summer pastime gave him a brief respite from the every day grind of minor league baseball.

In 1961 he was promoted to Richmond of the International League and was named the league's rookie of the year. As a shortstop for Richmond he hit .315, drove in 42 runs and led the team in hits with 176. His efforts led to a call up to the Yankees late in the season. He made his major league debut with the Yankees as a pinch runner for Binghamton Shrine member Johnny Blanchard on September 3, 1961.

In 1962, the switch hitting Tresh was the starting shortstop on Opening Day, since regular shortstop Tony Kubek was in military service with his National Guard unit. Tresh beat out his farmhand friend, Phil Linz, to replace Kubek. Linz, a Binghamton Triplet for one whole at bat during the regular season in 1958, often would be stuck one level below Tresh as they both came up through the farm system as shortstops. As the Yanks prepared to play the Giants in the World Series that year, Linz explained to Huston Hunt, a reporter for *Sports Illustrated*, "My friend Tom has the stronger arm—and he has the precedent. Twice before, in Richmond and in Binghamton, he won the shortstop job over me."

Tresh finished the season hitting .286 with 20 home runs and 93 RBIs, and was named the American League Rookie of the Year.

"Tommy was just a wonderful guy and a real plus for us, filling in for Tony the way he did in 1962 was so important. We couldn't have won that year without him," recalled Bobby Richardson about Tresh's rookie season. When Kubek returned to the team in August, Tresh became the starting left fielder, joining Mickey Mantle and Roger Maris to form the best outfield in the American League.

The baseball community had high expectations for Tresh after his fabulous freshman season, as he and Mantle were often mentioned in the same sentence, and not just because he played left and Mantle was in center. Both came up as switch hitting shortstops and were moved to the outfield, and both were handsome young men from Middle American states who could hit for average and power. Though Tresh had a fine career, he never fulfilled the expectations of the fans. "I always felt badly for him that he was always being compared with Mickey, just because he was a switch-hitting shortstop who moved to the outfield, " noted Bobby Richardson.

Over the course of nine seasons Tresh played shortstop, third base and the outfield. His statistics fell off dramatically in 1967, after he suffered a knee injury in spring training and waited until the off season to have it surgically repaired. His career and knee were never the same from the moment he first injured his knee. His best season turned out to be his rookie season and his biggest thrill of his career came in that year's World Series.

On October 10, 1962 Tresh celebrated one of his biggest baseball moments. The World Series between the Giants and Yankees was tied at two games apiece. Jack Sanford, a 24-game winner, was dueling Ralph Terry and the score was tied at two apiece in the bottom of the eighth when Tresh came up to hit with Richardson on second and Kubek on first. Tresh hit a 3-run home run to thrill the Yankee Stadium crowd of over 65,000 fans and give the Yanks a 3 games to 2 lead in the series. The Yanks went on to beat the Giants in seven games, giving Tresh his only World Championship.

Tresh was a three-time AL All-Star and won a Gold Glove Award in 1965. He was traded to the Detroit Tigers in 1969 and retired from the game in 1970. Upon retirement, Tresh returned to Central Michigan to complete his degree in physical education--he had been working on it since he was first signed to a professional contract. "It took me only four terms to graduate," Tresh joked after he achieved his quest. "Eisenhower, Kennedy, Johnson, and Nixon."

While back in Michigan, Tresh owned and operated a Kentucky Fried Chicken franchise, and worked at his alma mater as an administrator in the alumni and placement office of the business school. He also served as an assistant baseball coach for 14 years.

On October 15, 2008 Tresh passed away from a heart attack.

Pete Van Wieren: The Old Professor and He's Not Casey Stengel!

Pete Van Wieren was the radio play-by-play announcer for the Binghamton Triplets in 1967 and 1968 and when you couple that with his being the play-by-play announcer for the Atlanta Braves from 1976-2008, it is surprising that it took so long for him to be inducted into Binghamton's Shrine, which did not occur until 2013.

Van Wieren came to Binghamton to join WNBF radio in September 1966, as a 22-year old from Manassas, Virginia, where he had been the news director for radio station WPRW. He came to Binghamton because it had a minor league baseball team, and the fact that the team did not then have a broadcasting contract with any radio station did not deter him. One of the first things Van Wieren did upon arriving in the Southern Tier was team with Jerry Toman, the Triplets' general manager, to sell radio time to sponsor the broadcasts.

Based on the work of Toman and Van Wieren, WNBF signed up for the radio rights to broadcast the home games of the Triplets in 1967. In the late 1960's finding a box score for the opposing teams in the Eastern League was problematic for Van Wieren. The only statistics that Van Wieren came across were the ones sent by the Eastern League on a weekly basis, which meant listeners might be hearing statistics that were a week old.

When Van Wieren mentioned his frustration at not having timely statistics to John W. Fox, sports reporter for the *Binghamton Evening Press* and Shrine Class of 2011, Fox indicated that the paper got all the box scores over the newspaper wire, but did not have space to print them. Well, pretty soon that meant Van Wieren was getting all the box scores on a daily basis as he would stop by the paper to get the daily box scores. His friends in the sports department at the paper would hang the box scores on a hook that became known as "Pete's Peg."

With an abundance of statistics, Van Wieren became known as the man to go to with baseball-related questions, laying the foundation for his major league nickname of "the Professor," for having so many facts at his disposal during a broadcast. Interestingly, Van Wieren was being called "the Professor" approximately 25 years after sportswriters had first given the nickname to Casey Stengel for his quick wit and overall baseball knowledge as manager of the Yankees.

Though Van Wieren only announced baseball for two years in Binghamton, his play-by play work there convinced Van Wieren that broadcasting baseball was where his future would be. While at Binghamton, Van Wieren learned the most important thing for him to learn as a radio announcer. When he had to fill in for the morning radio host, Jack Murphy, he was nervous. Murphy had the highest ratings in the area and Van Wieren did not want to send the ratings into nose drive. Murphy told him, "Just talk to one person. That's what radio is—just you and the listener." In his autobiography, "Of Mikes and Men," Van Wieren states, "That maxim stayed with me my entire career. Whenever I was on the air I knew there may be a million people listening. But I tried to talk to them as if they were one person."

In late 1970 Michael Burke, then the president of the New York Yankees, interviewed Van Wieren to be the radio play-by-play man for the Yankees. Though Pete lost out to Bill White and the disappointment was deep, the idea that he came so close to landing such a prestigious job increased Van Wieren's confidence in his career choice. Five seasons after losing to Bill White, Van Wieren was broadcasting baseball games for the Atlanta Braves.

For most of those years he teamed with Skip Carey and together they witnessed and told the story of the most successful period in Braves history, as the team won 14 consecutive Eastern Division Championships. Van Wieren and Carey were both elected to the Atlanta Braves Hall of Fame in 2004 and before his retirement in 2008, Van Wieren had won the Georgian Sportscaster of the Year Award 11 times.

Van Wieren is a trailblazer for the handful of Binghamton area sports announcers who have gone on to national prominence. Van Wieren heads a list that now includes Robert Ford, play-by-play announcer for the Houston Astros and ex-Binghamton Mets broadcaster; Dan Orsillo, play-by-play announcer for the Boston Red Sox and ex-

Binghamton Mets broadcaster; Karl Ravech, who is best known for his anchor duties for Baseball Tonight for ESPN; Bill Pidto, who has worked for both the MSG and ESPN networks; Trey Wingo, of ESPN's *Sportscenter* and *NFL Live* fame. Ravech and Pidto worked for WBNG TV early in their professional careers while Wingo worked for WICZ and WMGC.

Shrine On Deck Circle...

One hundred teams provide literally thousands of players to evaluate in making the selections for the Binghamton Shrine. The Shrine currently sits at 61 members but even a cursory review of Greater Binghamton's baseball history will find many more names that can be added to the fraternity. Some of the stronger candidates for the Shrine committee to consider in the ensuing years include:

Benny Agbayani is best remembered for hitting a game-winning home run against the San Francisco Giants in the 13th inning of Game 3 in the 2000 National League Championship Series, giving the Mets two games to one lead. From 1998-2002 he played in 383 major league games, hitting .274. His best year came in 2000, when he hit .289 with 15 HRs and 60 RBIs for the NY Mets. He had an impressive .391 on base percentage for Bobby Valentine in 2000. He played for Binghamton in 1995 and 1996, and in '95 he displayed his talent for getting on base as he hit .275 and had an on base percentage of .368.

Jason Bay debuted with the Binghamton Mets on the same day as Jose Reyes in 2002. Bay and Reyes stayed at a local hotel during their stay in Binghamton and walked to the ballpark together every day. In 108 at bats for Binghamton, Bay hit .290 with 4 HRs; he won the NL Rookie-of-the-Year award in 2004 and hit 222 home runs during an 11-year major league career.

Heath Bell had his problems in Binghamton in 2001, as in 61.1 innings he had a 6.06 E.R.A., but in 2002 he excelled, striking out 49 hitters in 38 innings and pitching to a 1.18 E.R.A. He has gone on to save over forty games in the big leagues three times in his career and currently has a big-league career E.R.A. of 3.39.

Jerry Coleman resumed his professional career after serving in World War II with the Binghamton Triplets in 1946, where he manned second base and hit .275 while playing in 134 games. Coleman played his entire 9-year major league career (1949-1957) with the Yankees, hitting .263 in 723 games. He also received the Ford C. Frick Award from the Baseball Hall of Fame and off the field was a hero as well, as he flew combat missions during World War II and the Korean Conflict.

Juanita Crabb never played an inning of baseball, but this ex-mayor of Binghamton led the charge to bring baseball back to Binghamton in 1992. As documented earlier in this book, her ceaseless lobbying efforts and negotiations enabled Binghamton Municipal Stadium to be built and the NY Mets to bring the Williamsport franchise to Binghamton.

Carlos Gomez hit .281 and stole 41 bases for the Binghamton Mets in 2006 and today is one of the best center fielders in the game, as in 2013 he hit .284 while stealing 40 bases and hitting 24 home runs and making the NL All-Star team. The Mets traded him to the Twins in February of 2008 for Johan Santana; other members of the Mets organization

157

that were included in that trade included Kevin Mulvey, Philip Humber, and Deolis Guerra.

Matt Harvey was called up to the Binghamton Mets in 2011, after making 14 starts in the Florida State League for St. Lucie, where he won 8 games and posted a 2.37 E.R.A. Harvey's success at Binghamton was harder to find, as he went 5-3 with an E.R.A. of 4.53. His work at Binghamton, however, prepared him for his sensational debut for the New York Mets in 2012, as he refined his secondary pitches while with Binghamton. Harvey started for the National League in the 2013 All Star Game at Citi Field.

Butch Huskey hit .267 over a seven-year major league career and hit 86 home runs and knocked in 336 runs. His career year came in 1994 for the N.Y. Mets, when he hit 24 home runs and knocked in 81 runs. Huskey had an outstanding year for the B-Mets in 1993, hitting 25 homers and driving in 98 runs while hitting .251.

Jason Isringhausen saved 300 games during a 16-year major league career and teamed with Bill Pulsipher and Chris Roberts to bring a championship to Binghamton in 1994, as "Izzy" went 5-4 for the 1994 Binghamton Mets with a 3.04 era over 14 starts. He came back to Bingo town in 1995 and simply dominated in April, making his return stay a short one, as in 41 innings he struck out 59 batters and only gave up 26 hits. He also dominated at Norfolk and he made his debut for the New York Mets on July 17th in 1995.

Mike Kinkade played parts of six years in the big leagues, from 1998 to 2003, with his best year coming in 2001 when he hit .275 with 4 HRs and 16 RBIs for the Orioles. Versatility was his strength, as he played in the outfield as well as the infield corner positions. In an 11-year minor league career, he hit .326 with 102 HRs. His career year came when he hit .366 for the Binghamton Mets in the 2000 season, capturing the Eastern League batting title, while also winning a gold medal for the U.S. that year playing on the Olympic Baseball team for Tommy Lasorda. Teammates on that gold medal team included Sean Burroughs, Doug Mientkiewicz, Roy Oswalt, Jon Rauch, Ben Sheets, and Brad Wilkerson.

Tony LaRussa only played 12 games for the Triplets in 1962, but then went on to manage in the major leagues for 33 consecutive seasons (1979-2011), winning 2728 games. He was elected to Baseball's Hall of Fame in 2014.

Rafael Montero has not made his major league debut as of this writing, but his success during the 2013 season for the Binghamton Mets make him a bonafide candidate for Shrine induction when he retires from his active playing career. In 66.2 innings for Binghamton, Montero won 7 games, striking out 72 and only walking 10! His E.R.A. was a stellar 2.43.

Tom Morgan won 67 games in the major leagues from 1951-1963 and was a mainstay of the pitching staffs for those strong Yankee teams of the 1950's. During the 1950 season he starred for the Triplets, winning 17 games and throwing 203 innings.

Rey Ordonez came up in the middle of the summer to play shortstop for the EL Championship 1994 Binghamton Mets and he supplemented his outstanding defensive play with a .261 batting average. His call up to the Eastern League enabled Edgardo Alfonzo to switch to second, giving Binghamton an outstanding double play combination in that championship season. Rated as the 17th best prospect in baseball by *Baseball America* at the beginning of the '96 season, Ordonez played in the majors from 1996-2004 and compiled a .246 lifetime batting average. He won three straight gold gloves for the NY Mets, from 1997 to 1999.

Jay Payton hit .345 for the 1995 Binghamton Mets and .279 over a 12-year major league career. In 2003, he hit .289 for the Rockies, with 28 home runs and 89 RBIs.

Bill Pulsipher posted 14 wins for the 1994 Binghamton Mets, leading them to the Eastern League Championship. He was at his best in the post season, no hitting the Harrisburg Senators in the playoffs. Elbow injuries shortened his major league career, limiting him to 13 wins in 106 games over a 6-year career.

Jose Reyes led the National League in hitting in 2012 with a .337 average and has been known as a "triples machine," as he has led the National League in triples four different seasons. In 2002, he hit .287 for Binghamton and stole 27 bases and played short with aplomb. In a 3-game rehab assignment with Binghamton in 2011, he hit .333 and won over B-Mets clubhouse workers with hugs and call outs of "Papi!"

Mickey Scott won 8 games for the Triplets in 1968 and went on to pitch in relief in 133 games in the major leagues during a five-year major league career that lasted from 1972-1977. A graduate of Newburgh Free Academy High School in 1965, he was drafted in the 17th round (335th player picked) by the New York Yankees in the same year. Upon his retirement from baseball, he made Binghamton his home, owning Mickey's Tavern for many years, which was located just outside Binghamton, and bartending at "Southside Yanni's" for many years as well.

Bill Stafford starred for the Binghamton Triplets in 1958, winning 11 games and posting a 2.25 E.R.A. while pitching 172 innings. He went on to win 43 games in the big leagues during his eight-year career from 1960-67. He beat the San Francisco Giants in Game 3 of the World Series, 3-2, as he threw a complete game, allowing only 4 hits.

Noah Syndergaard made his debut for Binghamton in 2013 and though he only threw 54 innings in 11 starts, his dominant presence on the mound merits him serious consideration for Shrine induction many years down the road, after his playing days are done. He struck out 69 and only walked 12 in those 54 innings, winning 6 games.

Michael Urda has been one of the owners of the B-Mets since the franchise became locally owned and is the spokesperson for the ownership group, serving as the President of the Binghamton Mets. 100 years after George F. Johnson was the "face of the Triplets," Urda is the "face of the Binghamton Mets."

Preston Wilson was hitting .286 with 19 home runs and 47 runs batted in for the Binghamton Mets in 1997 before he was packaged with Ed Yarnall and Geoff Goetz for Mike Piazza. Wilson was the ninth pick overall in the 1992 baseball draft and hit .264 with 189 home runs during his ten-year major league career.

Jim Weed started working for the Binghamton Mets in the ticket office in 1997 and has served as the general manager since 2010. Under his stewardship the franchise continues to be known as one of the most "fan friendly" franchises in all of baseball, which can be seen in the team's policy of letting season ticket holders have access to the stadium hours before the gates open and in overall player accessibility to the fans.

Paul Wilson won 40 games in the big leagues, during an injury-riddled career. He starred on the 1995 Binghamton Mets, going 6-3 with a 2.17 E.R.A, in 16 starts. Isringhausen, Pulsipher, and Wilson were referred to as "Generation K" by the New York media in the mid 1990's as fans pinned hopes of a Mets' rejuvenation on the promising minor league performances of this trio.

David Wright is still playing baseball so his Shrine induction is many years into the future, but the face of the Mets franchise already has his ticket to the Binghamton Shrine punched!

The write up here may end with Wright, but the list of candidates does not. Other names that will no doubt be discussed for induction in the future include George Banks, Zeke Bella, Jim Brideweser, Jim Coates, Brian Daubauch, Hank Foiles, Ken Gilchrist (announcer), Ralph Houk, Butch Huskey, John Johnstone, Don Lock, Mike Lum, Billy Meyer, Clyde McCullough, George Selkirk, Jerrod Riggan, Jason Tyner, Gus Triandos, and Jeff Walters—and this list is far from exhaustive!

Epilogue

From James "Grasshopper" Whitney to current Athletics' closer, Jimmy Johnson, with the likes of Daniel Maurice Casey, Eddie "Doc" Farrell, "Wild Bill" Hallahan, Johnny Logan, Jerry Toman, Danny McDevitt, Rob Gardner, and Ron Luciano coming in between, the professional accomplishments of these home-grown Shrine members remind us all that dreams can become reality when coupled with hard work, determination, and the willingness to fail along the way, no matter the size or smallness of the city or town that serves as one's hometown.

Professional baseball in Binghamton has had its peaks and valleys, disappointments and triumphs, but through it all baseball has been a resilient presence and a reflection of the community as well. Brockton and North Broad Streets in Johnson City have given way to Henry and Lewis Streets in downtown Binghamton and players now visit such establishments as *Di Rienzo's Bakery & Deli*, *Little Venice*, and *Amici's*, but baseball continues to be the nexus from year to year, town to town, and generation to generation.

Attendance figures show that baseball's popularity in this area peaked in the early 1990's when baseball returned. History shows that the last baseball championship, complete with playoff victories, for the Greater Binghamton Area was in 1994. Local historians will argue that the Greater Binghamton Area will never again see the success it had in the post World War II era, when Endicott Johnson was in full bloom and IBM was growing exponentially.

But baseball brings hope and hope often sprouts the determination that builds on successes and learns from failures. Community leaders today argue downtown Binghamton is now on the road to revitalization, pointing to the ongoing partnership with Binghamton University and the increasing number of small businesses that have populated downtown. Washington Avenue in Endicott, though no longer filled with thousands of noon time workers getting a bite to eat, has been tenacious in staying the course and providing small town shops and cultural enticements, along with its traditional Christmas parade. And just a stone's throw from where Johnson Field once stood, abandoned buildings like the "Old Victory" shoe factory are being targeted for redevelopment by the Broome County Land Bank.

We're at 100 years of baseball in Binghamton and counting. Area baseball fans are hoping the first place finish of the 2013 Binghamton Mets turns into a full-fledged championship in 2014, and community leaders are trusting that the story of baseball in Binghamton continues to inspire the revitalization of the Greater Binghamton Area, as well as the determination of its denizens.

A Photo Gallery of Baseball in Binghamton

In 1992, **Steve Swisher** won an EL Championship as the first manager for the Binghamton Mets.

Ken Oberkfell is smiling here, but not when SPs Jose Diaz, Scott Kazmir, and Matt Peterson were traded on the same day.

The video scoreboard displayed this graphic for **Edgardo Alfonzo's** 2008 induction. Note that the graphic is missing the last two letters of Edgardo's first name.

During his brief stay with Binghamton in 2004, **Scott Kazmir** wore number 32 and dominated the opposition, posting a 1.73 E.R.A. for 26 innings. NY Mets fans still wonder if 2007 and 2008 would have turned out differently if Kazmir had not been traded.

David Wright completes one of his 10 home-run trots for the B-Mets in 2004.

Quilvio Veras was in the Shrine Class of 2009; he played for the B-Mets in 1993.

Cory Lidle was in the Shrine Class of 2007. He won 14 games for the B-Mets in 1996.

Bobby Jones poses for a picture with Daniel Lunde in Port St. Lucie during spring training in 1999. (Photo courtesy of Jim Maggiore.)

Jose Reyes squares to bunt in 2002, before becoming a ML All Star in the majors.

Heath Bell has also gone from playing at Binghamton to becoming a ML All Star.

John Stearns led the 2003 B-Mets to a fifth-place finish in 2003, going 63-78.

Brook Fordyce and **Bobby Jones** formed a formidable battery in 1992.

Mike Kinkade hit .366 for the B-Mets in 2000.

Noah Syndergaard throws under the watchful eye of Frank Viola in spring training, 2013. Syndergaard won 6 games for the B-Mets in 2013.

Matt Harvey's 4.53 E.R.A. for the B-Mets in in 2011 did not foreshadow his 2013 ML year.

Curtis Pride, Shrine Class of 2012, hit .227 for the B-Mets 1992.

Jon Niese had a 3.08 E.R.A. in 2008 For the B-Mets.

Paul Wilson had a 2.17 E.R.A. for the B-Mets in 1995

From Left to Right: **Jerry Toman**, **Ralph Terry**, Eleanor Toman, and **Clete Boyer** on Induction Day in 2002 for Terry and Boyer. (Photo courtesy of Susan McCann.)

Carlos Gomez, who stole 41 bases in 2006, hits against Portland's John Lester in in the same year. (Photo courtesy of Jim Maggiore.)

Pat Kelly sits in the rocking chair he was given on his day on 8/30/1963. (Photo courtesy of the John Nuzzella family.)

A View from behind the plate at a Triplets game in the 1940's. (Photo courtesy of the Broome County Historical Society.)

The Triplets from 1950. **Frank Verdi** is in the second row, third from the left. **Dale Long** is in the back row, 4th from the right. (Photo courtesy of the Gilbert DeClerq family.)

Talking Baseball after a Hot Stove Dinner: Seated—Elston Howard and **Jake Pitler**. Among those standing: J**erry Toman**, Jerry Coleman, and **Stephen Souchock** (far right). (Photo courtesy of the Frank Saraceno family)

More Stove Talk: 1st Row: Tom Meany (P.R. rep), Ralph Houk, Yogi Berra, **John H. Johnson**, Tommy Richardson (EL President,), Claude Bell (fan); back row: Marvin Behr, Art Ditmar, **Jerry Toman**, Bob Turley, **John W. Fox**. (Photo Courtesy of the Frank Saraceno family.)

Johnson Field, from the corner of Broad and Brockton Streets. (Photo courtesy of *Broome County Historical Society*.)

Only two blocks north of Main Street, **Johnson Field** was within walking distance of the center of the village. Numbered above are items of interest discussed in this book. (Photo courtesy of the *Broome County Historical Society*.)

Whitey Ford on the left and Arnie Landeck on the right pose before a Triplets game in 1949. Joe McCann, Shrine Committee member, is behind Landeck in the photo.

Frank Verdi, Binghamton's own "Moonlight" Graham, was Ford's minor league roommate. (Both the Ford/Landeck and Verdi photos are courtesy of the Gilbert Declerq family.)

Bill "Moose" Skowron greets Joe Gennarelli during a break from a Hot Stove dinner. (Photo courtesy of the Frank Saraceno family.)

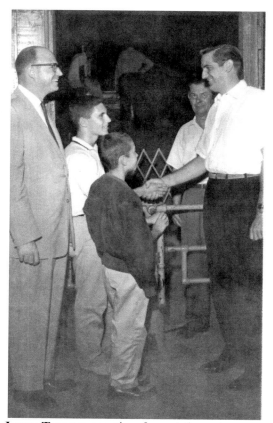

Fred Norman is on the left; Charlie Sechrist is on the right. (Photo courtesy of the John Nuzzella family)

Jerry Toman greeting fans at the gates to Johnson Field. (Photo courtesy of the Frank Saraceno family.)

In what looks like a very early call by the umpire, **John McNamara** is late with a tag in 1963. (Photo courtesy of the John Nuzzella family.)

Triple Cities Baseball Club --- 1947

Front: Freddy Bloom, Bat Boy. First row, left to right: Bob Gorbould; Bill Shea; Sam Masserini; Pete Kunis; Frank Bocek; George Wing; Tom Upton; Wayne Tucker; Marvin Crater; Bud Heslet. Second row: Bill O'Donnell, Trainer; Art Pollock; Harry Garbett; Tex Hoyle; Gale Pringle; Richard Martin, Public Relations; Lefty Gomez, Manager; Ed Kinney; Leo Venskus; Dick Kryhoski; Leon Hamilton, Business Manager; Bill Rodgers and Johnny Moore.

This '47 team photo was sold at the ballpark during the 1947 season. (Photo courtesy of the Gilbert DeClerq family.) **Lefty Gomez** was the manager of the '47 team.

Back Row L. to R.   Gene Monahan, Trainer, John Schroeppel, Dallas Jones, Ken Johnson, Geo Bechtold, Wes Rhea, Ed Gagle, Ron Klimkowski, Ross Moschitto, Ed Fiskland, Art Dawson, Frank Tepedino, Thurman Munson, Gary Jones, Jim Kennedy, Dave Senko, Batboy, Jerry Toman, General Manager.
Front Row L. to R.   Bobby Cantrell, Terry Ordway, Joe Pactwa, John Penderson, Jim Gleeson, Manager, Roger Dutton, Mickey Scott, Ron Boyer, Tim O'Connell.   1968 Triplets

The 1968 Triplets: **Gene Monahan** is at the far left; **Jerry Toman** is at the far right and **Thurman Munson** is the fifth from right in the back row. (Photo courtesy of the Frank Saraceno family.)

Steve Kraly won 19 games for the Triplets in 1953 and is currently the B-Mets scorekeeper. He also hit the baseball sign as a Triplet. (Photo courtesy of the Frank Saraceno family.)

Bill Stafford on the mound—note the baseball sign behind him, which **Charlie Keller** hit multiple times in '62. (Photo courtesy of the Frank Saraceno family.)

Pete Suder receives recognition as the player of the month in 1940. (Photo courtesy of the Gilbert Declerq family.)

NEW YORK **Mets** NATIONAL LEAGUE BASEBALL CLUB

Gerald H. Hunsicker
Assistant Vice President
Baseball Operations

September 21, 1994

Mr. Michael Urda
President
Binghamton Mets
P.O. Box 598
Binghamton, New York 13902

Dear Mike:

Your recent letter relating to the successful 1994 season in
Binghamton was much appreciated. Watching your club was one of the
few highlights in what has turned out to be a most difficult year
for our industry.

As I mentioned to you prior to the ownership transfer, our
minor league affiliates are our most important assets and we try
very hard not only to be successful on the field but to insure a
positive and professional environment for the development of our
players.

Binghamton has become one of the jewels of our system and we
all look forward to working with you and your staff in the years to
come.

Sincerely,

Gerald H. Hunsicker

P.S. Please realize we "spoiled" you this year. This kind of
talent unfortunately doesn't come along every year.

NEW YORK METS • SHEA STADIUM • FLUSHING, NEW YORK 11368 • 718-565-4372

Letter from Gerry Hunsicker congratulating Binghamton Mets President Michael Urda on
winning the 1994 Eastern League Championship.

Appendix A. Shrine Statistics

- ➤ Key:
- ➤ = Greater Binghamton Area resident (before or after playing days)
- ➤ **Bold underline** = Baseball Hall of Fame
- ➤ NA=Not Applicable
- ➤ - = No stats available

Note: Statistics in Appendix A and Appendix B taken from www.baseball-reference.com, *Eastern League 2013 Media Guide & Record Book*, and *Spalding Baseball Guides*.

1993 (3 Inductees)

Name	Years	HRs	RBIs	Average
*George F. Johnson				
Owner of Triplets	1913-1919	NA	NA	NA
"Wee Willie" Keeler , OF				
Binghamton	1892	2	-	.373
	1893	1	-	.294
Majors	1892-1910	33	810	.388
*Johnny Logan, SS				
Binghamton	DNP			
Majors	1951-1963	93	547	.268

1994 (0 Inductees)

No election due to AA All Star Game Held in Binghamton.

1995 (4 Inductees)

Name	Years	W	L	E.R.A
Ed "Whitey" Ford				
Binghamton	1949	16	5	1.61
Majors	1950-67	236	106	2.75
* "Wild Bill" Hallahan				
Binghamton	DNP			
Majors	1925-38	102	94	4.03
Tommy Holmes, OF		HR	RBI	Average
Binghamton	1938	6	62	.368
Majors	1942-52	88	581	.302
Eddie Sawyer, OF				
Binghamton	1935-38 1942-43	11	337	.310
Majors, Manager	8 Years	W	L	Winning %
1950 NL Champs		390	423	.480

1996 (3 Inductees)

Name	Years	HR	RBI	Average
*Ron Luciano				
Binghamton – No Stats				
ML Umpire	1969-1979			
John McNamara, C		HR	RBI	Average

Binghamton	1963	0	24	.226
Majors, Manager	1969-1996	**W**	**L**	**Winning %**
1986 AL Champs		1160	1233	.485
Stephen Souchock, OF		**HR**	**RBI**	**Average**
Binghamton	1941-1942	13	94	..317
Majors	1946-55	50	186	..255

1997 (3 Inductees)

Name	**Years**	**W**	**L**	**E.R.A**
* Steve Kraly				
Binghamton	1953	19	2	2.08
	1956	5	6	3.14
	1958	2	4	4.69
Majors	1953	0	2	3.24
Deron Johnson, OF		**HR**	**RBI**	**Average**
Binghamton	1957	26	102	.303
Majors	1960-76	245	923	..244
Thurman Munson, C				
Binghamton	1968	6	37	.301
Majors	1969-79	113	701	.292

1998 (4 Inductees)

Name	**Years**	**HRs**	**RBIs**	**Average**
John H. Johnson				
Triplets Business Mgr	Early 1950's			
Lee Thomas, OF		**HRs**	**RBIs**	**Average**
Binghamton	1956	2	25	.260
	1957	8	33	.262
	1958	17	88	.281
	1959	25	122	.304
Majors	1961-68	106	428	.255
Bill Virdon, CF		**HRs**	**RBIs**	**Average**
Binghamton	1952	2	46	.261
Majors	1951-1963	91	501	.267
* James E Whitney	**Years**	**W**	**L**	**E.R.A**
Binghamton	DNP			
Majors	1881-1890	191	204	2.97

1999 (4 Inductees)

Name	**Years**	**W**	**L**	**E.R.A**
Al Downing				
Binghamton	1961	9	1	1.84
	1968	1	4	3.48
Majors	1961-77	123	107	3.22
Bud Fowler, 2B		**HR**	**RBI**	**Average**
Binghamton	1887	-	-	.350
Majors	DNP			
Vic Raschi	**Years**	**W**	**L**	**E.R.A**

Binghamton Triplets	1946	10	10	3.16
Majors	1946-1955	132	66	3.72
Steve Swisher, C		**W**	**L**	**Winning %**
Binghamton, MGR	1992	79	59	.572
	1993	68	72	.486
		HR	**RBI**	**Average**
Majors	1974-1982	20	124	.216

2004 (4 Inductees)

Name	Years	W	L	E.R.A
Spud Chandler				
Binghamton	1932	8	1	2.76
	1933	10	8	4.23
Majors	1937-1947	109	43	2.84
* Eddie Farrell, INF		**HR**	**RBI**	**Average**
Binghamton	DNP			
Majors	1925-1935	10	213	.260
Bobby Richardson, 2B				
Binghamton Triplets	1953	3	55	.310
Majors	1955-1966	34	390	.266
* Bob Taylor, C				
Binghamton	DNP			
Negro Leagues	1938-1941	NA	NA	NA

2001(0 inductees)
All-time Binghamton Mets All star Team. No inductions this year.

2002 (2 Inductees)

Name	Years	HR	RBI	Average
Clete Boyer, 3B				
Binghamton	1957	12	48	.243
Majors	1955-1971	162	654	.242
Ralph Terry		**W**	**L**	**E.R.A.**
Binghamton	1954	11	9	3.30
Majors	1956-1967	10	213	.260

2003 (3 Inductees)

Name	Years	W	L	E.R.A
Fred Norman				
Binghamton	1962	3	5	4.89
	1963	13	14	3.89
Majors	1962-1980	104	103	3.64
Pete Suder, INF		**HR**	**RBI**	**Average**
Binghamton	1938	10	97	.278
	1939	4	25	.248
	1940	16	78	.301
Majors	1941-1955	49	541	.249

John Montgomery Ward	Years	W	L	E.R.A
Binghamton Crickets	1878	-	-	-
Majors as Pitcher	1878-1884	164	103	2.10
Majors as Hitter	1878-1894	26	869	.275

2004 (4 Inductees)

Name	Years	HRs	RBIs	Average
Johnny Blanchard, C				
Binghamton Triplets	1951	0	7	.183
	1955	34	111	.281
Majors	1955-1965	67	200	.239
Ken Harrelson, OF				
Binghamton Triplets	1962	38	138	.278
Majors	1963-1971	131	421	.239
Frank Verdi, INF				
Binghamton Triplets	1949	2	16	.252
	1950	1	52	.303
	1951	3	44	.270
	1952	2	67	.313
Majors	1953	0	0	0
* Jerry Toman				
Binghamton Triplets General Manager	1957-1968			

2005 (3 Inductees)

Name	Years	W	L	E.R.A
* Rob Gardner				
Binghamton	DNP			
Majors	1965-1973	14	18	4.35
Bob Grim				
Binghamton Triplets	1951	16	5	2.39
Majors	1954-1962	61	41	3.61
* Jake Pitler, 2B		HR	RBI	Average
Binghamton	1928	0		.285
Majors	1917-1918	0	23	.232

2006 (4 Inductees)

Name	Years	HR	RBI	Average
Bert Campaneris, SS				
Binghamton	1962	0	0	.364
	1963	0	12	.308
Majors	1964-1983	79	646	.259
Lefty Gomez		W	L	E.R.A
Binghamton	1946	0	1	5.50
	1947	0	0	9.00
Majors	1930-1943	189	102	3.34
W.B. KAY, OF		HR	RBI	Average

Binghamton Triplets	1914	4	-	.322
	1915	7	-	.378
	1916	2		.360
	1917	3	-	.314
	1918	1	-	.324
	1919	0	-	.308
Triplets/Wiles-Barre	1924	5	-	.314
Majors	1907	0	7	.333
Bobby Jones		**W**	**L**	**E.R.A**
Binghamton	1992	12	4	1.88
	1999	1	2	3.86
Major Leagues	1993-2002	89	83	4.36

2007 (4 Inductees)

Name	Years	HR	RBI	Average
Brook Fordyce, C				
Binghamton Mets	1992	11	61	.278
Majors	1995-2004	41	188	2.58
Charles Keller III, 1B		**HR**	**RBI**	**Average**
Binghamton Triplets	1961	19	104	.349
Majors	DNP			
Cory Lidle		**W**	**L**	**E.R.A**
Binghamton Mets	1996	19	10	3.31
Majors	1997-2006	82	72	.457
George McQuinn, 1B		**HR**	**RBI**	**Average**
Binghamton Triplets	1932	1	35	.319
	1933	7	102	.357
Major Leagues	1936-1948	135	794	.276

2008 (4 Inductees)

Name	Years	HR	RBI	Average
Edgardo Alfonzo, INF				
Binghamton Mets	1994	15	75	.293
Majors	1995-2006	144	744	.284
* Daniel M. Casey		**W**	**L**	**E.R.A**
Binghamton Bingos	1892	4	5	1.94
	1893	2	1	3.67
Majors	1884-1889	96	90	3.18
Joe Pepitone, 1B		**HR**	**RBI**	**Average**
Binghamton Triplets	1960	13	75	.260
Major Leagues	1962-1973	219	721	.258

2009 (3 Inductees)

Name	Years	HR	RBI	Average
Dale Long, 1B				
Binghamton Triplets	1950	27	130	.287
Majors	1951-1963	132	467	.267

* Danny McDevitt		W	L	E.R.A
Binghamton	DNP			
Majors		21	27	4.40
Quilvio Veras, INF				
Binghamton Mets	1993	2	51	.306
Majors	1995-2002	32	239	.270

2011 (3 Inductees)

Name	Years	W	L	E.R.A
Wally Burnette				
Binghamton Triplets	1953	21	10	2.10
Majors	1955-1958	14	21	3.56
John Fox				
Binghamton Reporter	1949-2010	NA	NA	NA
* Harry Lumley, OF		HR	RBI	Average
Binghamton	1910	-	-	.345
	1911	-	-	.323
	1912	-	-	.326
Majors	1904-1910	38	.305	.274

2012 (3 Inductees)

Name	Years	W	L	E.R.A
Gene Bearden				
Binghamton		15	5	2.41
Majors	1947-1953	45	38	3.96
Curtis Pride, OF		HR	RBI	Average
Binghamton Mets	1992	10	42	.227
Majors	1993-2006	20	82	.250
Bill Skowron, 1B		HR	RBI	Average
Binghamton Triplets		2	11	.246
Majors	1954-1967	211	888	.282

2013 (3 Inductees)

Name	Years	HR	RBI	Average
Willard Hershberger, C				
Binghamton	1933	2	58	.304
Majors	1938-1940	0	17	.316
Tom Tresh, INF				
Binghamton	1959	6	16	.243
	1960	16	51	.246
Majors	1961-1969	153	530	.245
Pete Van Wieren				
Binghamton Triplets Radio Announcer	1967-1968			
Majors, Atlanta Braves Announcer	1976-2008			

Appendix B. Teams of Binghamton

Note: Statistics in Appendix A and Appendix B taken from www.baseball-reference.com, *Eastern League 2013 Media Guide & Record Book*, and *Reach* and *Spalding Baseball Guides*.

Key:

> - ***Bold Italic*** indicates both first place division finish and E.L. Championship
> - **Bold** indicates Eastern League Champions
> - *Italic* indicates first-place finish for the division
> - Blank indicates no stats available

Note:

1) The Eastern League, when it was first formed on March 23, 1923 at the Arlington Hotel in Binghamton, New York, was a six-team league that was located entirely within New York and Pennsylvania. For the first 15 years of its existence the Eastern League was known as the New York-Pennsylvania League (not to be confused with today's NYPENN League). The original six members of the Eastern League were Binghamton, Elmira (NY), Scranton, Wilkes-Barre, Williamsport and York (Pennsylvania).
2) *Bingos* and *Bingoes* are both acceptable

Year	League	Level	Team	W	L	%
2013	*Eastern League*	*AA*	*Binghamton Mets*	86	55	.610
2012	Eastern League	AA	Binghamton Mets	68	74	.479
2011	Eastern League	AA	Binghamton Mets	65	76	.461
2010	Eastern League	AA	Binghamton Mets	66	76	.465
2009	Eastern League	AA	Binghamton Mets	54	86	.386
2008	Eastern League	AA	Binghamton Mets	73	69	.514
2007	Eastern League	AA	Binghamton Mets	61	81	.430
2006	Eastern League	AA	Binghamton Mets	70	70	.500
2005	Eastern League	AA	Binghamton Mets	63	79	.444
2004	Eastern League	AA	Binghamton Mets	76	66	.535
2003	Eastern League	AA	Binghamton Mets	63	78	.447
2002	Eastern League	AA	Binghamton Mets	73	68	.518
2001	Eastern League	AA	Binghamton Mets	73	68	.518
2000	Eastern League	AA	Binghamton Mets	82	58	.586
1999	Eastern League	AA	Binghamton Mets	54	88	.380
1998	Eastern League	AA	Binghamton Mets	82	60	.577
1997	Eastern League	AA	Binghamton Mets	66	76	.465
1996	Eastern League	AA	Binghamton Mets	76	66	.535
1995	Eastern League	AA	Binghamton Mets	67	75	.472
1994	***Eastern League***	***AA***	***Binghamton Mets***	**82**	**59**	**.582**
1993	Eastern League	AA	Binghamton Mets	68	72	.486

Year	League	Level	Team	W	L	%
1992	Eastern League	AA	Binghamton Mets	79	59	.572
1968	Eastern League	AA	Binghamton Triplets	67	72	.482
1967	*Eastern League*	*AA*	*Binghamton Triplets*	*82*	*58*	*.586*
1966	NY-PENN League	A	Binghamton Triplets	67	58	.536
1965	NY-PENN League	A	Binghamton Triplets	81	45	.643
1964	NY-PENN League	A	Binghamton Triplets	58	71	.450
1963	Eastern League	AA	Binghamton Triplets	65	75	.464
1962	Eastern League	A	Binghamton Triplets	60	80	.429
1961	Eastern League	A	Binghamton Triplets	75	64	.540
1960	Eastern League	A	Binghamton Triplets	70	69	.504
1959	Eastern League	A	Binghamton Triplets	71	68	.511
1958	**Eastern League**	**A**	**Binghamton Triplets**	**66**	**68**	**.493**
1957	*Eastern League*	*A*	*Binghamton Triplets*	*85*	*55*	*.607*
1956	Eastern League	A	Binghamton Triplets	81	58	.583
1955	Eastern League	A	Binghamton Triplets	75	62	.547
1954	Eastern League	A	Binghamton Triplets	70	70	.500
1953	**Eastern League**	**A**	**Binghamton Triplets**	**96**	**55**	**.636**
1952	**Eastern League**	**A**	**Binghamton Triplets**	**77**	**60**	**.562**
1951	Eastern League	A	Binghamton Triplets	69	69	.500
1950	Eastern League	A	Binghamton Triplets	81	58	.583
1949	**Eastern League**	**A**	**Binghamton Triplets**	**70**	**70**	**.500**
1948	Eastern League	A	Binghamton Triplets	58	82	.414
1947	Eastern League	A	Binghamton Triplets	52	88	.371
1946	Eastern League	A	Binghamton Triplets	51	89	.364
1945	Eastern League	A	Binghamton Triplets	56	81	.409
1944	**Eastern League**	**A**	**Binghamton Triplets**	**64**	**71**	**.474**
1943	Eastern League	A	Binghamton Triplets	74	66	.529
1942	Eastern League	A	Binghamton Triplets	80	60	.571
1941	Eastern League	A	Binghamton Triplets	68	69	.496
1940	**Eastern League**	**A**	**Binghamton Triplets**	**77**	**62**	**.554**
1939	Eastern League	A	Binghamton Triplets	71	69	.507
1938	*Eastern League*	*A*	*Binghamton Triplets*	*84*	*51*	*.622*
1937	Eastern League	A	Binghamton Triplets	67	69	.493
1936	*Eastern League*	*A*	*Binghamton Triplets*	*81*	*58*	*.583*
1935	**Eastern League**	**A**	**Binghamton Triplets**	**75**	**60**	**.556**
1934	Eastern League	A	Binghamton Triplets	76	62	.551
1933	*Eastern League*	*A*	*Binghamton Triplets*	*79*	*55*	*.590*
1932	Eastern League	B	Binghamton Triplets	69	71	.493
1931	Eastern League	B	Binghamton Triplets	76	64	.543
1930	Eastern League	B	Binghamton Triplets	67	72	.482
1929	*Eastern League*	*B*	*Binghamton Triplets*	*83*	*56*	*.597*
1928	Eastern League	B	Binghamton Triplets	83	57	.593
1927	Eastern League	B	Binghamton Triplets	57	81	.413

Year	League	Level	Team	W	L	%
1926	Eastern League	B	Binghamton Triplets	67	67	.500
1925	Eastern League	B	Binghamton Triplets	65	63	.508
1924	Eastern league	B	Binghamton Triplets	63	65	.492
1923	Eastern League	B	Binghamton Triplets	67	55	.549
1919	International League	AA	Binghamton Bingos	75	71	.514
1918	International League	AA	Binghamton Bingos	85	38	.691
1917	New York State League	B	Binghamton Bingos	33	20	.623
1916	New York State League	B	Binghamton Bingos	69	61	.530
1915	New York State League	B	Binghamton Bingos	79	44	.642
1914	New York State League	B	Binghamton Bingos	78	56	.582
1913	New York State League	B	Binghamton Bingos	84	53	.613
1912	New York State League	B	Binghamton Bingos	50	79	.388
1911	New York State League	B	Binghamton Bingos	63	77	.450
1910	New York State League	B	Binghamton Bingos	43	91	.321
1909	New York State League	B	Binghamton Bingos	61	77	.442
1908	New York State League	B	Binghamton Bingos	80	61	.567
1907	New York State League	B	Binghamton Bingos	51	83	.376
1906	New York State League	B	Binghamton Bingos	48	75	.390
1905	New York State League	B	Binghamton Bingos	46	77	.374
1904	New York State League	B	Binghamton Bingos	40	85	.320
1903	New York State League	B	Binghamton Bingos	52	72	.419
1902	New York State League	B	Binghamton Bingos	71	41	.633
1901	New York State League	C	Binghamton Bingos	69	45	.605
1900	New York State League	C	Binghamton Crickets	41	62	.398
1899	New York State League	C	Binghamton Bingos	56	55	.505
1895	New York State League	B	Binghamton Crickets	28	21	.571
1894	Eastern League	N/A	Binghamton Bingos/Allentown Buffaloes	23	60	.277
1893	Eastern League	N/A	Binghamton Bingos	48	55	.466
1892	Eastern League	N/A	Binghamton Bingos	38	18	.678
1888	Central League	N/A	Binghamton Crickets			
1887	International Association	N/A	Binghamton Crickets			
1886	International League	N/A	Binghamton Crickets			
1885	New York State League	N/A	Binghamton Bingos			
1878	International Association	N/A	Binghamton Cricket(s)			
1877	League Alliance	N/A	Binghamton Cricket(s)			

Notes
Introduction

1) *North and Brockton Street.* Site of Johnson Field, home of the Triplets from 1913-1968. Today the Johnson City Senior Citzens Center resides on this site.

Greater Binghamton's Baseball History

1) *In 1935 the New York Times Reported...* Mapes, Linda. "Johnson Field, A History," (Master's Thesis, available from *Broome County Historical Association*) Page 10.
2) *The use of my own private wealth...* Ibid, Page 11.
3) *...he enjoyed taking his friends to the World Series...* Ibid, Page 4.

Tales from the Shrine

1) *...no longer be active.* An exception was made in the case of Edgardo Alfonzo, who was making a comeback with the independent team, the Long Island Ducks when he was inducted to the Shrine.
2) *It was in AA Binghamton...* Interview David Wright had with Boomer Esiason and Craig Carton WFAN (1050) radio.
3) *Bill Virdon, 1960's World Champion.* Letter to Jim Maggiore in 2006.
4) *In a talk show in 2013...* Pete Rose interview with Chris Russ on Mad Dog Radio on XMRADIO.

Shrine Spinoff: Fan of the Year Award

1) *The common theme...* Through the years the front office of the Binghamton Mets has fulfilled numerous requests for fans to be married at the park. Joe McCann, current Shrine committee member married his wife, Sandra, at home plate on August 31, 2002. Joe's best man was a future bat boy for the Binghamton Mets, Ian McCann.

Binghamton: The Core of the Big Apple

1) *We played a lot of golf.* McGraw, Tug, and Joe Durso. "Screwball" (Boston: Houghton Mifflin Company: 1974) Page 47.
2) *When people think...* Roger Neel in talking to the Binghamton Mets Booster Club on September 16th, 2013.

Shrine Roster and Profiles

George F. Johnson
1) *And the headline...Binghamton Daily Republican*, Page 3.
2) *It is rather...* Mapes, Linda. "Johnson Field: A History" (Master's Thesis, Master's Thesis, available from *Broome County Historical Association),* Page 19.
3) *Funeral Services were held.* Ibid. Page 42.
4) *In the accounting offices...* "American League Baseball Club Financial Records, 1913-1950: Volume 7." The Baseball Library at the Baseball Hall of Fame.

Johnny Logan

1) *Sawyer could not convince the Yankees to sign Logan.* Buege, Bob. "SABR Baseball Biography Project: Johnny Logan." (http://sabr.org/bioproj/person/4140a710)

2) *He was one of the toughest players.* Ibid (Buege)

3) *After winning the World Series in 1957...* Ibid (Buege)

4) *Jake Pitler, Binghamton...* McCalvy, Adam. *"Milwaukee Baseball Mainstay Passes Away,"* for MLB.Com

5) *He was one of the toughest players...*Chapman, Lou. "Johnny Logan Recalls Old Days at County Stadium" (originally appeared in *Baseball Digest*, reprinted at www.mallardsbaseball.com

6) *I must have been very active.* See Buege.

"Wee Willie" Keeler

1) *He may have been small...* Baseball Hall of Fame web page for Keeler (*http://baseballhall.org/hof/keeler-willie*).

2) *He was also known to tire pitchers out by consistently bunting....*Smith, Robert. "Baseball's Hall of Fame" (United States: Bantam Books: 1965) Page 37.

3) *In 1903 he saw his average drop.* Skipper, Doug. "SABR Baseball Biography Project: 'Wee Willie' Keeler" (*http://sabr.org/bioproj/person/074d42fd*) 2011

4) *I was down to see the Niagara Falls.* Assael, Shawn. "ESPN: The File Blog – Willie Keeler Letters Show MLB In Infancy." September 28, 2010 (Letter from June 9th, 1892) (*http://espn.go.com/espn/otl/blog/_/name/assael_shaun/id/5625102/willie-keeler-letters-open-window-birth-baseball*)

5) *This manager is a stinker.* Ibid

6) *You don't want to say a word.* Ibid, letter from August 3rd, 1892

7) *...when he attributed his success in hitting...* Skipper, Doug. "SABR Baseball Biography Project: 'Wee Willie' Keeler" (*http://sabr.org/bioproj/person/074d42fd*) 2011

8) *Gentleman don't do that.* Assael, Shawn. "ESPN: The File Blog – Willie Keeler Letters Show MLB In Infancy." September 28, 2010

Whitey Ford

1) *We'd sit on that bus...* Ford, Whitey, with Phil Pepe. *"Slick: My Life In and Around Baseball"* (William and Morrow Company, INC. 1987). Page 42

2) *I was starting to strike out...*Ibid, Page 48

3) *It was the great Lefty Gomez ...*Ibid, Page 39

4) *But if you behave yourself...Ibid, Page 49*

5) *Dear Commissioner...*Baseball Hall of Fame Web Page: (http://baseballhall.org/hof/ford-whitey)

Tommy Holmes

1) *I played baseball as a kid...*edited by Curt Smith and published in cooperation with the Baseball Hall of Fame, "What Baseball Means to Me: A Celebration of Our National Pastime" (NY: Hachette Book Group, 2002)

2) *run far and wide to snag fly balls...* "Holmes hits .430 to Lead Triplets in First Six Games." *Binghamton Evening Press*, May 4th, 1938.

3) *In the bottom of the Eighth inning. ..*Baseball Reference Web Site, Post Season Box Scores (http://www.baseball-reference.com/boxes/BSN/BSN194810060.shtml)

Eddie Sawyer

1) *I mean over the long haul.* "Ed Sawyer Touts Sanicki as Tops: Phils pilot Compares Ed with DiMag," *Binghamton Sun.* Thursday, April 21st

2) *Sanicki injured his knee…* After his playing career was over he became a special education teacher in Cifton, NJ, winning a "Teacher of the Year Award" in 1974. "Edward Robert 'butch" Sanicki: Find a Grave" (http://www.findagrave.com/cgi-bin/fg.cgi?page=gr&GRid=19728)

3) *He was credited with…* Berger, Ralph. "SABR Baseball Biography Project: Eddie Sawyer" (http://sabr.org/bioproj/person/a54376db)

4) *Well my first pitch…* Roberts, Robin, with C. Paul Rogers III. "My Life in Baseball" (Illinois: Triumph Books 2003). Page 86

5) *He's still able to run down…* NY Times, September 23, 1997. Richard Goldstein (Sawyer Obituary). "Eddie Sawyer, 87, Manager of the Phillies' Whiz Kids"

6) *I'm 49 years old…* Ibid

Ron Luciano

1) *My Voice Is Perfect for Mime and My Face is Made for Radio.* Luciano, Ron, and David Fisher. "The Umpire Strikes Back." (Bantam Books, New York, April 1982), Page 4

2) *The fun came in between.* Stevens, Kevin. "Death of a Showman: Tier Mourns Ump Luciano" *Binghamton Press & Sun-Bulletin*, January 19th, 1995

3) *Luciano and Weaver teamed up to make history. See Luciano and Fisher.* Page 31-32.

4) *Talking and joking around…* Luciano and Fisher, *page 72*

5) *Making Decisions and working long games…* Ibid, Page 84

6) *The day they started throwing breaking pitches…* Ibid, *Page 145*

7) *It's Very Sad. Winheld, Mark.* "Baseball Celebrity Luciano Dies at 57," *Binghamton Press & Sun Bulletin.* January 19[th,] 1995

John McNamara

1) *I just try to throw strikes.* By Toniessen, Lowell. "Freddie (sic) Ready for Majors," *Binghamton Sun-Bulletin.* August 30, 1963.

Stephen Souchock

1) *A kid is so anxious.* Fox, John W. "Trips Carpenter Nailing Pitchers to the Wall, *"Binghamton Evening Press,* April 11th, 1957.

 2) *Unlike other fathers…* Olberman, Keith. "Where have You Gone, Steve Souchock?" *The New York Times*, September 20, 2008

3) *I remember Steve as a great hitter.* Sargent, Jim. "SABR Baseball Biography Project: Stephen Souchock"

Deron Johnson

1) *What's the story, Skip?* Fox, John W. "Trips Carpenter Nailing Pitchers to the Wall." *Binghamton Evening Press*, April 11th 1957

2) *Dad felt he had a job to do.* Newhan, Ross. "While Deron Johnson Battles Cancer At Home, his Son Dominick Gets a Chance with the Angels." The Los Angeles Times, February 19, 1992.

Thurman Munson

1) *Hello, my name is Dallas.* Tepedino, Frank. Story related in Voices of the Game Session in Cooperstown, NY. 2002

2) *Trust me.* Paterniti, Michael. "The House that Thurman Built," from Stout, Glenn. *Top of the Heap: A Yankees Collection.* Page 236

3) *When we were together in Syracuse.* Interview with Rob Gardner on February 6, 2014.

4) *Hey, are you guys OK?* Coffee, Wayne. "25 Years Later, Thurman Munson's Last Words Remain a Symbol of his Life." *The New York Daily News*, August 1, 2009.

Lee Thomas

1) *I want to give him a shot at the job.* "Hal Charnofsky sent to Triplets, who top Alexanadria, 5-3." *Binghamton Sun-Bulletin.* April 10, 1957

2) *He turned to his wife.* by Mcmillan, Brett. "Baseball Success Starts with Honesty for Lee Thomas." (brettmcmillan.wordpress.com). November 9th, 2012

Bill Virdon

1) *Binghamton was one of the steps*...letter from Bill Virdon to Jim Maggiore on 1-23-07

2) *The work of Bill Virdon*...by Slattery, Jack. "Virdon Fly chasing Pleasant Memory of Triplets' Season," *Binghamton Press*, 9-23-52

3) *I hope she's a right hander. Binghamton Press*, 1952.

4) *He probably helped my career as much as anybody.* Letter from Bill Virdon to author (Jim Maggiore), 1-23-07

5) *I want you out here tomorrow night.*" Gleason Warns Trips Pretzels Still Tough." *Binghamton Press.* September 20th, 1952.

6) *If one play*... "Triplets like to use Variety When hitting Home runs." *Binghamton Press*, 9-19-52.

Jim "Grasshopper" Whitney

1) *The 1878 Crickets*... Di Salvatore, Bryan. "Clever Base Ballist: the Life and Times of John Montgomery Ward." (Maryland: The Johns Hopkins University Press) Page 105

2) *Hop, skip, and a jump*... Gorman, Robert M. and David Weeks. "Death at the Ballpark: A Comprehensive Study of Game-Related Fatalities,1862-2007." (North Carolina: McFarland & Company, 2009)

3) *There were no restrictions*... Flynn, Kevin and Karen. "The Great Grasshopper." *Baseballhistory.com.* http://dcbaseballhistory.com/2013/10/the-great-grasshopper/

Bud Fowler

1) *Fowler has not, and will not*... McKenna, Brian. "SABR Baseball Biographical Project: Bud Fowler."(http://sabr.org/bioproj/person/200e2bbd)

Vic Raschi

1) *During the baseball season*... Gittleman, Sol. "Reynolds, Raschi, and Lopat: The Big Three and the Great Yankee Dynasty." (North Carolina: McFarland & Co, 2007) Page 44.

2) *Vic and Sally Rashi*... Ibid, Page 44

3) *Dear Vic*... http://www.findagrave.com/cgi-bin/fg.cgi?page=dfl&GRid=8471550&

Spud Chandler

1) *I pitched for my high school team.* Gomez, Vernona, with Goldstein, Lawrence. "Lefty Gomez: An American Odyssey." (New York: Ballantine Books, 2012) Page 162

2) *Manager George Selkirk*... "Jim Brideweser Headed for Triplet Camp: Rookie Flash, Two Others Cut by Yanks," *Binghamton Sun*, March 30th, 1950.

Al Downing

1) *I Never Say 7:15 Anymore*... Grant, Jim "Mudcat", with Sabellico, Tom & O'Brien, Pat. "The Black Aces: Baseball's Only African-American Twenty-Game Winners." (Farmingdale, NY; The Black Aces, LLC, 2006). Page 320

2) *There was a lot of talent.* Ibid, Page 322

3) *Every time I come back to Binghamton.* "All Stars Shine Bright for 12th Annual Jim "Mudcat' Grant All Star Golf Tournament" (web press release: http://www.smlny.com/all-stars-shine-bright-for-12th-annual-jim-mudcat-grant-all-star-golf-tournament/)

Clete Boyer

1) *Financially the bonus he got was great*... "Hard-hitting Ken Boyer brags about Little Brother, Clete—Clete Needs Confidence." *The Spokesman-Review*, May 7, 1961.The Associated Press

2) *Brooks beat me out of about seven gold gloves.* Madden, Bill. "Clete Boyer, Yanks' 3rd Man," *New York Daily News*, June 5, 2007.

3) *Defense wins ballgames.* Allen, Maury. "Yankees: Where Have You Gone?" (United States: sports publishing, LLC, 2004) Page 161.

Fred Norman

1) *Larry and Sparky loved us. Radio interview with Bill Lack* on "Redleg Nation Radio." https://archive.org/details/RedlegNationRadio86FredNormanPart2

2) *I was pitching against the Cubs.* King, John. "Standup Guy Pat Darcy talks about Game 6 and his Rookie Season." (http://www.thezephyr.com/patdarcy.htm)

3) *We won our last ten games that season…*Bill Lack interview.

Doc Farrell

1) *and over 15 rows….* Cohen, Marv. "Doc Farrell's Baseball Odyssey." (M C Productions, 416 Main Street, Vestal, NY June 2003). Back Jacket, Page 1.

2) *He's the best all around infielder…* the Ibid, Page 131-132

3) *Teammate of thirty-four players…* Ibid, Page 147

Ralph Terry

1) *With Willie McCovey…*Richardson, Bobby. "The Bobby Richardson Story: A Heartwarming Account of the Deep Personal Faith of One of Baseball's Outstanding Stars." (Pyramid Edition, 1966). P. 139.

2) *Beating the Yankees…* "Response to Jim Maggiore from a letter written to Mr. Terry in 2002. Question was "What was your most memorable moment in Binghamton?"

Pete Suder

1) *I wish you had.* Interview with Joe McCann. November 5, 2013

2) *Pete's a great guy.*, "Great A's Trio Gains New Honor: Joost, Suder, Fain Enter Lexicon of Baseball." *Connecticut Sunday Herald.* October 2, 1949

3) *Joost to Suder to Fain…* Armstrong, Richard Stoll. "Their Record Still Stands" from <u>Minding What Matters Web Blog</u> by Richard Stoll Armstrong (*http://rsarm.blogspot.com/2012/05/there-are-more-than-few-baseball-fans.html*) May 3rd, 2012 (Entire poem reprinted here, courtesy of Minding What Matters blog byArmstrong➔ All rights reserved. The photographs, articles, and poems in this Blog may be used with proper credits to Richard Stoll Armstrong, or to the appropriate person, when the authorship is otherwise indicated.

4) *On July 25th.* .."Triplets Beat Pioneers to Increase Lead to 4 and a Half Games." *Binghamton Evening Press*, July 26th, 1938.

John Montgomery Ward

1) I did not meet. "Helen Dauvray's Choice: To Be married this Morning to John M. Ward," *The New York Times*, October 12, 1887.

2) Was one of the … Di Salvatore, Bryan. "A Clever Base-ballist: the life and times of John Montgomery Ward." (Baltimore: John Hopkins University Press, 1999) Page 105

Johnny Blanchard

1) *I should have called for Eddie Lopat.* Rekela, George. "SABR Baseball Project: Johnny Blanchard"

2) *Hell, I can't play Mick, that's why I'm crying. Baseball-Reference.com*—Bullpen. (http://www.baseball- reference.com/bullpen/Johnny_Blanchard#Biographical_Information)

Frank Verdi

1) *We were eating chili…*Ford, Whitey, and Pepe, Phil. "Slick." (William and Morrow and Company, INC, 1987). Pages 42-43

2) *If some club in the majors…* Young, Dick. "Young Ideas" column. *New York Daily News*, October 10, 1970.

Ken Harrelson

1) I set the league record. Interview with Harrelson after his appearance at the Baseball Hall of Fame as part of the "Voices of the Game" segment on September 19, 2006.

2) Weaver would bang on… Handrinos. Pete. "Baseball Men: The Phenom" *The Birdhouse* web site (www.stlcardinals.scout.com). October 3, 2005

3) When I arrived, I was 17. Wulf, Steve. "The Hawk: A Nose for All Seasons," *Sports Illustrated.* January 20, 1986.

Jerry Toman

1) *I think any sporting activity...* Shay, Jack Edward, in collaboration with Betty Casey and Tom Townshend. "Bygone Binghamton: Remembering People and places of the Past" (Bloomington, Indiana: Authorhouse, 2012). Page 381.

2) *His love of baseball.* "Gerald Toman Obituary." *Pressconnects.com* web site. (http://www.legacy.com/obituaries/pressconnects/obituary.aspx?pid=159560162)

Rob Gardner

1) *It Seemed as after the first three innings...* interview with author Mike McCann, February 5 2014

2) *Never give up.* Note sent to author Jim Maggiore, November 2013.

Bob Grim

1) After his graduation from Franklin K .Lane... Though Grim is the only graduate of this now defunct high school who ever played in the big leagues, he is not the most celebrated alumnus who went on to achieve greatness in sports—that honor goes to William "Red" Holtzman, coach of the New York Knicks from 1967 to 1982, who was graduated from Lane in 1938.

2) But of equal importance... Behr, Marvin. "Grim's 3-hitter Tops Schenectady for Trips, 4-1," *Binghamton Sun:* June 6th, 1954

3) After my rookie year... Friend, Harold. "Bob Grim: The Pitch That Ruined the New York Yankees Rookie of the Year." (Bleacher Report: September 18, 2011) http://bleacherreport.com/articles/854498-mlb-the-pitch-that-ruined-yankees-rookie-of-the-year-bob-grims-career

4) He grew up. Liptak. Mark. "Flashing Back with Bob Grim." White Sox Interactive. (http://www.whitesoxineractive.com/rwas/index.php?id=3660&category=11)

Jake Pitler

1) *and the adjectives of "pepper pot"...* Bard, Stan. "SABR Baseball Biography Project: Jake Pitler." (http://sabr.org/bioproj/person/4b700caf)

2) *Jake Pitler and his Playground...* Moore, Marianne. "Hometown Piece to Messrs. Alston and Reese," 1956

3) *I happened to be invited by Jake Pitler...* Buege. Bob. "SABR Baseball Biography Project: Johnny Logan." (http://sabr.org/bioproj/person/4140a710)

4) *During spring training in 1947...* Rampersad, Arnold. "Jackie Robinson: A Biography" (New York: Alfred A Knopf, 1997) Page 163

5) *He's the indispensable man.* Ibid, page 228

Lefty Gomez

1) One of his Favorite Binghamton Stories... Gomez, Vernona, with Goldston, Lawrence. "Lefty Gomez, An American Odyssey." (New York: Ballantine books, 2012). Page 301

2) She excused herself. Ibid, Page 139.

3) In January... "Little Left to Be Desired as Gomez Joins Hot Stover," *Binghamton Evening Press*, January 26th, 1956.

4) None of the above are correct... Letter from Lefty Gomez to Clifford Rachline, representing the Baseball Hall of Fame. From the folder on Lefty Gomez in the Baseball Hall of Fame Library.

W.B. Kay

1) *The most remarkable game...* "Higgins Allows No Hits in Opener; Bingos Score 1-0 win over Utes" *Binghamton Evening Press*, May 1st, 1914.

2) *It is too early.* "Pilot Calhoun Lands 300 Class." *Binghamton Evening Press.* May 21st, 1914

3) *The third inning must have been...* "Bingos drive Pappalau to dugout; Annex Final Battle Albany Series." *Binghamton Evening Press.* June 18th, 1914

Bobby Jones

1) *I'm so happy for Bobby Jones.* Garza, Joseph. "Mets Initialize Giants." *Orlando Sentinel.* October 9, 2000.

Brook Fordyce

*1) It was just one side...*Jones, Tom. "Rays find bounty of joy in Fordyce." *St. Petersburg Times.* March 11, 2004.

2) It didn't look like blood. Barnes, Craig. "Catcher on the Rebound." *Baltimore Sun-Sentinel.* March 11, 2002

3) He's showing us the kind of ... Amore, Don. "Fordyce's Play Drawing Praise." *Harford Courant.* June 21, 1992

Corey Lidle

*1) The whole plane...*Newman, Maria and William K. Rashbaum. "Yankee Dies in Plane Crash, Official Says." *The New York Times.* October 11 2006.

Daniel Casey

*1) I was a left handed...*Faber, Charles. "SABR Biographical Baseball Project: Daniel Casey." http://sabr.org/bioproj/person/ec4f55fc

*2) If Seneca Falls...*For information on the annual Seneca Falls "It's A Wonderful Life Celebration," see http://www.therealbedfordfalls.com

Joe Pepitone

1) The bullet had struck a rib. Pepitone, Joe with Barry Stainback. "Joe, You Coulda Made Us Proud." (New York: Dell Publishing Co., 1976) page 61

2) I was hitting nothing. Ibid, page 81

Dale Long

*1) Some day somebody...*Holtzman, Jerome. "Dale Long's Record Home-Run Streak Grows More Important with Age." *Chicago Tribune.* May 29, 1986.

Danny McDevitt

1) I don't remember. Mayer, Bob. "Danny McDevitt: Ebbetts Field Finale." *The National Pastime: A Review of Baseball History.* Issue 24, May 2004. Page 84

2) He became good friends with Sandy Koufax. Ibid, page 86

*3) I realized....*Ibid, Page 86

Quilvio Veras

*1) In his rookie season...*Obrien, David. "Veras Out to Regain Form." *Florida Sun Sentinel.* April 29, 2997.

Wally Burnette

*1) He was one of the...*Baseball Almanac web page (http://www.baseball-almanac.com/deaths/wally_burnette_obituary.shtml), reprinted from the *Danville Register & Bee,* February 13, 2003.

Curtis Pride

1) The Tony Conigliaro Award is presented by the Boston Chapter of Baseball Writers Association of America in cooperation with the Boston Red Sox to Major Leaguers who have overcome adversity through spirit, determination and courage — trademarks of Boston Red Sox hero Tony Conigliaro. The award was established in 1990 by the Boston Red Sox in honor of Conigliaro and his legendary comeback from the beaning that nearly ended his career in August 1967.

Bill Skowron

1) When I was about... Goldstein, Richard. "Bill Skowron, Yankee Slugger in Golden ERA Dies at 81." *The New York Times.* April 27, 2012. (Note: Goldstein retold the story that Skowron told to John Tullius, the author of the oral history, "I'd Rather Be a Yankee.")

Willard Hershberger

1) Willard Hershberger, 29-years old. "Reds Catcher Found Dead in Hotel: Willard Hershberger Ends Own life." *Detroit Free Press,* August 4th, 1940.

2) A Very lovable human being. Nack, William. "The Razor's Edge." (*Sports Illustrated,* May 6. 1991)

3) I thought I had him completely talked out of it....I will take it to my grave. Ibid

Tom Tresh

1) *My friend Tom...* Horn, Huston. "It's the East vs. the West." *(Sports Illustrated, October 1, 1962)* http://sportsillustrated.cnn.com/vault/article/magazine/MAG1074146/3/index.htm

2) *Tommy was just a wonderful guy...*Madden, Bill. "Former Yankee Tom Tresh Dead at 71" (*New York Daily News*. October 16, 2008.)

3) *I always felt badly...*Ibid

4) *I took me only...*Woncho, Joseph. "SABR Baseball Biography Project: Tom Tresh," (http://sabr.org/bioproj/person/a1f535cd)

Pete Van Wieren

1) *...hook that became known as "Pete's Peg*. Van Wieren, Pete with Jack Wilkinson. "Of Mikes and Men" (Illinois: Triumph Books 2010) Page 24

Epilogue

1) *And a stone's throw...* Reilly, Steve. "County Landmark Wants to Redevelop Large Eyesores" (*Binghamton Press & Sun Bulletin*, October 17, 2013).

Bibliography

1. Allen, Maury. *Yankees: Where Have you Gone?* United States: Sports Publishing, LLC, 2004

2. Aswad, Ed and Meredith, Suzanne. *IBM in Endicott.* South Carolin: Arcadia Publishing, 2005.

3. Coates, Jim, with Douglas Williams. *Always a Yankee: A Pitcher's Story; Jim Coates, he beat the Odds to Become an All-Star and World Champion.* Infinity Publishing Company, September 2010.

4. Clavin, Tom, and Peary, Danny. *Gil Hodges: The Brooklyn Bums, The Miracle Mets, The Extraordinary Life of a Baseball Legend.* New York: New American Library, 2012.

5. Cohen, Marvin A. *Doc Farrell's Baseball Odyssey; Rubbing Shoulders with Greatness.* NE: Morris Publishing, 3212 East Highway 30, Kearney, 2003

6. Di Salvatore, Brian. *A Clever Base-Ballist: The Life and Times of John Montgomery Ward.* Baltimore, NY: The Johns Hopkins University Press, 1999

7. Ford, Whitey, with Phil Pepe. *Slick: My Life In and Around Baseball.* New York: William Morrow and Company, INC, 1987

8. Gittleman, Sid. *Reynolds, Raschi, and Lopat: The Big Three and the Great Yankee Dynasty.*

9. Gomez, Vernona, with Lawrence Goldstein. *Lefty: An American Odyssey.* New York: Ballantine Books, 2012

10. Grant, Jim "Mudcat" with Sabellico, Tom & O'Brien, Pat. *The Black Aces: Baseball's Only African-American Twenty-Game Winners.* Farmingdale, NY; The Black Aces, LLC, 2006

11. Interviews conducted: Joe McCann, Jim Weed

12. James, Bill. *The New Bill James Historical Abstract.* New York: FREE Press, 2001

13. Leinweaver, Mark, with Ryan Bradley. *Minor Moments, Major Memories: Baseball's Best Players Recall Life in the Minor leagues.* Guilford, CT: The Lyons Press

14. Luciano, Ron, with David Fisher. *The Umpire Strikes Back.* New York: Bantam Books, 1982

15. Mapes, Linda L. *Johnson Field: A History.* NY (Master's Thesis)

16. McCulough, Bob (as told to). *My Greatest Day in Baseball.* Dallas, Texas: Taylor Publishing Company, 1998

17. McGraw, Tug, and Joseph Durso. *Screwball.* Boston: Houghton Mifflin Company, 1974

18. Rampersad, Arnold. *Jackie Robinson: A Biography.* New York: Alfred A. Knopf Company: 1997

19. Rosario, Bill, editor. *2013 Eastern League 2013 Media Guide & Record Book.*

20. Pepitone, Joe, with Barry Stainback. *Joe, You Coulda Made Us Proud.* (New York: Dell Publishing Co., 1975)

21. Roberts, Robin, with C. Paul Rogers III. *My Life in Baseball. Illionois: Triumph Books, 2003*

22. Shay, Jack Edward, in collaboration with Betty Casey and Tom Townshend. *Bygone Binghamton: Remembering People and Places of the Past.*(Bloomington, Indiana: Authorhouse Publishing, 2012

23. Smith, Robert. *Baseball's Hall of Fame.* United States: Bantam Books, 1965

24. Stout, Glenn, editor. *Top of the Heap: A Yankees Collection.* New York: Houghton Mifflin Company, 2003

25. Van Wieren, Pete, with Jack Wilkinson. *Of Mikes and Men: A Lifetime of Braves Baseball.* Illinois: Triumph Books, 2010

26. *Voices of the Game* Series conducted by the National Baseball Hall of Fame in Cooperstown: Frank Tepedino, Ken Harrelson

About the Authors

Jim Maggiore has been a resident of the Greater Binghamton Area since graduating from Binghamton University in 1978. His writings on baseball have previously appeared in *Baseball Weekly*, *The Binghamton Press & Sun Bulletin*, and various editions of the *Binghamton Mets Baseball Program.* An Information Technology professional during the day, his hobby is writing on baseball; this is his first book. He has been a diehard NY Mets fan since his dad took him to see the Mets beat the Milwaukee Braves, 1-0, on a Charlie Smith single up the middle in September of 1965.

Michael J. McCann lives in Johnson City with his wife Susan and two sons, Ian and Shaun. He is a Johnson City firefighter during the day and baseball historian the rest of the time. This is his fourth book; previously he has co-authored *Hockey in Broome County, Baseball in Broome County, and The History of the Johnson City Fire Department.* One of his earliest recollections of a game is the 1974 Hall of Fame game when his father took him on a bus trip to see the Atlanta Braves take on the Chicago White Sox. He remembers that Hank Aaron played left field for the Braves and Richie Allen wrote words in the infield dirt at first base.

Mail Order Form

If you want to order more copies of "Celebrating 100 Years of Minor League Baseball in Greater Binghamton: Tales from the Binghamton Shrine," complete the form and mail as indicated here.

Item	Quantity	Cost
Celebrating 100 Years of Minor League Baseball in Greater Binghamton: Tales from the Binghamton Shrine		$10.00
New York State Sales Tax (multiply cost by .08)		
Shipping and Handling Cost ($3.99 for first book, $1.00 for each additional book)		
Total Amount Enclosed		

Mailing Address Where Book(s) Will be Shipped:

_____

_____

_____

_____

Mail this Order Form to:

Binghamton Mets Booster Club
C/O Binghamton Mets Baseball Club
Box 592
Binghamton, New York 13902

Please allow two to four weeks for delivery. Make checks out to the "Binghamton Mets Booster Club." Also, inquiries on the status of your order can be sent to Bmetsboosters@gmail.com. Stay abreast of all Binghamton Mets Booster Club activities via Facebook (bmetsboosters) and at bmetsboosters.wordpress.com